This Finer Shadow

Harlan Cozad McIntosh

Alpha Editions

This edition published in 2023

ISBN : 9789357941112

Design and Setting By
Alpha Editions
www.alphaedis.com
Email - info@alphaedis.com

As per information held with us this book is in Public Domain.
This book is a reproduction of an important historical work. Alpha Editions uses the best technology to reproduce historical work in the same manner it was first published to preserve its original nature. Any marks or number seen are left intentionally to preserve its true form.

Contents

INTRODUCTION .... - 1 -
CHAPTER I .... - 3 -
CHAPTER II .... - 8 -
CHAPTER III .... - 18 -
CHAPTER IV .... - 21 -
CHAPTER V .... - 33 -
CHAPTER VI .... - 36 -
CHAPTER VII .... - 46 -
CHAPTER VIII .... - 57 -
CHAPTER IX .... - 64 -
CHAPTER X .... - 70 -
CHAPTER XI .... - 81 -
CHAPTER XII .... - 89 -
CHAPTER XIII .... - 98 -
CHAPTER XIV .... - 105 -
CHAPTER XV .... - 121 -
CHAPTER XVI .... - 128 -
CHAPTER XVII .... - 158 -
CHAPTER XVIII .... - 167 -
CHAPTER XIX .... - 170 -
CHAPTER XX .... - 176 -
CHAPTER XXI .... - 182 -
CHAPTER XXII .... - 189 -
CHAPTER XXIII .... - 194 -
CHAPTER XXIV .... - 201 -
CHAPTER XXV .... - 209 -

CHAPTER XXVI .... - 213 -
CHAPTER XXVII .... - 219 -
CHAPTER XXVIII .... - 226 -
CHAPTER XXIX .... - 232 -
CHAPTER XXX .... - 236 -
FOOTNOTES .... - 240 -

INTRODUCTION

It is not always an unmixed advantage to an elderly critic of literature to be recognized as one of the Old School who is interested in extremely modern and daring young writers. But in the case of Harlan Cozad McIntosh this reputation of mine has won me the greatest and proudest pleasure a critic can have—the thrill of being among the first to announce: "Here, anyway, is genius!"

For from start to finish this extraordinary story holds you under a spell—that is to say, if you are, as I am, an obsessed devotee of the dangerous mole-runs of beautiful and desperate human aberration. I have no hesitation in saying that the character "Mr. Roberts" of this book is a masterpiece of portraiture, and an almost flawless presentation of one of those abnormal types of men whose subterranean and half-suppressed feelings lead to more tragedies than the ordinary reader of pathological fiction would believe possible.

But daring and terrifying as Mr. McIntosh's psychological flashes of insight are, they by no means cover the whole field of interest in this strange, and indeed I may boldly say, this unique book. There are passages of the most exquisite beauty, beauty of that rare, intense, evasive sort which, as the poet says, is like the lightning—vanished ere you can say "It lightens!" There is, indeed, in these poetic passages, so swift, so sudden, so startling a beauty that it sweeps the reader away, causing him to feel for a quick beat of time, as if he *were* the author!

Nothing could be further from a doctrinaire treatise on "the psychology of the abnormal" than this book. It is an exciting love story of the most healthy, natural and child-like simplicity; and that it is shot through and through by the purple threads of abnormal pity and terror enhances rather than lessens the tender freshness of this ancient theme.

The book is a terrible tragedy, and one that certainly in the fullest classical sense *purges our passions*; but tragic though it is, it is the extreme opposite of anything dispirited, dejected, disheartened or disillusioned. A fine, pure, fierce detachment from anything cloying, from anything voluptuously soft and sentimental, characterizes this "ill-starred" and yet so proudly "well-starred" young writer. The soul of the hero, obviously a reflection of the author himself, moves through these weird circles and ambiguous scenes, protected like Milton's lady in *Comus*, by the invisible guardians of a most unusual and indeed almost unearthly chastity. The moral of it all—if moral you want, and I am myself old-fashioned enough *always* to want exactly that—is no other than what we learn from Goethe as well as from Milton:

namely that *nothing*, however fascinating in its provocative phosphorescence, can really contaminate a soul "that has an instinct of the one true way."

Men and women who make the pathetic mistake of thinking themselves what is called "normal" ought all to read this tragic tale, so that they shall be *shamed*, not only into human sympathy, but into philosophical insight; whereas those of us who make no such claim, and are confessedly engaged in the hard struggle to get ourselves into order, will find in Harlan McIntosh's book just what we have been seeking in vain: a stark, authentic, unmitigated rendering of what it is like *really to be* what these complacently detached investigators analyze from so safe a distance! For myself, since I learnt about M. de Charlus in Proust, I haven't been so helped in my understanding of these strange matters as when destiny gave me the opportunity of passing my blind fingers—for we are all blind in these cases—over the mobile features of Mr. McIntosh's extraordinary creations.

JOHN COWPER POWYS

CHAPTER I

The sea's reaches moved blue and green from the western horizon to the Haitian coast. The small ship *Verda* disturbed the roll of water.

Martin gave the ship a little right wheel and she had her course, breaking the current. An offshore wind brought the jungle to him. He closed his eyes and felt its movement—the overcries of birds, animal musk and the heavy heat of clouds. There, facing the sun, lay a swan's feather of beach shining up to the darker ridges. Oceanward, the sea bent into the brightest corner.

It was after supper. He knew the sailors were lounging on the poopdeck. Rio, naked to the waist, handsome, with his broken chest and heavy shoulders, would be telling the younger seamen of One Beer Annie and her electric finger. Martin looked at the clock and at the compass. He struck three bells and stepped away as his relief entered the wheelhouse.

"Thirty-two," said Martin.

"Thirty-two," repeated the quartermaster.

"Steering thirty-two," called Martin to the mate on the bridge.

The officer nodded his head.

Later, on lookout, Martin leaned against the ship's apron and watched the sky ring blue to blue. On the coastal side the bright wing faded under the hills. Seaward, the sun pressed into mist—sustained by color. He shaded his eyes against the shrill line, saw it strike the water, burn and recede. Catching the rim, it held once and fell, breathing up softer lights. Flame, gold and scarlet in procession shifted to turquoise and a rolling mauve—slowly turning the crystal till darkness caught one star.

The distant light trembled in his eyes. He crossed the deck and faced the shore. An aluminum crust broke the dark shoulder of mountain, rising higher till its bright shale covered the swing of beach with moontide. Burning from the painting ran the moonspindle, striking the ship. Martin dropped his head and stared into the blue foam.

Above him, Orion swung easily past the foremast and returned; Polaris grew in the north; and behind him, the Southern Cross lay on her side. He grabbed the mainstay, pulled himself up on the apron and lay on his back. His eyes followed the moon as she came toward him, changing softly from flesh to white, round and white like the abdomen of a woman.

Silence, dead and liquid, held the *Verda* from both sky and sea. A restless mist, moving downward, obscured the stars. On the land side heat-lightning followed in sheaves. A thin black cloud raised the horizon. It built higher and darker as it rushed at the ship.

Martin pulled off his skivy-shirt. The heat covered his face with perspiration and he drew his arm across his forehead. Isolated on the fo'c'sle head, away from the ship and its crew, there was no proportion. The wind dried his throat and he bent under the apron to breathe, closing his eyes against the lightning. A wave smashed on the bow and sounded through the forepeak. He ducked lower under the steel cover and rubbed the salt from his mouth. The rain struck. Falling solidly, it hammered his back and shoulders until, at last, to ease the pain, he turned his side against the pressure. When he looked aft he knew that he was blind, seeing neither mast nor running-lights. Living in this vacuum of noise, without sight, he knelt on the deck with his head in his arms and tried to breathe through the falling water. Still and bowed he waited.

Abruptly the wind stopped, and the rain. He looked up and saw the retreating clouds uncovering stars behind him. The moon shone more brightly. The scent of the jungle was deeper and the man with the sword in the sky smiled as he swung past the mast. Martin stripped off his dungarees and wrung the water from them. The stiffening cloth was still moist when he pulled them on again.

He was surprised toward the latter part of his watch by a heavy, amused voice.

"Get your end wet?"

He saw Rio smiling at him.

"I did," he replied gravely.

Rio slapped his hands together.

"Why'd you go to sea?"

Martin rubbed his chin and looked away.

"I'm getting along," he answered.

Rio leaned on the rail beside him.

"A woman's place is in the home."

Martin felt himself beset by an out-of-time capriciousness. Yet he knew these words, so like the emptying of a fool's wounds, were no more idle than the turn of water and wind and all their purposes, though whistled through a child's melody. He knew also that certain eccentricities of men, of winds, of waters, must be directed and employed; therefore, without looking at his friend, he spoke to him.

"The boundaries of the home have been extended. The boundaries of your mind are arbitrary."

"That serves me up, I guess." Rio yawned. "But you ain't no seaman."

Martin sighted over the rail.

"Scorpio's tail light is out."

Rio, persistent, glanced at him sideways.

"You ain't happy here, and I am." He breathed the hot, moist wind and looked at the moon and the quiet length under it. "I'm happy. This is the kind of night I live for. It's clean and hot. It burns the yellow out of your blood. Some day," he nodded toward the island fading behind them, "I'm goin' to get a little shack over there with a shakedown roof, and maybe a small stove."

"So you're happy," answered Martin. "Happy!" he repeated in a louder voice. "That word doesn't belong on this deck."

Rio grinned.

"You're a Christian, then."

Martin stepped closer to him.

"I believe I am."

The lights of a ship came up on the port bow. Martin crossed the deck and struck two bells. When he returned he spoke abstractedly.

"I'd like to find a quiet beach myself. A beach that walks with you in the daytime and sings with you at night.... A place to rest.... But I can't rest."

Rio became confused. He put his hands on Martin's shoulders and for a second they stood motionless, like mildewed lovers in a gloom proportionately obscure. Then Rio whispered, "I'll do my bit, my friend. I'll take your last illusion."

Martin saw the fluid, hurt eyes and the bitter smile. He struck Rio's arms from his shoulders.

"How do you know that I still possess this 'last illusion?' ... Why do you follow me?... You call for the water and the heat. You're part of the land we passed and of your buccaneering ancestors. That doesn't include me. I'm a foreigner."

Rio looked at him with hatred.

"Meanin', my fine lad, I ain't part of you? Well, maybe I ain't." He brought one fist down on the rail, then pointed at the water. "Christ, you're wrong about it all, though. You ain't no sailor—but you *are* the 'part of.' I'm the foreigner. My father buccaneered from the pulpit. A hard-shell, hell-fire Baptist, he cheapened a pirate's trade with pennies out of a palm leaf.... I remember him well; a dirty man from the west, with green eyes and a thin beard. He showed me your English and your habits and shouted his bad theology. And all the time, my native mother, with the sound of the beach for religion, stared at him——" He turned clumsily, more like an anthropoid than a man. "I don't get myself, Martin. Maybe I'm starved. It's been a long time. I've lived in a monastery since a brown girl——"

"I hear every word," said Martin. "I hear 'monastery,' 'brown girl,' 'pirate'—but I can't put them together. I can't think logically. They're disconnected pictures."

"Keep your pictures." Rio moved closer. "I said I'm crazy to-night."

Now Martin could see an intentional grace, eager and sharp.

"Hold your Baptist's head then, Rio. That's not for us." Martin's waist was slim in the moonlight. He knew the night was wrong—something to fight or there would be a mistake. He turned away. "It's nearly eight bells, Rio, and the squarehead relieves me too fast."

Rio held his fist against the moon. His face seemed breaking.

"You ain't right, Martin, but you make me think you are."

He climbed down the ladder, walked across the foredeck and aft to his bunk. He took his bath in a bucket, put on clean skivies, turned in and tried to sleep.

On lookout, Martin watched dew form on the steel rail and rubbed his hand across it. The sun had burned his hair lighter than his skin; and as the moist wind pushed it from his temples, a smile, restrained by the unfathomable hurt of one who, for escape, has taken to the sea, formed on his lips. That he could dream well could be told by the changing color of his eyes according to that which was about him; and by the fact or the illusion that he saw great distances or none at all. His conversation with Rio had been a short but a disturbing one. At the climactic moment it had seemed obvious. Not now; and deliberately Martin turned his thoughts to the ocean. His union with the ship and all that was about him was brief and precisioned. Perhaps it was his quietness or perhaps a quality in the sky; but his silent figure was adjusted in the small cosmos. His eyes, indecisive of both moon and ocean, had found the properties of each. Thus, filled with iron and dull gold, he wore the uniform and restlessness of the tides and knew that although his own desire had been encompassed, it had not been lost. He pressed against the rail, his arms braced, his bronze hair damp against the deeper bronze of his skin. Through the clarity of a sudden, stern compassion, he swung around to where Rio had stood. In the recurring consciousness of the presence of his friend, he drew the solemn colors about them. Against his feet the steel plates trembled with the ship's engines. The wind changed. A thousand mirrors broke under the high moon.

CHAPTER II

Martin looked around the fo'c'sle, swung open the locker door to see if he had packed all his gear and looked under the blankets on his bunk.

"So long, boys," he said. "I'm shoving off."

The seamen at the card table and those lying in their bunks glanced up from newspapers and cigarettes.

"So long, Mart—So long. Take it easy."

He pulled his duffel-bag over his shoulder and walked up the ladder to the afterdeck. Languorous winds and the dark waters of streaming nights lurked in the corners of the bulkheads. Yet the knowledge of his late intimacy with these secrets had no quality of nostalgia for him. He was surprised at the indifference he felt on leaving the ship, all the more so because he had no reason for this coldness.

The chief mate saw him standing by the rail. He had often wondered about Martin—that strange sailor who had gone about his duties so quietly. That was part of it. He was so damned quiet. No wonder the other sailors hadn't liked that. He did his work well and was the best helmsman on the ship; but off watch, he had the air of a man looking for the unnecessary. He avoided the sailors with such instinctive thoroughness that it was obvious even to them that he intended no offense. It was more, thought the mate, as if he seemed to be thinking a great deal and never getting anywhere with it. Frequently, on sultry nights, when the mate couldn't sleep and had taken a turn around the 'midship deck, he'd seen Martin sitting alone on the afterhatch looking at the sky. The officer had a few books on psychology which he read instead of fiction; and therefore felt himself pretty well up on the distressed mind. He was a kind-hearted man, and one night he'd called Martin into his cabin to "sort of decide what made him tick," as he said afterwards. What was it Martin had said?... Something about the sea being a fine girl for a man, or some such rot; and said quite pleasantly. And when the mate had pulled him round to psychology, Martin had agreed with him that it was a nice vehicle for a malingering neurasthenic.... No—damn it!—the fellow had said that first, himself! It was easy to see the chap had read a bit. He addressed the mate's most ponderous terms with earnestness; but always he'd wound up in a theoretical mess that half sounded like a laugh. Still, one couldn't get upset over something that wasn't there; and certainly there was no laughter in Martin's expression. The mate was sure of it. It was a damned odd feeling though, to have him sitting there looking at you patiently with that peculiar, absent manner. He'd told Martin that it was best for the sailors to get along together and to yarn a bit and get things off their chests. And then the queerest thing happened. Martin had told him that good-fellowship was not only essential, but unavoidable; and from there on, he'd continued to speak in English; only what he was saying didn't make sense. It was like dumping words into a pot and shoveling them around with your finger. By God!—it was a strange feeling listening to that! And then Martin had gone.... Just the same, when the mate saw him with his duffel-bag beside him, looking out at the bulk of the city, it made him feel funny—sort of lonely for him. And he went over.

"New York in the winter is no place for a sailor, Martin, and you're paying off with very little."

"I know." He leaned toward the officer and spoke in a low voice. "I know. But there's something important to be found out, Mister. Important to myself, yes—and to you, and perhaps to more than both of us." He pointed beyond the warehouses to the pinnacles of the city. "That old line won't stay. But there's a basic pattern under it that will remain. That ought to be known. Damn it, Mister, I won't find it nor, perhaps, my son, but if we keep looking—" He picked up his bag.

Infinitely puzzled, the mate looked after him.

"That's that," he said to himself.

Martin went down the gangplank and, without turning, started for the city. He took the elevated to Chatham Square where he got off and asked a policeman for an address. The shock of change from the cleanliness and solitude of the ocean to this polyglot of grime and faces was physical; and he tightened up his nerves as though preparing for an explosion. A few minutes later he walked into Relief Headquarters, a rusty, high-walled building in the center of the Bowery. Policemen watched the group of applicants carefully. There were two lines of men, one set apart for seamen. Martin joined this group, noticing how strangely the sailors, tanned, alert and swaggering, contrasted with the white-faced, hopeless habitués. When his turn came a clerk, tired, frowning, looked up from his desk.

"Name?"

"Devaud."

"De what?"

"Devaud," answered Martin. "Vaud, as in vaudeville."

"Age?"

"Twenty-eight."

"Go to that desk." Aside, the man called to a case-worker. "Mr. Stein, here's another for you."

Martin went over and stood patiently in front of Mr. Stein who was fumbling with some papers. Stein had short-cropped gray hair which grew halfway down his forehead. It made Martin think of a Polynesian thatched hut. Stein's chin sloped backward so abruptly that he appeared more like a primitive man than one of the present. Only his fat lips and stomach were mellowed and sweetened by whisky and a rapidly departing youth.

"Sit down," he said. Then, smiling so that he showed a large area of widely separated teeth, he slowly drew in his smile and ended by regarding Martin almost beseechingly. "Sit down," he said again, folding his hands over his fat stomach. "We like to understand, to get closer to our more unfortunate brothers. We are here to help you adjust yourself. We hope to provide you with every facility for rehabilitation."

Martin felt a momentary irritation.

"Rehabilitation from what?" he asked, wondering what this empiric monstrosity was conspiring.

"Rehabilitation from—" Stein hesitated. He looked at Martin's dungarees. "Are you planning on returning to the sea?"

"No."

The case-worker took his pencil.

"I'm sure we can help you." He smiled again and nodded encouragingly. "It will be all right. Just sketch your history briefly." He slipped back into his chair, setting the flat convolutions of his brain at a receptive curve.

Martin reflected on his "history." The walls of this dirty place fell apart and memories came up in a flood.... His father—a story of the one professor, deathless in his circumference of knowledge; a man affectionate, yet untenable within the world, struck close in the mystery of his students; humble with his virtues, out of cognizance, and strong in the strength of those he guided, he lived apart and yet among the compasses of his direction.... His mother, carrying an exotic, foreign beauty into time as though indignant with maturities.... His white child-wife, her white child-fingers screaming on the piano against his inevitable demands.... Her death.... Then ships and oceans and the lust of palms....

"Your history!" Stein's sharp voice, bringing back the sharper walls and the honesty of where he was, demanded laughter. And Martin laughed until each memory was dead.

"My history?" he asked, wiping his eyes. "You wouldn't like my history. It isn't interesting enough. Case-historians would starve to death with me."

Mr. Stein sat up straight. He frowned and looked at his hands.

"Very amusing." He filled two forms rapidly. "This," he said, handing Martin one of them, "provides you with a hotel room for the duration of two weeks. And this," he continued, "allows you meal tickets at any of our restaurants to the value of forty cents per day for the same length of time."

Outside, Martin shook his head to free it from the mustiness of dismissed progressions and the impurity of this newer living. He glanced at one of the tickets. "HOTEL PINE LEAF, RESERVED ESPECIALLY FOR SEAMEN," he read. As he walked on toward the hotel he was stopped twice for a cigarette. One heavy-jawed fellow tried to strike up a conversation and offered to help him with his bag, all the time walking uncomfortably close to him. Martin shook his head and the man dropped behind, muttering.

The lobby of the Pine Leaf was one floor up. A man seated in one of the chairs which lined the walls, was snoring loudly. "He must be sick," thought Martin, for no one disturbed him. Martin leaned his bag near the desk and as he did so, a bull-necked sailor, his collar open, ran at him.

"Good God!" said the man. "We've grounded. Damn you, Captain! Keep her in the channel." He held his fist menacingly.

"All right," said Martin, stopping stock-still. "And now, look to your engines."

The clerk behind the wire netting regarded them worriedly.

"Go back to your cabin, Danny," he said. "We've taken on the pilot."

Danny, shaking all over, looked once more at Martin and returned to his chair.

Martin handed his slip to the clerk who turned it nervously in his hand.

"Danny's all right," he said. "Liquor took his ticket. He never jumped like that before, though. Kind of look out, will you?"

"He didn't mean anything." Martin smiled reassuringly. "I jumped like that once myself." He took his key and towel, packed his canvas up three flights of stairs and walked down the corridor to his room. It was a narrow, cell-like cubicle, furnished with a cot and a small locker. There was no light and the tiny window, high in the wall, admitted only a few indirect rays of sunshine. Martin sorted his gear, found his razor and went into the washroom.

Three men were huddled in a corner. As Martin lathered his face he looked in their direction and saw that they had a bottle of rubbing alcohol which they were diluting with warm water. After a good deal of grunting and shaking and laughing they held it to the light.

"Looks to me like Tri Gin," said one whose hands shook violently.

"Looks to me like smoke," said another, laughing and turning to Martin. "Have some smoke, Jack?" he asked.

Martin shook his head.

"Ulcers," he said, pointing to his stomach, and started shaving.

The men shook their heads sympathetically. This, they understood. They were dancing to the clapping of hands when Martin left.

In the low glim of his room he changed his shirt. He was about to lock his door when a lad ran frantically down the narrow hall, bumping into him. Martin held the boy coldly.

"Hide me," sobbed the lad. "It's Danny. He's had smoke—" the sobs continued. "Danny thinks ... for Christ's sake!—hide me!"

Martin shoved the boy inside his little room and closed the door, then took a cigarette from his pocket. A moment later, Danny put his head around the shadowy corner and walked slowly toward him. When he was closer, Martin struck a match and lit his cigarette abstractedly.

"Where is he?" asked Danny in a hard whisper. "Where's my little galley rat?"

"Speak American, buddy," said Martin. "This is an American vessel—not a Limey."

"Don't lie to me, you damned school-ship!" cried Danny, coming forward. "Where is he?"

Martin sighed resignedly.

"He's here, Danny—under my shirt. Come get him."

"Ah! That's better. I'm coming, friend."

He walked up close to Martin who dropped his cigarette. Danny shot out his right hand and grabbed Martin's shoulder; but feeling the broad, tensed muscle, he became suddenly quiet and stood for a long time running his hand up and down Martin's arm. At last, he started to cry gently. Then, and only then, did Martin throw his arm about him and whisper all the lonely, desperate things that sailors know; until willingly, Danny let himself be led into his own room. Martin got down on his knees and took off Danny's shoes. He covered him with a blanket, looked at him once to be sure he was sleeping and tiptoed out.

When he got back to his own room the boy was gone. So were his small camera and his pea-jacket.

He went out into the street and walked along until he saw a beer sign. He stood at the rail and kicked the sawdust angrily, thinking of his camera. As he took his glass he caught his reflection in the large mirror above the bar and burst out laughing; for his head seemingly rested between the enormous breasts of a nude which had been painted on the wall behind him. Amazed at this unsuspected liaison, he turned to regard with favor the immense mural. The lady reclined, supine and indifferent to the ardent glances of the drunken men about her. Her bottom rested on a couch of lurid green and one arm, disproportionate, held aloft a wreath of garden spray and roses.

Martin was still laughing when a little white-haired man with a thick nose and red eyes walked over to him.

"Ahoy, sailor," said the little fellow, and blew two sharp notes between his teeth. "Ship ahoy!"

"Ship ahoy," said Martin.

The little man giggled.

"I like you, mate." He held out his hand, his eyes watering happily. "I'm a sailor, and my name's Old Crackin. When my old lady's sick—when she's havin' babies—*I* don't take no tea for the fever. *I* don't wait."

He turned and pointed to the mural. "I git mine from *her*." His eyes dimmed in affection as he stared at the naked lady. Then he smiled again at Martin. "I can spell too, mate," he added proudly.

"Spell CAT," said Martin.

"K-R-Double T," said the old seaman, an ecstatic glow on his face.

"That's right," observed Martin, in a tone of approbation. "Can you spell DOG?"

"Sure I can!" Old Crackin answered promptly, looking as if he could scarcely contain himself for joy. "G-R-Double D," he recited, and held out his hand once more.

Martin saw the running sores between the old sailor's fingers. He smiled at him, called the bartender, asked for a beer and paid for it.

"Drink up," he said and left.

The little man looked at his beer and drank it slowly, bitterness and necessity in his expression.

The nearest Relief restaurant was at the far end of the Bowery. Martin walked along, sticking to the edge of the sidewalk, glad that his dungarees were clean. The horizons of the sea outlined the figures of the people about him. They moved down the street, slack-mouthed, too tired to be desperate. Martin saw them as an old river, full of eddies and currents—muddy, yet retaining the purity of utter despondency.

In a doorway, out of the late afternoon sun, a man lay sleeping as though drugged. And at one corner three men were drinking openly from a bottle while a policeman passed them without interest. A long-haired, wild-eyed fanatic, his shirtfront covered with dark stains, addressed an amused group of loafers on their sins, vividly painting the atrocious hells that awaited them, and turning only to spit at the passing cars. Whenever there was a momentary lull of traffic he would spit on his own thin coat-tails in his excess of hatred. This brought the most hilarious laughter from the crowd. A thick-set drunken woman with one stocking dragging the pavement brought the preacher's fury to such a height that he rushed at her, his mouth wide open. She swung at him sluggishly, missing his chin by a narrow margin; whereupon he ran around her in ever-widening circles as she continued her forward movement in dignified arabesques.

Martin walked on more slowly, attempting to find a stronger sedative with each horror he passed. A man lay stretched across the sidewalk. His mouth was bleeding, his trousers were open and a slow trickle of urine ran down to the curb. The crowd, apparently oblivious, walked around him and continued down the street. In his rising emotion, Martin nearly stopped. He wanted to cover and protect the man—wanted to carry him to some safe doorstep. But his hesitation was brief; for he knew that this was the accustomed vagary in a clouded, forgotten street—knew that he would be jailed or put to trial as a mischief-maker or a madman if he tried to block the immutable routine of such a land. And so he went on to the restaurant with his heart completely hypnotized because, alive, it could not bear the awareness of such a state.

Noise and confusion were in the cafeteria. A line of men moved slowly past the counter, carrying their trays and pointing to the food they wanted.

Martin picked up a tray, shook off the greasy drops and looked at the signs. They read:

BREAST OF LAMB!	FIFTEEN CENTS.
HAM AND BEANS!	FIFTEEN CENTS.
EGG!	FIVE CENTS.

"Ham and beans!" he shouted against the noise of rattling plates and cups.

The boy behind the counter ladled out a large plate of beans, dropping a slice of boiled ham upon them.

"Milk," yelled Martin.

He carried his tray to a vacancy on the long, marble-slabbed table.

An old man, bent, unshaven, was scavenging the plates for food that others had left. Martin reached in his pocket for a meal ticket. A boy sitting nearby pulled at his elbow to stop him.

"Don't be a sucker," he said. "It's the old guy's racket."

Martin handed the ticket to the old man. He felt irritable as he sat down next to the boy.

"He can take it, and to hell with him," he said.

The boy laughed.

"I felt like that when I paid off. Now, I'm Red, the Cockroach—and a tighter one you'll never find in the galley sink!" He talked on rapidly, going from one subject to another and his freckled nose was so impudent that Martin had to smile with him. At last, the boy pulled off his cap, showing his dark red hair. "That's why they call me 'Red.' And," he continued, putting his hand in his pocket and pulling out a fistful of tickets, "that's why I'm 'Red, the Cockroach.' How's shipping?"

"I'm not trying to get out," Martin replied. "No butter?" he added, looking at the stale, brownish bread.

"No butter," answered the boy, nodding his head. "And watch the beans. See those black fellows?" He pointed to Martin's plate. "They'll come up."

"We'll leave them," said Martin, running his fork through the pinkish mixture.

The boy had thrown his cap on the floor. He picked it up with a nervous gesture and got out of his chair.

"I'm going for a stick of weed," he said. "Do you want to blow one up with me?"

Martin shook his head.

"I'm a drinker," he said. "I'll put a beer behind yours if you care for it. I'm not hungry enough yet to manage this." He stood up, pushing his plate to one side.

"It's a hell of a racket," said Red, as they walked out together. "They make plenty on this garbage."

It had grown dark. Under a streetlamp, Red looked sideways at Martin.

"My connection is around the corner," he said. "It's Chilean Hay—good stuff."

"Sorry," said Martin. "I'm a drinker. I don't object to Marihuana, but it depresses me; gives me bum kicks, you know."

The boy shrugged.

"O.K.," he said. "There's my connection." He nodded to a man watching them from a doorway.

The fellow met them and looked suspiciously at Martin.

"It's O.K.," said Martin's friend. He took two cigarettes and handed back a quarter.

"I'm hot," said the fellow, and walked away.

"He's right," said Red. "The law has his number. They know he's peddling."

"That makes it nice for us." Martin glanced cautiously around him.

"We're O.K. The law don't bother the consumer. Here!" Red pointed to a dimly-lighted alley. "We can blast it right here."

"Isn't it rather open?"

"It's all right," said the boy. He lit a cigarette, puffed on it and held the smoke in his lungs. Talking jerkily, he let out the smoke.

"There's just two kinds of men in the Bowery," he said. "Weed-heads like me, and they're smart. And lushhounds—" he stopped talking.

"Like me?" asked Martin.

Red took several more puffs from the cigarette, jigging on his heels.

"There it is," he said. "I got it." He laughed uncertainly. "Come over to the Square with me. I know where we can make a couple of bucks."

"How?" asked Martin before he thought.

"Hustling," answered Red.

"Hustling what?" insisted Martin, already in.

"Anything from gin to Jesus," said the boy dreamily. "Or in a pinch, an Old Auntie."

"No. I'm turning in." Martin felt suddenly tired.

Around the corner, Red faced him.

"It's as soft as roses," he said. "Just as soft as roses." He walked to the curb, peered over the edge, and stepped carefully across the street.

CHAPTER III

The *Verda*, due to sail the following day, lay in port. Her lines were coiled and her deck chipped. The houses had been cleaned and the captain's deck and the bridge were freshly painted. She was neat and lonely, pushing against the wharf with tired swells. She was not the same ship that had smashed against a storm-driven wave with a ferocity equaling that of the ocean, or had tolled deftly under the charge of a freak sea. She was aloof, nearly desperate amid the deluge of cans and boxes and other flotsam that swept the harbor. She was a dead creature, with the look of a coffin about her; and all the ships alongside were the same.

Below, in the *Verda*, the sailors were busy in the washroom. Tired by a day in the holds they opened some beer. A young ordinary seaman, restrained by weeks at sea, jumped around the room noisily and popped a towel at one of the men.

"Pipe down!" someone yelled at him.

The boy, unlistening, wrapped a towel around his waist, grabbed another, put on wooden sandals and ran into the fo'c'sle. Rio was sitting on his bunk, his chin in his hands, staring straight before him. Exhilarated by the beer and the cold bath, the ordinary danced forward and snapped the towel, flicking it against Rio's cheek. Instinctively, the big sailor jumped to the boy's side, his fingers spread. The ordinary turned pale and backed away. At this, Rio's eyes cleared. He regarded the lad as though seeing him for the first time and without a word, returned to his bunk. The ordinary took one more frightened look at him, went back to the washroom and was soon laughing again.

In the fo'c'sle Rio was silent. The other sailors began to drift in, but no one spoke to him. He sat on his bunk with his chin in his hands, thinking about Martin. He remembered the night on lookout, the ship's foam and the low constellations. He remembered lights over Haiti and a young, impulsive face. Martin hadn't understood. He knew what his friend had thought. By God!— he'd thought it himself for a minute or two.... Why had Martin got off in New York at this season? It would soon be winter. He didn't have any money. His body was conditioned to the tropics. His clothes were light and his blood thin. He would sleep in a flop house, eat bad food and get sick from that cold east wind.

Rio got up from his bunk and went to his locker. He put on a new suit and new shoes. He packed his gear except for his sea boots and oilskins. These he laid on a bench. Then he put on his overcoat and a new hat, picked up his bag and walked out of the fo'c'sle.

None of the sailors had said anything while he packed. But when he had gone, the young ordinary looked around with wide eyes.

"For gosh sake!" he said. "What's he doin'?"

No one answered him. An old sailor picked up Rio's sea boots and inspected them.

"There's a god-damned hole," he said.

An able-bodied seaman lit a cigarette.

"He blew his cork," he said to the smoke.

"It's his own cork," answered the old sailor.

"Yeah," said the A.B., picking up Rio's oilskins and hanging them by his own locker.

"Let's get a game," suggested the ordinary, shuffling a pack of cards.

"Get your game with the black gang," said the old sailor. "Them lights're goin' out."

"So'm I," said the A.B., pulling on a blue jacket. "There's a bag on Sand Street that thinks I'm papa."

The ordinary stopped him.

"Loan me a dollar, Al. An' I'll go with you."

The A.B. laughed.

"A dollar?" He laughed again without looking.

"I'll pay you back in Panama," said the ordinary.

"We don't get no draw in Panama," said Al, and left.

Some of the men followed him and the others climbed into their bunks. The lights went out. The old sailor snored uneasily through the bitter ghosts of his life. In the bunk above him the young ordinary tried to forget Sand Street. He wanted to think about a secluded little valley on the Pacific coast—so far away. He remembered the thick smell of clover and the believing, fresh eyes of a girl he had left—for this? His bunk felt damp and he turned wearily.... His shipmate was on Sand Street now. There would be light-haired women and dark-haired women. There would be dancing and an orchestra.... The boy rolled on his stomach and held a pillow tightly against his eyes. The darkness brought fields and sunsets; branches and yellow, curving rivers. Memory covered Sand Street—Sand Street with its gin-mills, its red mouth and perspiration. The boy held the pillow tighter. Smelling the girl's lips and the clover—dreaming of the bright, soft land—so far—his mother, his sweetheart, he went to sleep.

CHAPTER IV

Martin had lived in the Bowery a week before he realized that the sounds and odors seemed less offensive to him; that his acquaintances and his surroundings appeared less brutal. Each night in the hotel some man died loudly in his bed. It was an incident. Martin felt himself in a husk through which no poison could penetrate. One day, in an effort to regain his lost perception he left the street, crossed old Italian town, passed barren, rock-like buildings and looked for the first time at Washington Square. He walked across the park, holding it all—the grassy air, the fat babies, the old men with tanned, bald heads and individualities he'd never seen before nor understood. On one bench he saw several of his comrades on Relief. They were sitting quietly in the warm, fall sunshine. "Talked out," thought Martin, "and glad of it." He passed them, nodded, smiled and wondered why they thought him so apart, youthfully looking at them for an answer instead of at himself. He then crossed over to the circular pool in the center of the Square where boys and girls were romping in the thin spray of the fountain. In the anticipation of the approaching colder weather when the water would be stopped and this late play ended for a time, they seemed more active than usual. "Why is it," Martin asked himself, "that I feel kinship among the antitheses—these gay children or the devil!"

One child, like all the others but for thinner legs and an abundance of pale freckles, looked up at him and asked if he would watch her shoes and stockings while she waded. This responsibility was heartening; and he sat down on the edge of the pool while she went in rather cautiously. The child seemed even more fragile among the vigorous ones who were shoving each other and kicking up the water. For a long time Martin watched her. "She might have been my own little daughter," he said aloud at last; and immediately the mist seemed to fall more heavily from the fountain and the play to become more violent until he wished it over with. The thought of home—a child—serenities attendant, brought the conflicting inquiries of his life more sharply before him and he brooded. A few drops of cold water in his face stopped the course of these reflections and he looked up frowning, his eyebrows raised. It was the little girl. She was laughing at his discomposure.

"You looked funny," she said.

"Did I?"

"Yes. That's why I threw the water. You looked cross. Did I keep you too long?"

"Not at all," he answered, smiling at her. "You know quite well that wasn't it at all. Furthermore, I shouldn't be astonished if you *did* know, right now, why I was cranky."

This amused her again.

"You're the funniest person I ever knew," she said. "You talk like a teacher."

"I'm not a teacher; I'm a pupil," Martin replied. "And I'm funny because I study funny things."

"What kind of funny things?" asked the child, looking excited.

"Many things. I study lady tigers that take off their stripes every night and put them on in the morning quite differently and——"

"Why do they do that?" interrupted the girl.

"So they will be in style," he continued seriously. "And I study dentist birds that repair alligators' teeth; and mice that fly upside down."

"Why!" exclaimed the girl somewhat indignantly, "I never heard such stories in my life!"

"That isn't half," said Martin. "Be very quiet now. Don't move. Do you see that fly that lit on my knee? He's looking for something to eat. There. He's found it. Maybe I spilled sugar on my pants this morning. But do you see what he's doing before he eats? He's washing his face with his forelegs."

The little girl watched carefully and saw the insect dip its head and bring its arms across its face like a brush. Suddenly she waved at it and the fly spun away.

"I can't stand them," she said.

"Just the same," Martin nodded, "it washed its face."

"It isn't as funny as the tiger," the girl concluded. "Tell me how a tiger can take off its stripes. Does it hurt?"

"Of course not." Martin stood up. "I have to go now."

The little girl put on her shoes.

"I wish you'd come again to-morrow. If you do, I'll bring my ball."

"That will be fun," called Martin as he walked away. Going back to his hotel he thought of this blue-eyed youngster and how great it would be to tell her fairy tales every night and buy her sandals and her frocks. And with this picture came once more the vision of all the rest of it—a wife's head on his shoulder, a fireplace, and yes—a pipe. He wondered then where in the world a finer shadow was leading him—a search for mysteries without substance or reason. At that moment he was a tired and a lonely man, quite willing to exchange a pound of mysticism and ideals, hard-won from depth to depth, for one ounce of level complacency. But after the first bitterness had worn off he was the same desperate young lover of the physiostatic tides of force that subtly pull and push until out of sheer pity they permit the frail skeleton to slip up on the sands of its desire where the hollow star, so followed, lies desolate and discontent.

The next day he was glad to see the child again. Her good humor freed him—was pure liberation from the constriction of the Bowery. She called out to him at once.

"Hello, teacher."

"I'd rather you said 'Martin.'"

"Is that your first name?"

"Yes."

"And you don't mind if I call you that?"

"Of course not."

"Well," she said deliberately, "my name is Alice."

"A pretty name." Martin appeared abstracted.

"I don't like it. But I can't help it. I'd rather be called 'Betty.'" She held out her hand. "Here's my ball. Let's play by the Arch."

They bounced it back and forth until Alice was tired.

"You can't throw it on top," she declared, sitting down on the curb.

Martin examined the light and badly worn tennis ball and measured the distance to the top of the great Arch.

"You're probably right," he agreed. But he gave a mighty heave and the ball just rolled over the edge where it remained. This amused Alice; but Martin was annoyed. He stood looking up at the top ledge of the Arch for several minutes. At last, however, he said, "Come along," for he remembered a drug store near by in which he had seen some tennis racquets.

A policeman had been watching them play ball and Martin thought the observation had been casual; but when they made ready to leave the park the suspicion on the man's face had become so obvious that it brought Martin up with a start. From surprise, he changed to anger; and when they passed the patrolman he stared with such fury at the officer that Alice questioned him. Martin did not answer her, but talked on rapidly about the tennis ball. Then he began to reconsider the situation. It was true that the policeman had been justified. This was New York—a thick, practical city with an imperative demand for the protection of its children. Martin's anger abated; and when he and Alice reached the drug store he deliberately put an end to his thoughts and premonitions and bought her a fine, new ball. The matter-of-fact way she took it pleased him more than any thanks she could have given him; for it meant he was accepted as a friend.

The little girl insisted that he return to the park next day, explaining that he should use her present first. And when she went dancing away, Martin smiled so broadly that the intense, deft lines of his face were strangely softened. This mood remained until he reached the Bowery, but in his room was completely lost in its solitude. Apprehension for his friendship for this child turned the channels of his mind toward new rivulets, each more forbidding than its predecessor, until he realized there was no oasis of sweetness in the barrens of his choosing. His temporary home, his very style and itinerant manner of living were contributory fences to the land beyond the streets—a land he felt he had invaded. He decided to tell little Alice that he was going across the ocean again, where there were bees that neither stung nor gathered honey, where lady tigers—and then, more tired than he knew, Martin slept.

He saw Alice first the next day and called out cheerily. But the little girl was quiet. She was holding the new tennis ball in both hands and her eyes were lowered.

"What's the matter?" asked Martin, surprised.

She looked up hesitatingly and Martin was shocked by the expression on her face. He found it difficult to analyze, but there was hurt, and fear, and he thought even horror there.

"My mother told me to never play with you again," said Alice, and her voice was so thin and far away it sounded like a tiny pipe. "Mother said to give this to you," and she held out the new tennis ball.

Martin put his hand around it. He was not looking at Alice anymore, nor apparently thinking of her; for his vision was directed beyond—at a disassociated blot of ugliness upon the sky; and he spoke so softly that the girl could but faintly hear.

"A voice like a reed in an Indian wind," he said. "Like a tender, Indian reed." Then, without addressing the child, he passed her and walked, with eyes implacably bemused, toward the corner of sky that held the dark and obscene smudge.... That afternoon, upon a street he'd never seen before, he remembered curiously it had been the first time he had cried in a great while.

In the PINE LEAF, next morning, his eyes were clear, his skin bright in the sun; but with all of it, he counted every measure of his heart. This was a dead passage—a ship without wings—men beside him shaving without faces. There was no hastiness in his action, though; and with impassible restraint he left the Bowery, its fretful entrances and lanterns thick with sickness.

He went uptown to the Relief Employment Station and stood in line again. Behind and before him, such pitiful neatness would formerly have brought the thought of laughter or poor tears. No more.

A counselor interviewed them quickly. There was a card on his desk marked MR. ROBERTS. Martin studied him with concentration, knowing that this man through whom he might be placed demanded understanding, subtle coyness and perhaps, beauty; for he saw a person hesitant in sex and yet requiring it; a man lurid of cheek, yet pale; a contradiction with a flush abnormal as its pallor. The look of Roberts was more theory than fact; although Martin thought, amusedly, that certainly this personage, most elegant, existed almost regally. The counselor's eyebrows, alert and thin and dark, commanded all his face. His deep-set cheeks and bold, firm chin absolved too bright, too wide a pouting lower lip. His hair, compressed and black, cut strongly in his temples and took away the color from his eyes. "This masterpiece," thought Martin, "should be done in platinum; with alabaster, ebony and careful points of gold." And then, he found that he was next.

Roberts glanced at him.

"Sit down," he said. "Are you waiting for a ship?" His eyes opened wide, closed intimately, then opened wide again.

"No," said Martin. "I want a job ashore."

"Have you had college experience?"

"Yes. Five years."

Roberts grew cautious.

"Really! Post-graduate work?"

"No. I was never graduated. It was off and on."

"Why?"

Martin hesitated a moment.

"I suppose because the electives interested me much more than the requisites."

Roberts spoke impersonally.

"A diploma is quite valuable in getting a job," he said.

Martin smiled.

"That's right."

The adviser looked at him questioningly.

"I wasn't trying to be rude," said Martin, "but the situation appeared somewhat ridiculous."

"I can well imagine," answered Roberts, smiling back at him. "I wish everyone out of a job could develop the same sense of humor."

"It isn't a sense of humor," replied Martin. "It's a form of embarrassment. I used to see little girls act this way in school."

The counselor nodded.

"An acute analysis," he said.

"I didn't mean that," Martin added quickly.

"Of course not." Roberts was thoughtful. His eyes had assumed a knowing look. His voice was unprofessional and the color in his cheeks had become more prominent. At last, he picked up a card. "What kind of work do you prefer?" he asked.

"I've done a good many things."

"Have you specialized in anything?"

"No."

"That's curious. One would think that a young man with your intelligence would——"

Martin interrupted him.

"I'm not intelligent," he said. "I'm imaginative. Sometimes it gives the illusion of intelligence." Then, slightly bewildered by his own statement, Martin reflected on this uncalled-for abstraction until he forgot where he was and sat absently, with an appearance so unusual that Roberts, who was watching him keenly, spoke one word half under his breath; and Martin, taken from his musing by the unexpected character of the exclamation, said sharply, "What was that?"

But the adviser, disregarding the question, shrugged his shoulders—basilisk in state once more.

"Are you really ingenuous," he asked, "or are you kidding me? One would think that a young man of your—education—then, would have prepared himself to meet inevitable economic problems."

"No." Martin shook his head. "I'm not ingenuous, either. I'm conscious. I'm too conscious; it makes me brittle. Nor am I kidding you. I told you the truth. It is curious that I didn't adjust myself. I tried to think about it occasionally but it didn't do any good. Other things seemed more important."

Roberts was listening intently.

"What other things?" he asked.

"Oh—pretending. Sometimes other things; but mostly just pretending."

"Pretending what?"

"Pretending that I was everything except what I am—that things were different from what they are. I thought that life would move on and somehow carry me with it. I have no way to substantiate this; but all my life I've known that the finish was illusive—that it was best for me to float with the current until an eddy whirled me into my right course."

"Have you struck the eddy?"

Again Martin felt the intimacy of Roberts' tone and frowned.

"Perhaps you misinterpreted my question," said the adviser coolly. "I asked if you were in your proper medium."

Martin flushed and started to rise; but Roberts lifted his hand in a gesture of restraint.

"I really know how you feel," he said gently. "Perhaps that's why I spoke as I did. In your capacity as a job hunter, however, there can be no room for individual conflict; particularly in your relationship with one who, understanding, offers both his professional facilities and," he said more slowly, "his friendship—" all the time looking directly at Martin with the strange color coming and going as he spoke.

"Cheeks—like a lost woman," said Martin, trying to stop the sentence before it was out of his mouth.

Roberts stared at him for a second in astonishment. Then he went into uncontrollable laughter.

But Martin remained unsmiling.

"I'm sorry I said that," he remarked severely. "I really can't excuse it or explain it."

"Well, I'm not sorry," said Roberts, leaning forward. "It's the first genuine fun I've had in a long time. I'd like more of it. But I'll confess—it's disruptive to the morale of the office." Still amused, he glanced around him. His speech was high and unbalanced. "However," he went on, becoming more practical, "I'm going to get you a job."

"Well—" said Martin.

"No, no," insisted Roberts. "I'm glad I'm in a position to help you." Once more, he looked swiftly around him and continued in a lower voice. "I think it's wonderful to be able to help people. Don't you?"

"Yes."

Roberts hesitated.

"It's about the only thing there is in the world," he said in a still lower tone. "Isn't it?"

"Yes."

He wrote his address on the card and handed it to Martin.

"I want you to come to my residence this evening. There, we'll work out your economic destiny." He smiled faintly.

Martin accepted the card, smiling also, wondering if he really looked this subjective and, if not, why Roberts' obvious attitude.

"Very well," he said, facing with curiosity a phenomenon before its occurrence. "What hour?"

"Nine."

Martin stood up and nodded slightly. It seemed to him that the employees were watching him evasively as he left.

The great city arose with Martin and marched to its hysteria of noon. Then, slowly falling till evening, burst into flame, quieted and slept. Gigantic presses told of her neurosis. In this immutable turning flashed black lines of the growth of the disease. Its people, wooden-eyed, marionette, accepted with grimness; their minds numb and evasive. They held their buildings higher in the air—pointed them like caricatures of things that had gone, of things still to come. But their thoughts were buried. Hidden under music and dust and smothered in light, the precious balance died....

The moon, free of clouds, shone through the blinds and into the living-room of Roberts' apartment. A crystal vase, without flowers, directed the dim light into a corner. Small ebon figures held out their arms. Roberts was wearing a dark Russian blouse. To Martin, he appeared more fabulous and crystalline than in his office. His flush was constant—so determinate that Martin guessed it artificial, noticing however, that the native, restless color had moved into his eyes. There it remained, fluctuating and searching until it seemed disturbingly like the luminant phosphorus of uncertain, yet violent leaves and shadows Martin had avoided in the tropics. Roberts had been ambiguous throughout the evening and Martin felt that he knew him no better. But he watched the adviser closely—watched each apparent banality for a *double entendre* and speculated upon the inevitable. He countered each triviality; and made no attempt to acquiesce in a secretive understanding.

Roberts now grew silent for long intervals. With a compelling, but a quiet vision, he observed his young friend. The room had become warmer and frost was forming on the window panes. Once, Roberts arose and ran his finger across the glass, leaving a clear, narrow trail from which fell small drops of moisture.

"It's colder outside," he said.

"Much colder," replied Martin.

Roberts came over and sat down near him.

"Then I take it the warmth of our civilization has its appeal after all?"

In a different fashion Martin confused the scene in as remote and complex a pattern as his friend. Deeply muscled by the sea, he nevertheless was finely drawn as a lady's slipper and as quick of kicking to the notice. Roberts was aware of this and other features that, to him, were more demanding and elemental; for in his bleached eyes Martin carried the ocean; there was the smell of salt about him—and, Roberts thought, in a sort of painful hysteria, probably sand in his hair. His face, out of the Indies, with its stain from the sun and from his youth, should not hold dignity; and yet it did, in such a steady, high intensity that Roberts caught his breath on it. Martin rubbed his foot over the rug.

"'Warmth'—of your civilization?" he repeated. "I'm astonished."

"Perhaps the word was ill-chosen," answered Roberts. "But whatever our qualities may be, I hope that you prefer them to those which emanate from the fo'c'sle of a West Indian freighter. Now, it is my turn to be astonished. Why did you say '*your* civilization'? Are you not—" Roberts hesitated, "one of us?"

"I'm a seaman. We don't fit in anywhere on land." Roberts changed—seemed more severe in the passing light.

"This bold and masterful deception of all seamen is, to me, Martin, a shabby thing. I see it as a trite avoidance of each standard which, although sometimes unbeautiful, is present in the world. Such life, irrelevant and irreverent of all doctrine, is but a switching of responsibilities—a turning of the back that's shielded by mere boastfulness. In honesty to myself, I must admit that there's a careless beauty in its physical, sweet shape—the wrap of dungarees—and forgetfulness in song. And yet, it's impotent. Quite sterile in its loveliness.... And finally, I see the man—the dungarees—the very songs in pity." The color surged into Roberts' cheeks and he leaned nearer. "You've abused yourself, Martin. There's been dishonesty in plenty for yourself. And what, dear boy, quite comes of it?"

"Perhaps I do it to hear you drain yourself," said Martin dryly.

Roberts answered with immediate fierceness.

"I don't believe I've ever talked this way before. But I'll use your method now, Martin. You need a job. From your card I noticed that you've been a printer. Can you operate a linotype?"

"Yes."

"Then I'll arrange things. Now, in heaven's name—let's leave this miserable economic status. It's impossible."

Martin frowned slightly.

"But isn't that why I'm here? You said—"

Roberts' blue eyes became darker.

"Why not quote our professional introduction literally?" he asked. "You were trying to amuse yourself, not help yourself. Why did you do it? Why do you do it now?" With difficulty he restrained his anger. "A job should be considered first, before this premature folly." He stopped, put out his cigarette and waited, only to be startled by Martin's sudden laughter. He raised his shoulders arrogantly. "You are entertained then, by emotion?"

"No," said Martin. "Rather, by a grotesque episode."

"Grotesque?" Roberts seemed more contemptuous than indignant.

"Indeed," said Martin, inflamed by this dry attitude. "Grotesque. Absurd. A farcical horse-opera of a lost decade revived in different ribbons, different sex. This renovated melodrama is enough to make one sick!—a pale girl with a stack of mortgage documents fastened in her long, blonde hair, arguing for her virtue with a Russian blouse!"

Roberts listened with fascination. His eyes became solicitous. The tenor of the room altered swiftly.

"You *could* have been, Martin," he said in a breath and quite excitedly. "Yes, you could have been." And then, between his lips, and with no intended insult, Roberts spoke the same one word that he had whispered to Martin that afternoon.

Martin looked at the man and knew this exclamation had never been so used. Without changing his expression he reconstructed Roberts' face from the fragments of thought that had suddenly charged the room. The pink, hairless mask moved closer—without eyes, without nose, with a single hole in the lower part and a single, dreadful sound protruding.

Along the blinds lay a few ravelings of light. The face regained its natural shape. Only an undermovement of greediness and a distant, crying sound remained.

Roberts walked over to a cabinet and brought back a colored liqueur which he offered to Martin, pouring it slowly and meticulously into Holland glass. He was once more the host, aloof, charming, courteous.

"How do you think you will like your job?" he asked. "I'm sending you to a friend of mine—a Mr. Jackson. He'll see that you get along."

"There's no reason to lie," Martin answered. "I won't like it. It'll be wretched—sitting there, pounding a machine that is more efficient than I am."

"Then tell me—why do you want a job ashore? Why don't you go back to sailoring? Or, do you really like that sort of thing after all?"

"It's a free life," Martin answered slowly.

"And this is not?"

"I don't know. But your evaluations interest me."

Roberts became genuinely curious. All of the coldness left his face and only the deeper lines of his integrity remained.

"What is it that disturbs you, Martin?" he asked gently. "The past or the future? Or the shadow behind the lamp?"

"I imagine the shadows are worst."

"You intensify them, don't you?"

"Perhaps I even create some of them. We demand contrast."

"Mmm." Roberts, his head nodding loosely, studied him. "You have something in your eyes, Martin," he said. "If you were a woman I would forget my business, my complacency. I would want to run away with you—if you were a woman."

Martin hesitated a moment before answering.

"If I were a woman—you would not be interested," he said at last.

Roberts' face grew white under the rouge.

"You are candid. But my temperament should not disturb our friendship."

Martin leaned over, closing his hand about the adviser's wrist and holding it tightly.

"What do you mean by 'temperament'?" he asked.

The insolent red came back into Roberts' cheeks.

"That was young, Martin, my lad. It was cruel." Then, sensing the flux of blood upon his wrist more keenly, he felt curiously strong. Happiness, nostalgia and strength merged and fused until his mind turned slowly and hung staring down upon the stages of his life. Two pale stars drifted upward and dimmed. Roberts looked into his mother's eyes.

CHAPTER V

Rio lay on a bed in a room on Fourteenth Street. He was in a bad humor. A back tooth ached and he sucked hot smoke from a cigarette against it. The Relief authorities had told him that Martin had signed up, but had disappeared without report. Had he left New York, or had he found a job? Had he changed his mind and caught a ship—Martin was too slippery for an idea to hold on to. Rio's irritation increased.

"He never was solid," he said to the girl sitting across the room.

"What do you care?" she answered. "You ain't in love with him."

Rio dropped the cigarette butt, pressed his thumb on the coal and rubbed it into the floor.

"Don't get mad now, sweetheart," the girl said. "I try to be funny. And that's more than you done."

Rio sat up, took his coat and left. There was another chance. Martin might have registered at the Employment Station. Rio walked along Third Avenue, watching faces, stopping frequently to glance inside the saloons. A long line of men, waiting outside one of the Relief restaurants, attracted him. One of the men held out his hand.

"Two for a nickel, buddy," he said, holding his fingers over the meal-tickets.

"Three for a nickel, pisan," said Rio, walking on.

It was late afternoon when he reached the Employment Station. Roberts was at his desk when Rio approached. He was turning over the cards in some files and did not look up immediately. Rio, a rollicking expression in his eyes, put his hands on his hips and began to pose slightly. He looked like a male bear under morphine. The adviser glanced at him briefly, saw the attitude and dismissed it.

"Come back to-morrow. It's five o'clock," he said.

"I don't want to sign up," answered Rio, grinning now. "I'm lookin' for a shipmate."

Roberts shook his head.

"They'll help you at Central Relief Headquarters. This is Employment." He spoke peremptorily.

"I know," said Rio. "He signed up over there and never checked out, but he ain't around. I thought maybe he found a job here."

"Five o'clock," Roberts repeated, looking annoyed. "My secretary will check over the list for you."

"His name is Devaud," insisted Rio. "Martin Devaud. He's a sort of young guy."

"Devaud?" Roberts' eyes were round. "Have I heard the name? A thin, crippled fellow?"

"No."

Roberts took a pencil and filled in a blank card.

"We aren't permitted to give information concerning these men, but if such a person should ever come in, I'll give him your name."

"My name's Rio."

"What shall I tell him you wanted—if I see him?"

Rio stuck his thumb against his chin.

"You don't need to tell him nothin'." He leaned on the desk.

Roberts looked at him stiffly. The color surged into his cheeks.

"Is that all? I'm accustomed to accepting, not giving information. Unless you give me the particulars I need, it will be impossible to coöperate with you. Is this boy wanted for any misdemeanor?"

Rio's face turned a heavy red.

"This boy ain't wanted for 'any misdemeanor.' This boy's a friend of mine. He's on the beach. I want to see him."

Roberts dropped the card on his desk. He showed the stamp of discipline.

"Have you ever been thrown out of anywhere?"

"Not by ten like you."

"Fortunately there are gentlemen here vested with that privilege." The adviser nodded across the room at several policemen.

Rio laughed.

"Fortunately? Gentlemen?" He walked away, then turned. "I'll see you later, Mister!"

Roberts watched him leave. Powerful brute, he thought. Rio! A shipmate. A friend. How good a friend? Roberts put his finger to his lips. Certainly not a good contact for Martin. Damn the intimacy of the sea—like prison, like Devil's Island, holding men together, destroying all the niceties of camaraderie.... Were those stories true about men on ships? A sordid subject exaggerated out of all proportion—still, some of it must be true. That big fellow. Was he? He had been unwarrantedly excited.

Rio left the Station. Mr. Fish inside would look good with his teeth out. Strictly fruit, huh? By God, these governors! Well, what of it?... Where to look now? Martin wasn't trying to ship. He wasn't at the Hall or on the docks. He wasn't on Relief. He hadn't got a job at the Station—or was Roberts lying. "Gentlemen here vested with that privilege!"

Rio took a train to Forty-second Street. The bright, flashing lights of Broadway shut out the early stars. The hurrying expanse of faces had less individuality than waves. There was no bond between their eyes and his, impassionate. They were as eternal, as indestructible as ants. They passed him, died, were born and passed again; a long, driving throng, pale and imperishable, typed and counterparted into immortality. Rio turned away, disgusted. Martin wasn't there. He'd die in such a sea. God bless sailors and their drifted lives.

Rio returned to his room and lay down on the bed, nervous from its quiet. He saw the unused pitcher—one of dignity; with whiteness and good height. It made him slightly sick. There was a girl's bag on a chair; and one article, too intimate, beside it. He rolled over. Suddenly the doorknob rattled.

"What is it?" he called out, impatiently.

Two girls walked in, smiling, red-cheeked.

"Hello, Rio," one of them said. "Did you find your buddy?"

"No."

"That's too bad, Rio."

"Look here," said Rio, unsmiling. "This is amateur night. Now beat it."

CHAPTER VI

Martin worked into the routine of the printing plant. There were thirty linotypes around him, shielding him with their clamor. He found retreat in their noise and liked to feel that he was a lever or cam, bending or turning inconspicuously in the tide of words. He hid his revulsion as an automaton and mixed his sweat with the oil of the machinery. There was an acrid taste of hot lead in the air, a taste of ink, the taste and rattle of matrices. Martin could feel his shoulders bend into the machine—could see the horizon shrink to the area of light on his copy. Type, type, type—up with the line. Feel the grinding of the fellow, pressing, digesting. Out with the slug, searing hot and good to calloused fingers.

When evening came and work was over, Martin straightened his back and went to the wash-trough. The gritty soap smelled good, like candy. He associated it with freedom. Outside, he felt like running—jumping a hydrant, racing a car. He wanted to shout at the slanting sunlight.

He lived uptown, at one of the most inexpensive club-hotels for men. The rooms were clean and, from the standpoint of his present earnings, the cost was reasonable. Most of the residents were hard-working fellows who needed a place to sleep. Martin read the recreational program; but women were not included in its itinerary, so he remained in his room or walked up and down the street.

He sat in his room, thinking to a point and back. The period seemed interminable. The break, the nervous ejaculation that would throw him out of this treadmill seemed further away than before. He remembered the sea and ships upon it, hot rain, salt and rust and bubbling, rising life. The memory filled his nose and lungs and mind.

"God damn," he said, and struck the wall with his hand.

The buzzer in his room sounded and he went to the house-phone in the hall to answer.

"Hello, Martin. How are you?"

"Hello, Roberts."

"I have a surprise, Martin. There's a little party and I'd like you to come with me. Just a few people. Would you like to?"

"Yes. Yes, I'd like to."

"Good. I'll come by for you. It will all be very informal, very casual."

"Indeed it will," said Martin.

"What's that?"

"I said, indeed it will."

"What do you mean?"

Martin could feel Roberts' eyes over the wire, slightly protruding, and his eyebrows moving gently up and down.

"I meant nothing. When will you be here?"

"Oh. Soon. It's unexpected."

"Thanks," said Martin. "Till then."

He went back to his room and shaved. Next he put on one black sock and one gray one—not for style's sake, nor to be eccentric. When he was dressed he looked earnestly in the mirror.

"Pale," he said. He sat down on the bed and stared at the wall. It seemed a long time to him before Roberts rapped on the door.

"I'm glad to see you," Martin exclaimed with relief. "It's you all right—you and your intolerable verve."

Roberts laughed.

"Good heavens! What finery!" he cried, looking at Martin's suit, which was pressed.

Roberts was wearing a Derby. There was a narrow beaver collar on his dark topcoat and under the fur was a light, silken scarf. He carried white knitted gloves. He stood for a few moments in the doorway looking at Martin. Then, throwing his hat and gloves on the bed, he went over to the mirror and adjusted his scarf, observing himself carefully.

Martin lay back in his chair and watched him, a twinkle in his eye.

"You're beautiful, all right," he said.

Roberts turned around and nodded seriously.

"I know I am," he answered. "But there is more character than feature—that's what pleases me."

Martin laughed good-naturedly and got out of his chair.

"Both qualities are necessary for complicity with women, aren't they?"

Roberts gave him a slow, cynical smile and they left.

Martin was sorry that he had accepted the invitation to the party when he met his hostess, for her immoderate greeting brought about a sudden loneliness within him. Among the guests this feeling of desolation grew stronger. Their faces and smiles seemed vaporous and foreign. One large fellow grinned persistently, his eyes unfocused. Only the hostess retained her buoyancy. She bounded from person to person with an amazing levity. There were sentences all over the room, but they were incoherent, more porous than the faces. Feeling helpless, Martin went to a corner and sat down. One of the guests sang "*The Bells of St. Mary's*" backwards, and Martin began to doze.

Through his discomfort he heard a new voice. Clear, apart from the conversation, it held his attention. He opened his eyes. Near the fireplace at the other end of the room, on a large divan and leaning far back into it, sat a blond young man, his legs crossed. In spite of his careless attitude, Martin was conscious of the earnestness with which the other regarded him. Fully aware of Martin's observation the man continued to look at him squarely. At last he sat straighter, brushed his hair into place with a sweep of his hand and gave Martin an unusually provocative smile. Its good nature was genuine, but Martin kept to his own melancholy and somber stare. He had never seen a man with such apparent knowledge of his blood and caste, nor one so youthfully wise. Altogether, Martin saw in him a weathered, inbred prototype of himself, an experienced apprentice. It was the soil, the rash, the water Martin needed; and he continued to stare like a child absorbed. It was not until the young man turned to his companion that Martin realized that a woman as individual—more quickly individual, held his strange friend's arm. Under Martin's continued gaze she placed her other hand upon the blond man's sleeve and looked up at him questioningly.

In the half-light of the room Martin could see her profile—could feel the intensity of her womanhood; and it caused him to forget, momentarily, her companion. Holding her throat that way, the way her breast rose under her satin gown, the unnatural silver in her dark hair caused Martin to speculate—to wonder at his own abreaction. He felt awkward and indecisive, yet withal, an inconsiderate urge and tightness under his collar. He could scarcely restrain himself from walking over and speaking. But he stayed quiet instead, and felt hot and cold at each thought, and finally decided he would just go away from sheer itching. When at last the woman did turn to look at him he continued to stare at her for a moment the same way he had done with the young man. Then he found that his thoughts were going down the satin dress to the slim waist and hips that seemed to be moving under his watery eyes, and down at last to her stockings.

"It isn't her legs," he thought. "It's her stockings and every damnable, secret place they lead to." Looking up again he saw her young clear lips, tattooed;

and, he imagined, caps of equally bright color under her dress. Her eyes were the most beautiful of all of her, and yet the worst; for Martin, in amazement that they should translate his idiom so perfectly, felt that they were turning him inside out so that each thought and desire could be read plainly. However, there was something else about the woman that made him want to go away, or come, or do anything as long as it was she who sent him away, or took him in.

"I'm mad," he said. "She's nothing but a brood-mare. A wild, teasing brood-mare stamping for me. But I wish I had her in the grass where she should lie." And he turned his flushed, wet face toward Roberts who was approaching.

"At whom are you looking?" asked the adviser, suspicion in his tone.

"I was watching," Martin answered.

"Where are you looking?" persisted the adviser.

"I believe I should go home," said Martin briefly.

Roberts looked around in the direction of Martin's stare and smiled without amusement.

"Come along," he said, sighing and taking his friend by the arm. "Either one was inevitable, I suppose."

Without answering, Martin walked with him to the couch where the young man and his companion were sitting.

"I want you both to know Martin," said Roberts. "He was just going home on account of you. I wonder what he meant, Deane," he continued, ignoring the young man who stood up, smiling unconcernedly. "What did he mean, Drew?" he asked, this time of the man; and without waiting for an answer, sat down rather sulkily, peering from under his eyelids at Deane as though he was displeased, for Martin and Drew had moved a short distance away from the divan and had begun to talk together.

Deane looked at Roberts with understanding, her brilliant lips open, her cool, dark eyes filled with indulgence.

"Your friend looks interesting enough," she said. "Why does he upset you? Isn't he your protegé? Dear Ella," she glanced toward the hostess, "intimated as much."

"Damn her fat tongue," said Roberts. "But," he continued wearily, "I wish he were, Deane. I'm part of him and he doesn't know it—or pretends not to.

I gave him a rotten job. A job full of grit and lead and ashes and he won't—he won't———"

Deane seemed a little contemptuous.

"No?"

Roberts shook his beautiful head and turned away despairingly.

"A young girl in her first romance," said Deane, speaking now with an undertone of anger.

"You only think me so," went on the adviser, still desperate. "But I've waited for this a thousand years and it goes in one bleak night to my one dear friend," he looked up at Drew who was still standing before Martin, "or," he ended bitterly, glancing once more at the woman beside him, "to you. I tell you, I know him, Deane. I saw it in his eyes. He was watching you so. I never saw him watch me that way. Never!"

Deane looked at him in amazement.

"You?" she cried. "Watch *you*?"

Roberts, observing her, sat straighter, became more haughty.

"Yes," he said quietly. "He never looked that way at me. And *I'm* mad because of necessity and not an empty wish! It's the bone of me—it's my flesh and the rancor of centuries!" He stood up, trembling.

"Drew!" he called commandingly. He was white, beautiful and Satanic in his rage.

Drew started, looked around at him and the two young men stepped nearer.

"Roberts!" cried Drew in consternation.

But the adviser merely waved his hand.

"Roberts!" said Martin slowly. His eyes half closed, and in the space where the iris showed came a harsh light as if misdirected robots were moving behind the lashes. His face, still burned by the sea, became intent. It was as though he were concentrating upon a floating object. Motile, sensitive lines drew around the corners of his eyes and turned from rust to white. Under this stare, Roberts faltered in his attitude of severity; and wheeling suddenly, without excuse, his hands half out, walked swiftly across the room to the buffet where he stood, leaning one arm upon it.

Deane sat quietly, watching Martin. There was now a look of contempt upon his face. It formed about the fine cheeklines, which by themselves seemed to curl until the face solidified and grew articulate with sour flutes of madness. He took a step toward Roberts and Drew caught him by the arm.

"What is it, Martin?" he asked. "In heaven's name, don't look that way! Be careful! Everyone is watching you. Stay here with us!"

Abruptly, Martin sat down with Deane, so close that she could feel him tremble. She looked up quickly at Drew, who nodded, and with a brief, inscrutable smile, left them and went to Roberts.

As he waited for Roberts to speak, there was a tactfulness and grace about him which the adviser could not evade.

"Drew," he said at last, "listen to me. It's dreadful." He paused to look steadily at his friend. "I can't work without thinking about him. I can't eat. It's a damnable obsession! And to think!—with such a shameful lad!"

Drew appeared listless.

"Is that the word, Roberts?"

"It's the smallest I can think of."

Drew took a purple flagon containing a cordial from the buffet, holding it so that he might find its color from the room's dim light.

"No," he said, "'shameful' is not the word. Rather I should say," he hesitated, "'shameless.'"

Roberts regarded him carefully.

"What is your interpretation of that word?"

"The usual one," said Drew slowly. "A lacking of, Roberts. Not a diverting of."

"You think then, that he has no moral sense at all," said Roberts, as though in agreement.

Drew tilted the flagon, observing the changing violet lights as the clear, thick drops of the liqueur ran individually down the neck of the bottle.

"It isn't this important, dear," he said. "It *can't* be this important." He was still observing the flagon. "Do you know this amazing drink?" he asked. "It comes from a small flower that grows only in the Bavarian Alps, and at an altitude of between four and five thousand feet. This very discriminating blossom is called the 'blue dormant.' ... A boy once pointed out to me the place where they grew," he said reflectively.

"Oh! Damn you, Drew!" said Roberts miserably. "Answer my question. You've often told me that you, yourself, were unmoral, not immoral—are you drawing a likeness?"

Drew replaced the Gebirge Enzian and faced Roberts, sincerity in his voice.

"You were terribly upset and I chatted a bit. That's all. I don't even know what I said, and I don't believe you meant what you said."

"Oh, I do." Roberts nodded his head grimly. "Indeed I do. Look over there." He motioned slightly in the direction of Martin and Deane who were speaking intimately with each other. "Do you see that, my love?" he went on contemptuously. "As catching as flypaper and as promiscuous. And yet I can't help myself. The very way he looks at Deane puts arrows into me." Suddenly Roberts' eyes filled with tears, and half choking, he turned from the guests and from Ella, who was hovering nearby and who seemed frightfully amused. Instinctively, Drew stepped close to him, his protective shadow encircling the bent shoulders of his friend, hiding the quiet sob.

When Drew had gone to Roberts, Deane placed her hand on Martin's for a moment, then withdrew it gently, without speaking.

"It was a kiss," thought Martin. "She's bringing me across the river.... A proud woman, with her hair like the lights of a ship.... A woman sheltered, but one inalienable to love.... I wish she'd smile again.... God help me! She's on my trail like a hound! I might as well have spoken through a trumpet." Turning toward her he said, "I really shouldn't have come here. I feel out of place. But," he hesitated, "I thought that it might be ... and it is," he added shortly.

Deane started to touch him again, then stopped, for Martin looked so eager and shy that she became the same way.

"Damn it!" thought Martin. "What a trip!" ... "Well," he said aloud, "it shouldn't have been."

Deane laughed softly. Martin could see the black diagonal stripes across her red kid slippers and this cabalistic signal took his thoughts back wantonly to the Church where so often as a child he had released his theological rut into the dark precipices of the Cathedral. Those fearfully sweet memories came sharply into his mind now and he remembered how the vast, swelling notes of the organ had lifted him up and rocked him into peacefulness. Nostalgia overcame him as he continued to gaze at the little red and black slippers. Then he grimly blocked these crevices of the mind which exude a flavor too ghastly even for the pith and stench of the undersoul, and he spoke again, this time without thought or conception.

"I mean," he said, "that for a long time the parties I've gone to have been so apart from this sort of thing—that is, apart dimensionally. The people were plain and simple. There were rivers, mostly yellow, and bushes and trees to lend informality, and all the music came out of parrots. Once, along such a river-path, I met a man with a nose as broad as my fist. His dark skin had such heavy needlework upon it that it was beveled like tooled leather. His feet splayed like a water-creature's. We couldn't speak each other's language, but we both understood food. It made us friends. We had mashed rice, water, and some kind of grape he'd brought out of the forest over his shoulder." Martin stopped abruptly at Deane's curious look.

"I'm sure there was that and more in the tropics, Martin," she said deliberately. "There was the Right Honorable Lord Jesus stamping through the jungle."

Martin, embarrassed and yet amused, looked steadily at Deane.

"Such things can, and should be reduced," he said. "I'd have been impatient, myself." He hesitated, unable to keep from staring at the soft line of her throat where each shadow lay like a bruise upon her skin. This intimation of her feeling for light, of limbs too tender, made him lift his intense eyes to her own which were even more brilliant. "Please," he continued, "will you please let me take you home?"

Now, Deane saw him differently, with more excitement. What an enigma! And what a charming transition from his faint braggadocio (or was it!) to this straightforward question. She knew that he was waiting for an answer, yet she was silent. Silent while they kept turning their heads to reassure each other like naughty children in the cool green brush and willows by a railroad track. They knew. They understood completely; and Martin, in this Roman anticipation, shivered; and when at last they did stand up to separate only for a moment they still seemed to cling together helplessly. Once, as they crossed the floor, Martin paused, and Deane, aware of his intention, went on alone. She disappeared into the hallway, and the sight of her sweet entirety, her gown, the thought beneath it made Martin caustic and erect. Only then did he look around to see that Drew and Roberts were observing him. As he came up to them, Drew greeted him warmly, but Roberts held his face away.

"We were talking of compassion," said Drew, smiling. "It takes sophistry, Martin." He turned to his other friend. "Isn't that true, Roberts?" he asked.

"It takes common sense," said the adviser.

"It takes that, too," said Martin. "It takes sophistry and common sense and a hundred other things. But I prefer to leave it to the Giver."

"Right," said Roberts angrily. "It takes the god-damned miserable Giver!" Then more softly, "Deane Idara is a remarkable woman, Martin. You realize that she has recently suffered a severe shock?"

"No! A shock, you say?"

Roberts' eyes shone above the sudden pallor of his cheeks.

"Yes," he said. "She lost her husband only a very short while ago."

"Why did you tell me that?" asked Martin rapidly. He tried to quiet himself, but he bit his lip and looked at Drew rather wildly. "I understand death. I too have died. I too have seen intimate death." The phosphorus shone again in his eyes. "Cowardly remark!" he said under his breath.

The adviser seemed to draw within himself, growing even more pale. He spoke sarcastically.

"Do you mean that you, too, Martin, have lost a husband?"

Martin glanced again at Drew who was standing motionless, expressionless, then back at Roberts. He could scarcely move his lips.

"I'm going home," he said. "Goodnight, Drew. And goodnight, Roberts."

"Goodnight," Drew answered, holding out his hand to detain the adviser who was automatically following. "Goodnight, Martin," Drew called after him again. Then, "Roberts!" he whispered uneasily, still holding his friend's arm. "You don't have even the foundation! *Won't* you be sensible?"

Deane Idara was standing at the door. Martin's shadow fell across her face and they left the apartment. Outside, the air was high and pointed with light. Crisp new stars whizzed over them, brightening the street. Martin could feel her arm get tighter and tighter, and his own breath became heavier until in the darkness between corner-lamps he swung her round to him and kissed her cold little wet lips. With his arms around her and the feel of her lips becoming warmer under his, he whispered, "I'll kill you. Oh, by God!—I'll kill you, I love you so!" And then he kissed her again until he felt himself just going away as he had thought he would. Deane was pressing as tightly as she could against him, but her head seemed to fall back too loosely and Martin kept saying, "I'll get a taxi, dear. I'll get a cab." He waved at several until one stopped, and after they had climbed inside he pulled Deane to him and asked, "Where are we going, dear?" She kissed him, and Martin could feel her breath on his cheek. The cab driver slumped down in his seat indifferently and lit a cigarette. "Where are we going, Deane?" Martin asked again.

"Not far," she answered, nodding to him feverishly. "Tell him to drive up the street. It's one sixty-nine...."

Her apartment was dim and motionless. A long window faced the line of city buildings. Martin and Deane stood before it, breathing the soundless air. In this black and white panorama he felt indistinct, separate from his identity. He had removed his topcoat and he imagined he could feel Deane's skin against his, so tight was her black gown. They stood by the window, holding each other in a sensuous embrace of expectation—of change of clime. Then he thought of her stockings and her sacramental slippers. They were furiously beautiful and revealing against the rug. Martin put his hand within her blouse and held it there while she pressed closely to him. He unslipped a button, then another, and another. "I've buck fever, Deane," he whispered hoarsely.

Deane shook her hair, her eyes blazing.

"You helpless bastard," cried Martin to himself.... "Let's break it, Deane," he whispered to her once more. "Let's break it completely," and he pulled the loosened gown from her white shoulders. "And here's mine," he went on, continuing the motion until his opened shirt and singlet were flat against her breast. "We'll call it the wild black clogs of Belgium, dearest," and he clenched his hard brown arms around her waist. Without speaking further he took her hand and led her into the adjoining room. He sat down on the gray paneled bed, pulling her surely beside him. Deane saw the slight trembling of his lips and the heavy expression of his eyes which stirred her with an intoxication that was close to fear. She was drawn by the swift pace of his emotion, yet held back by the certainty of his demand. Even as she was thinking, the rapid heartbeats against her became more rapid and the pressure of Martin's hands brought so definite a response that all vaporous abstractions were forgotten and she knew herself in an immediate physical presence. Wanting Martin as she did, the knowledge of his action brought no idle gestures; and she was quiet, with eyes half closed as she felt herself lifted, then rested, with Martin's arm for a pillow. Infinitesimal beads of moisture formed on Martin's temples as his hand caught the rim of her stocking, but the warm, soft flesh above it made him cry out softly. The very lights seemed tenderer and the very shadows kinder as these two lovers held each other. The night was penetrated by a question, by a sob; and all the cruelties and perversions of humanity were justified by this union—natural, unashamed and magnificent in simplicity and passion.

CHAPTER VII

Roberts waited near the printing plant the following afternoon. When Martin came out he went swiftly to him, holding out his hand. There was haggardness and strain—a formation of new lines in Roberts' face.

"I could hardly wait till you were through work to-day, Martin," he said anxiously. "I have been terribly distressed over last night. I feel that it was my mistake—entirely my mistake. I was overminded by my zealousness—or," he hesitated, "by my jealousy. You know how I feel about you. You do know, don't you?"

Martin, following his emotion, rather than the outposts of his mind which usually warned him, was drawn to Roberts by this speech, so painful and revealing.

"For God's sake, Roberts," he said, "there wasn't any mistake. But if there is anything deserving such a name, we'll forget my fault, and yours."

Roberts sighed with relief.

"Then you *will* forgive your old mother?" he asked contentedly.

"I forgive myself and you," repeated Martin.

Roberts did not hear, or hearing, did not understand. A strong impression of brotherhood made his hands tremble. A feeling of careless happiness exhilarated him. The vision grew clearer and his heart tried gallantly to keep pace with his mind's picture of the Affinities, striding hand in hand against the foolish tide of intolerance and misunderstanding. He took Martin's arm and started down the street, a new freedom in his eyes.

"We are going to have dinner together to-night, Martin."

"I'm sorry, Roberts, but I have an engagement."

Roberts laughed.

"Oh, you'll come, all right!" He swung on to Martin's arm. "We'll have the most glorious dinner of our lives. We'll put the table by the radio and have our sherry with Bach—yes, with Bach. But you may have Delius with your Chablis." He shook his finger in Martin's face and laughed again. "I warn you, however, our Benedictine will call for Wagner! The renegade!—The impious Pretender! We'll swing his stomach like a bell over our Benedictine."

Martin's cheeks were sucked in. He seemed ready to laugh but his eyes were shaded.

Roberts, still chuckling, glanced at him carelessly in his merriment and was astonished.

"Martin!" he cried.

"I'm sorry. Some other time I'd like to. But to-night, I can't come."

Rage, a positive hatred, shook the adviser. Words of reproach and anger were about to be spoken when he was deterred by the same quality in Martin's face that had quieted him before. This time, even in his shame, he tried to analyze the reason—to connect and precipitate Martin's features into the symbol that stopped his fury. He felt that it was an earth-impression—a breath of old winds—a shade of substratum clay—a distillation neither spatial nor timely. He saw Martin's face in retrospect as the outline of a rising mountain crag, lonely within the moon; or as the shaping pseudopods of cloud that are confusing in their similarity to some ancient clot of memory.

But Roberts was not easily defeated. He spoke evenly.

"We *must* have dinner together to-night."

"I have an engagement," repeated Martin.

"An engagement! *Our* dinner is important."

"My engagement is the kind you can't break."

"Really!" A supercilious expression flitted across Roberts' face and his one sharp word carried an air of volubility.

Martin, looking straight ahead, made one more effort.

"Won't you walk down this way with me?" he asked.

"But this is a special dinner," protested Roberts, following him.

"I'm sorry. I'm really sorry."

"Oh, I see. I didn't realize your social program was so strenuous."

"This is the first thing of its sort," Martin replied.

"First thing of its sort?" Roberts laughed shortly.

"Yes," Martin answered. "That was awkwardly put."

"Yes," said Roberts, a mimicking expression on his face. "Yes, yes."

"Let's not break this, please." Martin spoke earnestly.

Roberts' voice acquired a superior tone.

"I can't help it, Martin, if your sense of values is unintelligent," he said.

"I wish you would understand."

"I do understand." Roberts held his finger in the air warningly. "Don't let some transitory illusion make a fool of you, dear boy."

"'Transitory illusion?'" asked Martin absentmindedly. "It has a history and a future."

"Deane Idara is a clever woman," observed Roberts. "But you have a job."

Martin smiled queerly.

"Doesn't my job depend upon my work?" he asked.

Roberts stopped abruptly and faced him.

"I can tolerate rudeness, but not unkindness," he declared with dignity.

Martin took the other by his arm.

"I want to be as good a friend as you've been to me, Roberts," he said, trying to speak calmly. "Every contact, economic or social that I have, you've made for me. I'd not be myself if I were unappreciative. That's not it alone, though. We have many things together—food—and music—isolate cynicisms—and all these have their place. You understand. You know, also, that even with the best of friends, sometimes a path divides. Certain diversions, certain loves, are found impossible in common."

"But love is what I need," said Roberts quietly.

"That element is fugitive."

"And still I need it."

"The whole world does," insisted Martin.

"But I, especially."

"It's too difficult, Roberts."

"Nothing is difficult," he replied. His voice was sorrowful. "Martin! Break this date with Mrs. Idara."

"It has more than precedence, Roberts."

"I demand it."

"Then," said Martin, a feeling of exhaustion coming over him, "I'm afraid there's no alternative. I turn down here."

Roberts' wide blue eyes looked white in the twilight.

"We've been fools, Martin. We should never quarrel. Let's forget all this. Come on." He was like a small boy pulling at Martin's arm. "We'll have wine and chicken. We'll have mushrooms."

It might have been a sob.

"I can't."

Roberts, blinded to Martin, stared at him. Then he turned swiftly. His eyes darkened in the first lights of evening and he walked hurriedly away.

Roberts' face superimposed the view from the window where Martin stood with Deane. Its expression was somber and equivocal. Through this skeletal haze they watched the city's significant pantomime—the silhouettes and flashings, the play of shadows below them.

"You've seen Roberts, haven't you?" asked Deane quite suddenly.

Martin looked down at her bright sandals. She was wearing a deep blue hostess gown, nearly the color of the evening sky. A burnished cross, held by a woven cord, fell from her throat and lay between her breasts, and again Martin saw the silver within her hair as mast lights over the water.

She picked up a cigarette and lit it for him. Around the tip, the moist red paste from her lips left a scarlet ring. She put the cigarette in Martin's mouth.

"Yes," he said, holding the smoke in his lungs, "I've seen Roberts. But he has no place up here."

Deane looked at him strangely.

"He disturbs me, Martin. I don't like him."

"He disturbs, me, Deane. He wanted me to have dinner with him to-night. When I told him I had an engagement he knew it was with you. One wheel in his brain spins on an eccentric."

"What can he do?"

"He can kill the copper goose—cause me to lose my job. And it's all wrong. We like each other. We should have been good friends. I admire him. He has a mind, and my brand of humor. The first time I saw him at that Relief place I was attracted to him. I wanted to know him better."

"But couldn't you see that he was—different?"

"You call it 'different.' Roberts calls it temperamental.' Rio would call it———" He stopped.

"Rio! Who is Rio?"

"Oh. Rio? He was a shipmate. An individual. Sometime I'll tell you what I know about him.... But to get back. I did know that Roberts was different. I believe I knew it the first time I saw him. It didn't interfere with my admiration for him. I was lonely. Hard work on ships had surfeited me with the physical. I didn't hesitate at the specter of consequences—although I did anticipate them. I believed that I could handle them. I couldn't. You see, Roberts was convinced that I, too, was 'temperamental.'"

Deane made an impatient gesture.

"He had no reason to think that."

"Perhaps he did," said Martin thoughtfully. "Perhaps he had a combination of reasons. First of all, I took no pains to hide my interest in him. Perhaps he misunderstood the motive. And then, there are gestures and expressions that are open to suspicion. The line of demarcation in such friendships seems variable. Roberts wanted me to belong to his group, and whether the misconstruction was artificial or genuine, he arrived at a conclusion. Tell me what you know about him, Deane." He turned to her impulsively.

"Then I must tell you of his mother, Martin. She was as luxuriant as himself and more. She was pure crystal with the same high febrile cheeks, but an attitude so strong that I always felt his should be less. I'm sure though, that no one could touch her but himself—at least, I felt she swept along in an invulnerable carriage of glass, indifferent to any but her son. William Roberts finds his coloring from her, and his bearing, and his remarkable beauty; for," Deane observed in reminiscence, "he wears a tie or scarf the way she wore her pearls, as though they were a part of her throat. They were glorious pearls—a small dark strand with a diseased, slow luster, indistinct in tone, but so inseparable from her body that when her skin assumed the radiance we see in Roberts, they followed her as though they loved her. What her husband meant to her before his death seemed of little importance; for her life, so obviously, was contained in Roberts' glance, his frown, or contradictory expression. These two were more like complementary figurants intent upon each other in their mutual demand than like a mother and son. That he adored her showed in every action—from the way he placed her shawl—" Deane looked at Martin briefly, "from the gentle manner with which he drew her shawl over her exquisite, proud shoulders (it was like a caress!) to his affectionate concern over trivialities—her slightest expression, or even guarded undertones that no one knew except themselves. Once, I saw them when he became aware of a woman speaking—I knew it was without intent—and then I saw his mother's strength. She never moved— no line of her face changed; but everything in the room became alive and hard. To me, it seemed that the tender pearls around her throat turned into steel. The woman who had been speaking with Roberts became confused, faltered, and he seemed ready to rise from his chair. But at this, his mother smiled faintly and spoke graciously to the other woman. It was all right, apparently; but I was chilled and felt ever so glad when the party broke up.

Shortly after that, Martin, the mother died, and I am sure that part of Roberts went with her." Deane was speaking intensely, with a fixed, unusual look toward Martin which he accepted steadily. Since he would not speak, she made a curious remark. "This, you knew, Martin—not the way I told it; but you knew."

"Yes," he answered. "Yes, I knew." He turned from her, staring out of the window into the darkness.

The doorbell rang.

"It's Drew," said Deane. "No one else would come here at this time—— unless——" she looked at Martin, and for a moment seemed to be less assured. Then she lifted her head. "No! *He* wouldn't—Roberts wouldn't dare! I'd better answer."

Drew entered and kissed Deane lightly on the cheek.

"You're lovely," he said, holding her arm affectionately and extending his left hand to Martin who, embarrassed, knew of nothing but to squeeze the delicate, closed fingers.

Drew smiled faintly and sat down, crossing his slender legs.

"I just left Ella, poor girl," he said, with a sigh. "She wouldn't have a doctor. So she called me."

Deane looked at him in surprise.

"Ella sick? Why, she seemed very well last night. Should I see her?"

"I shouldn't bother," said Drew, smiling faintly again. "I gave her a bromide and devotedly held her hand till she went to sleep. She'll be all right in the morning."

"But what happened?" insisted Deane.

Drew leaned forward and spoke more seriously.

"I'm glad both of you left when you did," he said. "Roberts drank consistently—a thing he's never done before, and left in a stagger, vowing he would never see Ella again. He spoke rather madly in his apartment, too. I stayed with him most of the night." Drew sighed once more. "Of course, both of you are to blame."

"It's ridiculous!" said Deane, her dark eyes brilliant with anger. "Is Roberts out of his mind?"

Drew did not answer, but settling back in his chair, took from his pocket a gold cigarette case inlaid with an exquisite Mosaic design in various metals, opened it, and without offering its contents to the others, selected a rather bulky cigarette which he lit at once, before returning the case to his pocket. A singularly aromatic odor was first noticed by Martin. He looked at Drew in surprise. Then a wisp of smoke floated toward Deane who wrinkled her nose.

"One of your disgusting cigarettes," she said. "I don't see why you smoke them."

"It's a beautiful herb," replied Drew contentedly. "Martin understands it."

"Of course," said Martin.

"Will you smoke?" Drew inquired of him, reaching for the case once more.

Martin smiled slowly and shook his head.

"But I can see it in your eyes," persisted Drew.

Deane looked at Martin excitedly, then turned to the other.

"Please, Drew, don't ever offer Martin hashish."

"Ah!" said Drew, slightly amused. "So you know!" Then, taking a long, deep draw on the cigarette, he let the smoke escape in little puffs from his mouth and nose. His attitude became more languorous. The timbre of his voice changed and he sighed. "A quiet night," he said. "My lovely friends.... You *are* lovely, aren't you?" he continued, speaking carefully.

"Yes," answered Martin, studied and frowning. "Lovely."

Deane reached over impulsively and laid her hand on Drew's.

"Won't you put it out, darling?" she pleaded. "I hate to insist, but it gives me a feeling of———"

"Of apprehension," supplied Drew, rising slowly and slowly crossing the room to the open window. He tossed out the half-smoked cigarette, then returned, partly on his tiptoes.

"I wish you wouldn't smoke like this," said Deane quite urgently. "It gives you bad dreams. You hate yourself, too."

Drew raised his hand with a listless movement.

"Later—perhaps. But now everything is very sweet." He smiled dreamily. "This clarity, after my extreme confusion, forgives an old sin. An image!— memories unfolding that bring a figure more alive than you.... A splendid figure.... Burning with clandestine color.... Unfaithful!... He tried, though, more than I...." Drew leaned back again, resting his head against the chair. His lips were partly open and there was a flush of pleasure upon the high oval of his cheek.

Deane arose without a word and went into the kitchen. Martin imagined that she was making coffee. As the aroma came into the living room, Drew opened his eyes, looked at Martin and shivered.

"A good awakening," he said, smiling nervously.

"Yes," said Martin. "The cigarettes are mild."

"Too mild," said Drew. "I should have eaten the salve, but I was afraid. I was nervous from spending last night with Roberts. It was terrible to see him act the way he did. He cried out once. It was like a bellow." Feeling slightly dizzy, Drew stopped talking for a moment and wiped his forehead.

Martin waited quietly.

"This evening," Drew continued, "I went to my bedroom and took the jar from my cabinet, holding it as though it contained radium. I was uncertain, as I always am on approaching this Nirvana; but to-night I was afraid. As I removed the lid, exposing the ointment, its ungodly musk affected my breathing. There was something sinister in its appearance. I peered deeply into it, and the jelly seemed to glow and change from a dark green to a paler color. It trembled and faded to a lighter shade, and stayed that way. Then the odor poured afresh into my nostrils. I felt staggered and closed the lid." Drew shivered again, then relaxed in his chair, while Martin watched him.

Deane brought in three steaming cups of coffee. Martin drank his hurriedly, taking the hot liquid in large swallows. Drew sipped his, while Deane's remained untouched.

Seized with excitement after this fresh stimulant, Drew arose suddenly, put down his cup, turned to Deane and said, "I must go. And I know you will understand, Deane, if I ask Martin to leave with me." With feverish haste he put on his coat and Martin, with an expressive look at Deane, followed him from the apartment.

As Deane fastened the door after them she leaned upon it for a moment, her forehead resting against the panel, her small hands tightly closed.

Drew and Martin walked swiftly up the street, for the cold night breeze whipped in from the Atlantic. Martin turned down the brim of his hat and put his hands into the pockets of his topcoat. Drew looked around at him.

"Would you like to be at sea to-night?" he asked.

"I was just thinking about it," answered Martin. "There isn't a bad night on land but that I think of the men on ships."

The air seemed to exhilarate Drew and he spoke again, enthusiastically.

"Will you answer a rather intimate question, Martin?"

"If I can."

"Well, don't be angry. But are all the stories that seamen tell—I mean the tall tales—just fancy, or are they mostly true?"

"That's a trade secret," said Martin thoughtfully, noticing that Drew's classical manner had become more feminine since they had left Deane's. Then, as though suddenly changing his mind, he added, "Yes, Drew. Most of them are true. You don't have to exaggerate or romance about the sea. It gives you a bellyful whether you want it or not. Of course, all the adventures that sailors tell about probably didn't happen to them. But they happened some place and to someone. I have a good collection of tales I've swapped, and I couldn't tell you right now the true ones from the borrowed."

Drew took Martin by the sleeve and they came to a halt. There was a curious, understanding expression in Drew's eyes.

"I like you very much," he said. "Please don't misunderstand me, Martin, but I think a great deal of you. I'd like to know you better—to have your friendship."

"You have my friendship, Drew." Martin held out his hand and was surprised at the other's firm, steady clasp.

Drew nodded his head in the direction of a subdued, blue glow on the opposite corner.

"There's a cocktail lounge," he said, "where once in a while I go when I'm tired of routine. I've never taken anyone there before, but I'd like you to come with me this evening. It's very quiet—a place where one can rest or think as he desires. Will you?"

"I'd be glad to," Martin answered simply, still wondering at Drew's eagerness.

A waiter hurried to them as they entered.

"Mr. Noland," he said, bending his head slightly before Drew. Then, glancing at Martin with mild, respectful curiosity, he led the two men to a small booth in a remote corner of the lounge where he received their order and left quietly.

Martin was attracted by the room—its lighting, the suggestion of avidity. Directly across from them, and near the wall, a fountain sent up a soft golden spray from its center, around which individual columns of multi-colored water rose and fell. A mural, hung just behind the fountain, caught its indiscreet fires. There, the lights blended into a seeming gradation of silver fungus until only the sharp blue antlers of a stag, at the top of the painting, stood out thirstily over the water.

Martin looked away from the fountain. Drew was watching him with a reflective expression, with such a gentleness foreign to men's eyes that Martin was immediately intent. For there, in Drew, he saw the central, fine equation between his friend and savage, weeping Lesbos. The two united, defying by extreme cunning and deceitful fingers a dogmatic scythe of science which uses the symbol X for one impossible of definition. And what he saw beneath, caused Martin to tremble and lean back in his seat, with his heart beating faster as though the secret had been upon his lips or in his mind. However, that fever which comes upon a man as he sights dimly before him the object of his life's search—the feeling that it might kill if the secret was discovered, left him suddenly. Vaguely he knew that he had touched the edge of it, and that was all. In one way he was glad that the revelation had not come to blind him. He was not ready. Nor could he, by any trick he knew, even follow. There were years before him, other trails to entice him, so he argued. And as he opened his eyes, rather painfully, Drew, concerned and full of question, brought him round again to sanity, and not a mind deliberately drugged by the spin and shuttle of the fountain's aimless *carrousel*.

The waiter came at this moment and set the glasses upon the table. Even the man's crisp, white hair seemed a part of the scheme of the lounge, Martin thought. Fancies, ridiculous and uncalled-for, occurred to him in succession until he wished that he could stay quiet forever with Drew, whom he trusted most of all in this irrepressible hysteria. However, the waiter withdrew quickly enough, resting his hazel eyes only for a moment upon Martin, who spoke to Drew with a restrained irritation.

"Was this intended?" he asked. "It seems, Drew, to be something planned." He waved his hand impulsively. "All this," he continued, "is native to you and unfamiliar to me. It has—it has a quality—" Martin stopped talking.

Drew picked up his drink.

"I suppose it does have what you say, or suggest," he answered. "I've felt it many times. But it was not defined to me before to-night. I came here to rest, because it was restful; but I shall never come here again, because you have given it a suggestion of intimate life which is offensive. It wasn't planned at all, Martin, and I was never native until you said so." Drew leaned forward frowning, puzzled. "What kind are you?" he asked. "You, Martin, could vulgarize the very Church." He sipped his drink, although Martin left his own glass untouched. "Prosaic as it may be," Drew went on, "it is not myself with whom I'm concerned. It isn't myself, or Roberts, or even you that I am most deeply worried about. It's Deane." He lifted a finger, decisive, commanding. "In her you have found sweetness, tenderness and passion—a physical, well trained animal. Don't speak!" He held his finger warningly again as Martin's brooding shoulders straightened. "You've talked uncannily enough, Martin, to make even me wonder. I love your thoughts—the upside down philosophy that makes me laugh when I believed I could never laugh again. But Martin, you surely won't abuse this powerful—yes, this beautiful gift with Deane. Don't misunderstand me, I beg of you once more. It isn't evil, Martin, to use a weapon at your command. It isn't really that you're a devilish anti-Christ, as I first thought." Drew lowered his voice, speaking almost frantically. "It may be that you are even Christ himself. You have your Cross and finally you'll rest there. For you are no more invulnerable than the Man on Calvary, who under pressure—under striated clouds asked for an end of it. Is there anyone *you* can ask in that intolerable moment?" Drew wiped his forehead, drank deeply and spoke again, although he avoided Martin's flaming eyes. "I repeat," he persisted, "'that intolerable moment!' And it matters very little whether you consider me a fanatical, abusive priest, or—" and now the spray from the fountain seemed to lean toward Drew. Heavy lines of moisture which he failed to notice, covered his forehead. "Martin," he said, "I know Deane. I love her 'in my fashion.' I—I too, was taken from a medium of ordinary happiness into this rarefied, spiritualistic land you understand so well." Unable to speak further, Drew brushed his handkerchief across his eyes and placed his hands upon the table. To his astonishment—almost to his grief, he saw them tightly gripped by Martin, who seemed to hover over him, transfigured....

They got up and put on their coats. With surprise, they noticed that the shutters of the lounge were drawn and that the bar was untended. Alone in a corner, the white-haired waiter sat dozing. Drew pressed a bill into the hand of the sleepy attendant and opened the door himself. Out in the street the wind was blowing harder than ever and a pale green light clung like a heavy paste to the eastern horizon.

CHAPTER VIII

Martin left the typographical plant. He thought he was a funny one. Being fired made him feel a little childish. It might be hurt or anger, or it might be something more esoteric. He didn't know. But his face was colorless and his eyes gleamed unnaturally.

"I guess it isn't anything to sigh and fret about, 'dear boy,'" he said. "It was Roberts, of course; and I can't buck him. This city's even more of a machine than I had thought." He walked until he was thirsty, went into a restaurant and had two cups of coffee. Then he walked some more. He stopped in at another restaurant and tried to eat. He couldn't. So he had a third cup of coffee and decided to call up Roberts. The conversation was pertinent.

"It's Martin Devaud. Is Mr. Roberts there?"

"Hello, Martin. It's myself."

"I'm fired. May I see you this evening?"

"Come at six."

"Right." And they hung up.

Martin continued to walk. His throat was dry and he yawned frequently. As evening approached he grew more and more nervous. Several times he lost his bearings and with some difficulty he found Roberts' street. In the elevator, which was warm and a little close, he tried to keep himself from shivering.

Roberts was dressed in black trousers and a white shirt, starched, but open at the collar. He greeted Martin extravagantly, then seeing his pallor, so unnatural, he brought out whisky and soda.

Martin held up his hand.

"No soda," he said.

Roberts' eloquent features absorbed at once the harshness of Martin's despair. He understood. Nevertheless, propriety made him ask, "Straight? That's dangerous."

"Straight, please. And it's not half so dangerous just now for me as being sober."

Roberts shrugged his shoulders.

"You may take the bottle, if you care to, and lie down with it," he answered petulantly.

Martin looked him straight in the eyes.

"A drink will suffice," he said.

Roberts flamed and quieted and the color came again.

Martin smiled a little maliciously as he watched him.

"What a story, or picture!—if you wept in all that brilliance!" he said calmly.

Roberts poured his own glass to the brim with whisky and drank it before he answered. His eyes were hot—completely without modulation.

"Drink yours!" he commanded, pouring another.

Martin took the glass to the window and threw it, whisky and all, into the street.

"May it kill!" he said, whiter-faced than ever.

"You talked to me once of melodrama," said Roberts acidly. "I've never seen it so rampant, so unorthodox, so uncontrolled. I've had enough! Tell me—tell me—or by God!——"

"I want to know if you had me fired," said Martin, simply.

Roberts became placid at once. He waved his slender hands and, half-closing his eyes, smiled patronizingly.

"Surely you do not—" he began, when Martin cut him off.

"Surely, hell. I wondered. I thought it was probable."

Roberts still watched him from under his lids.

"I don't understand."

"I said I'm fired."

"Well?"

"I want to know why."

Roberts folded his hands. It was almost a gesture of dismissal.

"I talked with your employer, Mr. Jackson," he said. "The conversation, I must say, was disappointing. He told me frankly that your work of late had been lax." Roberts cleared his throat. "I've been somewhat afraid of that. You can't burn the candle at both ends, Martin. The social and the economic won't mix."

"Roberts—save your platitudes for a darker night!" Martin was glaring at him. "So that was really it! You intimated as much at one time."

Roberts went over to him, touching the back of Martin's hand with indescribable tenderness.

"Are you tired enough now, my friend, to have a drink with the one man in the world who sees you in your entirety?" he asked.

"Yes. I'll drink," said Martin wearily, leaning back in a chair and closing his eyes. He took the glass from Roberts, holding it loosely, and drank from it without thinking.

Roberts now put his hand on Martin's head.

"I have given my time to place you," he said gently. "You would not rebuke me for that."

Martin felt the lassitude of the whisky, of the words; yet some fundamental stroke of his own blood kept him from acceptance. He seemed to hear a bold, ancestral cry, and sat straighter.

"You're modern, Roberts. You have a modern sword."

"I've never hurt you, Martin. I've tried to help."

"Of course. But your body is too demanding."

"Meaning?——"

"I won't fence. I've seen an ugly mind—an inexpensive one."

"Devaud," said Roberts, in a sharp, clear voice, "you don't belong among civilized people. One can't talk to you decently without your making an unpleasant issue. You're a confounded savage and worse, because you have the instruments of this superficial world, too. And all of your cruelty—yes, you're cruel!—and I suppose all of your vices are tucked under your fine exterior. No wonder Deane is intrigued! But if she could see you just as I see you now, with that brutish look in your eyes, then——"

Martin interrupted him.

"Don't mention her name," he said, in a low, moody voice.

Roberts moved away from him quickly.

"Martin—did you make this appointment to build, or to destroy?"

"Neither. I just wanted you to know that my understanding belongs to you."

"Then it's the only thing that belongs to me." Roberts spoke bitterly. "Martin! For the last time I ask you to forget a cycle that has brought you only unhappiness."

Martin got out of his chair.

"You should never try to be clever with me, Roberts. I respect the frank demands of the body. Petty intrigues disgust me. Your intricate desires have overruled your intelligence. As an invert I respected you. As a subverter I find you intolerable."

Roberts walked toward him, motioning, his head shaking. His shining black hair fell across his face which had turned from red to a lurid purple. The white part of his eyes took on the same color. His appearance was that of some monster in a fable.

"I'll—" he said, "I'll not—I'll not—" his head bobbed up and down. "I will never let you——"

"You're prodding yourself sick," said Martin in disgust. "You're jarring the very devil out of yourself," he flung at him and left the room, his shoulders swaying.

Martin went to a liquor store and bought a gallon of wine. In his room, he sat down on the edge of the bed, kicked off his shoes and began to drink. Half-drunken, he lay back and soon fell asleep.

He awoke in the late morning. He knew his position. The contact had been broken. Sick from the evening's drinking he got out of bed and looked at his face in the mirror. His cheeks were pale and there was an unhealthy expression in his eyes. He felt his heart. Its methodical, heavy beat disturbed him. He poured a glass of wine and drank it swiftly. The nerves deadened. His apprehension died and he stood again before the mirror, regarding himself calmly. He shaved and dressed, took another glass of wine and went out, going directly to the typographical plant.

His former employer was writing. Martin looked at him vaguely, hesitating before his desk.

"What is it, young man?" asked Jackson, glancing up with impatience.

"No one told me why I was fired," said Martin indistinctly. "Will there be anything later?"

His condition seemed a little pitiable to Jackson, although, the employer told himself, such individualities really belonged outside the mathematical régime of commerce. One had to dispose of them accordingly.

"There will be nothing later," he stated firmly. "You were inefficient. I can see no reason for returning you to this Company."

"I want to work," said Martin. "That's the reason." His fingers rubbed the top of the desk and he looked unsteadily at the man behind it.

Jackson arose.

"You're drunk, Devaud," he said. "It is not a question of personalities. Good-day."

Martin gave him a perplexed look. The impeccable tailoring of his employer's suit had suddenly become offensive to him. Completely bewildered by this strange revulsion, Martin turned and walked out of the room.

"Good-day," he said, and went down the steps and out into the street. "Good-day," he kept repeating into the ears of astonished passers-by. He stopped, after he had wandered awhile, before a restaurant; for he smelled the aroma of coffee. Then he shook his fist at the window.

"*That* won't split this illness!" he said, and walked on, mumbling.

In his room he sat down once more on the edge of the bed. His mind, levitated by wine and discouragement, projected itself. Images rose before him. Secretive, luxurious women were in his fantasy. He drank again and went to bed. He slept, awakened, washed his face and slept once more, reality and the dream becoming as one. Day and night passed.

The sun rose, slanted, fell over the windowsill and crept up the bed into Martin's eyes. He awakened, his heart pounding. He stood up and finished the last of the wine.

"Internal application only!" he observed. Repeatedly the mirror drew him. "Poison if taken externally," he continued amiably; then seeing the foolish expression on his face, turned away in disgust.

He looked at himself again.

"Emancipation!" he shouted. "To business! To weaving, undecipherable sex and even my own hot mouth!" In amazement he looked into the crypt of his eyes. That soft sound of weeping.... "From the ceiling," he cried. "Not from these French fried lips!" He went back to bed.

In a dream he placed his hand on his hard body.

"The unborn," he whispered, breaking his hand on himself. "Modest child of onanism.... One daughter who will not ride the world on her ruby-jeweled bird's nest!... One lad who will not ride the world on a bird's nest!"

He awoke and looked at the ceiling. The room was death. Outside, snow was falling, flakes padding the window. He stared into the darkness. To escape without struggle—his body falling—and then, rest—infinitely deep and sweet.... His imagination stretched steeply into awareness. Not into chaos or unreality. The wind pressed snow on the window, through the window and into his arms. He felt the cold. Holding his hands into the air, he prayed....

"God!"

No bright arm of light; no sound of wings. It was four in the morning and his terror had grown to a deadening satisfaction. The rose shadows of steepled city buildings at night rang dimly in his court, their inner warmth full of promise and engaging noise. He looked out of the window, and shook his head.

"Too young and stupid, my infantile prince," he said, and touched the gooseflesh on his arm, kissing with faint disdain its embarrassed nubs. "Back to bed again to sleep and jump like a poisoned cat." And another day waved her dreaming, blue hands, regretfully——

Martin knew an alternative in that purple morning. A gun—the shot—the quick flutter of his hand.

"No," he whispered. "Too demure. Fruitful, but demure."

Outside, the sun blended into trucks and the yapping noise of turning wheels. He dressed and went into the street, stopping at the nearest bar. And strangely, in all his tiredness and fear, arose the man as he had been—straight from the ocean, with clear eyes that had watched the sea so often, and with hand half-raised as though holding the helm of his ship. It was momentary; but the bartender stood looking at him quietly and with respect.

"A Guinness's Stout," said Martin.

"A nip or a pint, sir?" asked the man.

"A nip and a pint."

The black liquid hung to Martin's glass as he raised it to his lips. The stout ran through his dry throat and into his stomach, washing away the starved slime. It spanged against his knotted intestines, loosening their disgusted quiver. It broke the cordy fold of nervous tissue.

Martin bent over the bar, touched by its rustic intimacy. Out of its shining, wooden face arose the image of Deane, slim-throated, filling the mist. She moved closer. Martin mused over the bar and drank, and drank again. The liquor sank to his nerves and he awoke.

Deane forgotten?... Her bell-like gown drifting over his teeth—sprung from the fog—outlined in the smoke of his thoughts....

The subway was crowded. Meaty faces lined in pink, pale array before him. A woman, mother of too many, rubbed a glove over her nose, worry misting her eyes, a dustpan supporting her neck. Across from her perched a she-gazelle on meatless haunches, hair and breasts correctly arranged. The train stopped and Martin went up the stairs into the cold wind. He entered a building and walked down the hall to Deane's apartment.

She opened the door and stood before him, a bright, tremulous blur. He swayed a little and she caught him by the shoulder, assisting him into the room. He tried to stand straight, smiling gently through his brackish eyes.

"It's all right, Deane, but I can't stop my mind," he said. "I can't stop it from turning." He licked the dry scale of his lips. "I can't do it." He closed his eyes tightly to keep in the moisture and talked on rapidly, glibly.

From the window came the city lights. Deane sat in a chair, brooding, a frightened look on her face; for Martin's hysteria grew in the strength of evening. His motions became more selfish. Every idea turned upon itself.

"Somewhere," he said, "there is a worm. A relentless worm canting my words, embarrassing me—deep, vicious and blinding."

"What do you want me to do, Martin?" All of Deane's tolerance—her understanding and affection were contained in this question; but he was deafened with pain and apprehension and all the seeds of disaster which fall, germinate and grow so swiftly in certain poisonous gardens. He put his hand across his face.

"Let's get a doctor," he said. "A magical doctor ... a sorcerer ... a doctor for a sorcerer."

Deane nodded her head. And if he could have seen her then, in the gown he loved and with all the concern in her eyes, it might have taken him from this evil spell. But he was blind and sick and walked like a dead man; while in his agony he cried, "No! Nothing! Get nothing!" Tormented, he went across the room to her, and as he faltered, Deane caught him in her arms.

CHAPTER IX

Martin felt the hum of an elevator, fresh air in his face and the movement of an automobile. He knew that he was talking too much to an individual he'd never seen before, and suddenly found himself in a long bright corridor that smelled of medicine. He was helped into a semi-darkened room and felt a glass between his lips. He thought of Roberts, swallowed and choked.

"It's ether," he said.

"No, it isn't," said the nurse, standing by him and trying to get him into bed. "It will be good for you."

Martin saw her for the first time. Then he felt himself falling. The nurse steadied him, and suddenly everything was clear. He felt well, stimulated. He wanted to talk some more.

"So! Martin finally reaches Hell! Our pathological bundle of yeast becomes animate in Bedlam!"

"*Won't* you get into bed?" asked the nurse. "You will be sleepy in a minute."

"All right." He stood up, swaying. "Martin in Hell. Being tucked in bed by an angel with wide hips. Coasting to sleep with a bellyful of ether. A true Nirvana for a true aesthete." He stopped talking. Again hysteria struck him. But this time it was soft and languorous and he held it tightly as it moved in his groin. His breathing was quiet.

The nurse sat beside him in the darkened room. He breathed slowly now, beginning to jerk and posture. He held his hand in the air as though emphasizing a dream.

In the early morning he awakened. His hand moved over the side of the bed, reaching for a bottle of wine. His fingers went back and forth over the rug. Then he opened his eyes and saw the woman sitting beside him.

"Are you my nurse?" he asked.

"Yes, I'm your nurse. Won't you go back to sleep?"

"I hurt," said Martin. "I hurt all over, but my back is the worst. And I need a drink."

"What would you like?"

"Whisky. A big one."

"I'll get your medication," said the girl, and left the room.

Martin looked around him. A hospital—neurotherapy; adjacent to a madhouse! Weakened your resistance in one and shipped you into the other!

His body ached and his mind still turned. On with the medication!—and then what? From dipsomania to dope in twelve treatments. Bring on the bed-straps. Damned efficient nurse, that one—watching him jump around. Patient. If only his back wouldn't hurt so terribly. Must be the kidneys. Need flushing. Why not use a plunger? Imagine that immaculate nurse astride him, pounding his gizzard with a plunger!

The nurse returned with two glasses. One was full of orange juice. The other she held away from her nose.

"More ether?" asked Martin.

"It isn't."

"Well, ether or not—down the hatch!" And taking a deep breath he swallowed.

The nurse steadied him once more and he pressed his head into her breast, breathing sharply, like a man struck in the throat. He allowed himself to tremble. His feelings changed from sick horror to quietude and a faint elation. He let his head drop on the pillow. This time the paraldehyde brought relief, but no immediate sleep. Words kept ringing in his mind and he talked on, without cessation. The nurse listened to him, laughing occasionally. In the morning's light, Martin slept.

When he awoke, the nurse was gone. He was alone on a bridge with madmen. He was afraid. Afraid of what? Afraid of fear. A word sounded in his mind—phobiaphobia, fear of fear. Nothing tangible to fight. The deep-seated root of the worm in his imagination. His feeling of isolation became complete, unbearable. He got out of bed and walked into the hall. A student nurse looked warily at him as he approached—unshaven, with bloodshot eyes, his unfastened robe trailing.

"Where's the head nurse?" he asked. "Where is she?"

"Here I am."

Martin turned on her, white faced and trembling.

"For God's sake, nurse. Is this a hospital? Get me a drink. Get me something. And don't leave me alone."

She helped him into bed and brought the same medication. Sober, terror-stricken, Martin could not face the shock of the incredible drug. The nurse held him, and again Martin drank, feeling the same shudder and movement of the deep-seated tissue. He reached out and felt the woman's arms. A sharp, sweet odor in his nose prolonged his trembling. The nurse wrapped a blanket around him, leaned over and kissed his damp forehead. Martin rested, watching her move quietly around the room. Was her kiss a gesture of sympathy? He met her gentle brown eyes and knew she understood.

The greater part of the next two days and nights he slept, only awakening to drink the bright, relieving poison. The third day he remembered Deane—her laugh, the surge of her skirts; and each thought was a torment.

That evening two psychiatrists came to talk with him. One, his own doctor, young and solemn; the other, the consulting physician, mature, shrewd, Olympian. Martin explained his fears, bringing up the residue of his experiences. During his story he caught fragments of remarks from the older man. Suggestive words such as *masochism* and *sadism* set fire to his imagination. When they left him without comment he was more lonely and fearful than before. In desperation he entered deeper into his mind, finding new horror with each analysis. By night the momentum had grown to such an active fear that the nurse did not dare leave the room. Martin followed her with his eyes.

The special night nurse came on duty, fresh, buxom and cheerful. Martin drew new hope out of her vitality. As he watched her straightening his bed he felt resentment at his own weakness. What was he?—to be fussed over and coddled like an old dog. He watched the strong shanks of the girl move steadily around the room. A curious thought entered his mind and he laughed. The nurse turned and looked at him, fearing new hallucinations.

"No," said Martin, "I'm not hysterical. Come here and sit on the bed."

"I can't," said the girl.

"Well, then," said Martin, "pull that chair closer and sit here."

She did as he requested, and Martin reached out for her hand. It was soft and warm. He pressed it tightly, looking into her eyes. The girl's cheeks flushed but she did not pull away. Martin looked up at the ceiling, each fresh thought bringing anger—the keen, strong happiness of anger. This young animal beside him had given him a new perspective. He turned again to the nurse and held her hand more tightly, stroking it, and explaining his movements with his eyes. He reached out for her waist and smiled to see her pull away. She was afraid. Not he. What did he have to be afraid of? Phobiaphobia? How foolish! This complex, that complex——

"Listen, nurse," he said. "I'm cured."

"Yes. You seem to be much better."

"Better nothing!" cried Martin. "I'm well. There isn't anything wrong with me. I was drunk."

The girl stared at him for a moment, then put her hand on his shoulder.

"I've never believed the things you've told me," she said. "At first, I thought there was something a little bit—" Her cheeks turned red and she laughed. "But now, I know you're just a normal man."

Martin thought of the woman he loved. Deane! He could go to Deane now. There was nothing wrong. He thought of his doctors. Surely they had known. They had left him with that fear—its implication of neuroses and reference to disgusting complexities. How many lay that night, fed with bromides and sedatives; crucified on theories!

In the morning when the psychiatrists returned, Martin raised his head from the pillow.

"Good morning."

The young doctor nodded his head briefly, blinked his eyes and faced the light from the window, his face expressionless.

"Good morning. Did you sleep?" asked the older physician, in a perfunctory tone.

"Very well indeed," Martin said. Then sitting up a little straighter, he added, "Doctor! I don't want to anticipate a diagnosis, but I'm not sick. You understand that I merely gave a history of the fantasies and sublimated desires that are in all our minds, but which we are rarely dyspeptic enough to publicize."

The older doctor watched him furtively. Martin saw that he resembled a spider, and grinning to himself, thought that there were probably a few cobwebs about him. But in the younger doctor's eyes he saw concern and liking, and even the faint touch of friendship.

"What do you mean?" asked the older man at last.

Martin climbed out of bed, put on his robe and stood before the consulting psychiatrist.

"You understand."

"You have been a child," said the physician sternly.

"You understand," repeated Martin.

The psychiatrist took firm hold of his shoulders. There were furious lights about the man—not understanding; merely curiosity and hatred for something unintelligible. He tightened his grasp on Martin's shoulders, shook his head angrily and stormed out of the room. But the younger doctor, with all the suns between his eyes, observed in formula Martin's pulse and all the rest of it, dismissing his patient with a friendly, sympathetic nod as soon as he could.

When Martin left the hospital it was snowing. The medication had destroyed his orientation. He leaned against the wall of the building for a moment, then tried to walk straight while he looked for a taxi.

Inside the cab he wrapped his coat about him and held his ankles from the cold air. Sick from the drugs and weak from lack of food, he thought once more of Deane and smiled. He was tired, but he had won.

When he arrived at the apartment he stopped just inside the door. There was a woman sitting in a chair. Who was she? Where was Deane? Was this woman alive? For her face was pale, and her eyes, too large, too dark, seemed to have lost all comprehension.

"What is wrong?" he asked excitedly. "What is it?"

Deane did not answer but sank down in her chair, covering her face with hands that trembled.

Martin felt sick. The air in the room suffocated him.

"Deane! It's Martin!" he cried.

Her hands dropped to her lap.

"I talked with your doctors," she answered simply. "I talked with them for two hours. I was ashamed—humiliated."

"Ashamed of what? Ashamed of me? Why! I'm all right now!"

"I spoke with your doctors," Deane repeated, as though in fatal acceptance. "It was horrible."

Martin took off his coat. He had on no shirt. He looked past Deane for a moment, leaning heavily against the wall.

"They have taken my girl." He spoke bitterly. Then in a louder, more distracted voice, he repeated—"*They have taken my girl.*"

He continued to look about him as though in a daze.

"What have they done to you?" he kept asking. "Damn them! Collaborators with madhouses—sucking my giddy ideas, engendering the malingerer. They've doped you with psychological jargon, hypnotized you with fine phrases.... Breeders of hypochondriacs! I'm not afraid of them any longer, I have nothing but contempt for them. I wanted the clear advice of mature, impersonal intellects, and I meet with personal vindictiveness."

"They said you have a persecution complex," replied Deane. "They tried to help you." Her throat was dry and the room was spinning round.

"'Persecution complex!'" repeated Martin with a contemptuous gesture. "It's contagious. It's a disease—an indiscriminate application of words typing an individual, placing him in a box, granting him the elasticity of brick. They are dealing with humanity—not with bricks. What do these rigid intellectualists know definitely, after all? Stumbling about in the most infantile science of the lot. A befuddled group of astrologers of the mind. The more competent admit they know little—admit that while they do the best they can, that often they must strike out blindly, hoping that nature will effect a cure."

Deane's eyes did not change; but the delicate lids, with their heavy lashes, gave a sudden, nervous flicker. What was this perspiring man talking about? She still felt sick. He didn't have on a shirt. If she could only rest. She knew that her mind was bleeding. Each of Martin's words opened a new point in her brain.

"They are dangerous because they are clever," he went on. "And some of them are diabolical. Theirs is a subtle lechery. They love this parade of erotics. Orgasms by proxy! Intelligent, perverted and ruthless!"

Deane now looked steadily at him. The ice locking her mind moved restlessly.

"They do good, Martin. Not everyone plays with love and pain the way you do."

"Let me rest, Deane. I want to rest." He leaned for a moment against the divan and then got up. "You're the only one I care about," he said wearily. "Can these ponderous technicians, with their burden of world-pain give you happiness? Can you let their hard lines of conduct, which apply to the diseased, disturb our concept of life? Top-heavy and non-elastic—surely they cannot appeal to your ideas!"

Deane knew that he was splendid in his agony. She wanted to kiss his cheeks. She wanted to forget his tiredness, his indictment of psychiatry. She felt that his imaginings were unfair; untrue; those of a sick man. She knew that he had talked bravely and fought desperately for her. She felt all these things. But she stood up and turned away.

Martin knew. He put on his coat and smiled at her. He wanted to tell her that he loved her. Instead, he left the apartment.

CHAPTER X

Rio went down to the Seaman's Institute for breakfast. He had come to a conclusion about Martin. He felt that it was useless to look for him. And Rio needed the sea. It would be easy to get a ship.

The Mediterranean?—Algiers on a hot night, a skiff rubbing its brown keel on a plaque of sand. Turpentine.... South America?—Through the deep night wind one single light on Tierra del Fuego, an invalid blonde on the cruise ship, port of Rio.... Intercoastal?—The French "Babee" Quarter in Cristobal, water changing under the heat.

Rio scuffed his shoes on the concrete floor and looked up moodily. Then he saw him. Martin was sitting alone at one of the small tables. Rio pushed back his chair and walked over to him.

"Well," he said, looking at Martin's white face. "Well."

"Hello, Rio." Martin raised his cup, but the coffee spilled before it reached his lips, and without drinking, he replaced the cup on the table.

"You're a fine guy," Rio was frowning.

"Yes."

"Try again."

"No."

Rio took his arm and they went into the street. In Rio's hotel, Martin lay down on the bed. The other sat beside him.

"You ain't quite so funny now," said Rio.

Martin nodded.

"Where you been?"

Martin raised himself on his elbow.

"I've been playing bats with a visitor from Saturn. You know it has many moons. The visitor told me all about them."

"Yeah," said Rio dryly. "You only got one. But it ought to be kicked."

"It has been," said Martin.

"You son-of-a-bitch."

Martin couldn't manage sympathy and started to cry. He didn't make any noise and there were no tears. There was just a choking, helpless movement as he looked steadily at his friend.

Rio got up, lit a cigarette, then sat down once more on the bed and put the cigarette between Martin's lips.

"I know all about it, buddy," he said. "Once in Dairen I piled off a ship...." He looked away as dreamily as a big ape.

Martin laughed inside to see this fellow trying to be tender, but he listened to the story and it made him feel better. Finally he sat up.

"One night in the tropics, Rio, you told me I wasn't a sailor. I knew you were right, so when we came into New York I got off. I went on Relief and met a man named Roberts at the Employment Station. He was intelligent and interesting, but he was like this—" Martin held out his arms.

Rio nodded.

"However, that didn't make any difference," Martin continued, lying down again. "And later, he got me a job."

"Now ain't that pretty," said Rio.

"He got me a job," Martin went on, "and asked me up to his place. Anyway, to make this a good yarn, along came the girl. I liked her. Roberts' vanity was hurt. Perhaps he even liked me. But I thought I loved the girl."

"You do."

"All right, then. I do."

"So?"

"So Roberts had me fired."

"So?"

"I got drunk and the girl told me I was through."

"You weak punk," said Rio.

Martin hit him in the face. It was a glancing blow off Rio's nose and there wasn't any drive behind it. He tried to get in another one, but Rio shoved him back on the bed and held his shoulders down. Martin saw that the big sailor was grinning.

"It's all right, buddy," said Rio. "How about some food?"

Martin looked at his friend's nose. There was a trickle of blood coming from it.

"All right," he said, still watching the blood which was dripping over Rio's lip.

"Here's a couple of nickels," said Rio, laying a bill on the bed. "Get some sleep and some food."

Martin sat up again.

"Where are you going?"

"Down to the docks."

"What ship?"

"The *Steeldeer*."

"Where's she going?"

"Around the Loop."

"Any chance to make her?"

"The crew's signed on."

"I'm sorry to see you go." Martin couldn't stop the hurt in his voice.

"I ain't goin'," said Rio, not looking at him. He left the room without further explanation and Martin went to sleep.

It was Saturday afternoon and the office force at the Employment Station had gone home. Roberts alone remained. He was writing when he heard someone come in. He did not look up.

"My name's Rio."

The adviser threw down his pencil.

"I remember you," he said, regarding the man in front of him with intense annoyance, "I might add—unfortunately. I have no desire to see you. I have not seen your friend."

"But Mr. Roberts. I got some news. I seen him. I seen Martin, the cripple." The big sailor laughed. "He was thin, at that."

Roberts went around the desk and faced Rio.

"Get out," he said.

"But Mr. Roberts!" Rio was still smiling. "I like you." He rubbed his face gently against Roberts', who moved back in astonishment and disgust.

"I said, *get out!*" The adviser spoke between his teeth.

"But I like you, Mister." Rio put one hand back of Roberts' neck and the other across his cheekbones. The adviser tried to move but the pressure stopped him. He stood quietly, his eyes looking frantically back and forth, the color in his cheeks flickering. Rio squeezed harder. Above the hand on his face Roberts could see his torturer dimly. The pain changed to lassitude and Roberts wasn't afraid anymore. He remembered that he had dropped his Derby on the street a night or two ago. He had intended to send it to the cleaner's, but had forgotten it. He could not condone such negligence. Then he went to sleep.

Rio looked at the man he was holding. Roberts reminded him of an old sailing vessel on which he'd once made a trip. She'd struck a reef off Cocos Island. Rio had watched the ship from the beach. Her stern was up and her sails dead. A red anchor light flickered like this man's eyes before she sank in shoal water.

He carried Roberts to a chair behind the desk. Then he left the Employment Station, went to a phone booth and looked up Deane Idara's address.

At the Employment Station Roberts heard someone in the hall. He tried to open his eyes, although it didn't make any difference. It was probably that fellow returning to make sure that he had killed him.... Again came the strange fancies. It seemed to Roberts that he was chasing his Derby which was now being driven violently down the dusty street by the wind. Thump—thump—thump it went along the sidewalk, and at each corner, when he thought he had caught up with it, the wind would rise, and he would have to dash after the hat, trying desperately to retrieve it before the wind got hold of it again. "The cleaner can never make it right now," he kept thinking dismally. "The dirt will be ground into it." And once more, the hat made funny, hollow-sounding noises as it turned over and over on the pavement. Suddenly the Derby changed shape—growing enormous, building out misshapen shoulders, becoming a terrifying bulk which turned on him. Stricken with horror, Roberts fled before the onslaught of the monster. Thump—thump—thump— A janitor walked into the room.

"Mr. Roberts!" he cried. "Mr. Roberts!" He ran to the telephone and tried to dial the operator, but his hands were shaking too much.

The adviser knew how he looked. He knew that his mouth was open. Perspiration was pouring from his face and hands. He fought off the darkness. He got his mouth closed. With consciousness came pain—a sharpness at the base of his neck that made him sick.

"Leave the phone," he commanded sternly.

The janitor hesitated.

"Leave the phone," Roberts repeated. He could move his arms now and was able to sit straighter in his chair.

The janitor picked up his broom, looked at the adviser again and started sweeping. Roberts was writing when the janitor left.

Rio got out of the elevator and was approaching Deane's apartment when an elegantly dressed young man stepped from her door, closing it behind him. The sailor's anger rose at the thought that this woman should betray his friend, as so it seemed. And when the two men neared each other in the hall they both hesitated as if by mutual agreement—Rio, still in his murderous rage, Drew in curiosity. They were barely moving as they started to pass each other. Rio scowled, then stopped a moment to stare at the other, who merely lifted his eyebrows and looked at the small bouquet in his own lapel, smiling as if he had a notion. Rio's face became red. Thoroughly embarrassed at his mistake, he could not help but smile back. His healthy, undisciplined grin allayed any possible apprehension on the part of Drew who continued down the hall.

Rio found Deane alone. He thought he had never seen a woman so foreign to him—so sweetly unattainable that for one slow instant his deep native blood rebelled, reached out in mind, then caught itself. He held his cap when he sat down.

"I won't be long, Mrs. Idara," he said. "My name's Rio."

"Martin has mentioned you, Rio," answered Deane. "I thought it was you."

The big sailor glared at her.

"I just left Martin. He's sick."

"I know." Deane looked away.

"I'd help him, Mrs. Idara. But he don't need me."

"He doesn't need anyone but himself, Rio."

"He needs a good woman," answered Rio coldly.

Deane looked straight at him.

"That is—a stupid one?" she asked.

For a moment Rio stared at her helplessly.

"You're right," he said at last. "I can't talk. But Mrs. Idara, Martin ain't the first to break his neck over a woman—only mine died, and her skin wasn't your color."

"I'm sorry, Rio. I'm sorry it had to happen to you." Deane made a little gesture of sympathy.

Rio thrust his head forward.

"That'd work better on a live man," he said bluntly.

"Is Martin alive?" Deane spoke as if to herself.

"He's crazy," answered Rio, "but he ain't dead. And he never lost all his bearings till he met you. He even handled Roberts."

Deane was astonished.

"You know Mr. Roberts?"

Rio twirled his cap in his hand.

"Yes, ma'am. He's a friend of mine."

"You're a friend of both Martin and Roberts?" Deane asked incredulously.

"I can get along with anybody." Rio looked at her and some of his hatred appeared in his eyes.

"You love Martin very much, don't you, Rio?"

"Maybe. He said so one night. The way you and him throw that word around, though, it means anything."

"I intended it to be a good word, Rio—a brave word."

Rio grinned. Deane thought it was the strongest, most vicious expression she had ever seen. She wasn't afraid, but such clear hatred made her hesitate.

"Rio," she said finally, "I love Martin. But I won't let him escape the world. It isn't fear that makes him try it, but he has a quality of evasiveness that clears him from all reality. It has been convenient for him at times, but some day it will destroy him. I love him too much to let this happen." Deane was tired. She felt older. She didn't even know that her eyes were full of tears.

Rio stopped smiling and stared at the floor. Suddenly he got up and went over to her.

"I made a mistake," he said.

He put on his cap and Deane walked to the door with him.

"Rio," she touched his arm, "tell Martin I need to see him. Will you?"

"I'll tell him, Mrs. Idara." Deane's hand against his arm upset him. He wanted to kiss her. That moment he hated Martin. "I'll tell him," he repeated, and walked down the hall, looking surprised.

Martin was sleeping when Rio returned. He awakened and saw the big sailor looking down at him.

"What's the news?" he asked.

"I seen Mrs. Idara. She wants to talk to you."

"You saw Deane?" Martin sat up.

"She wants to talk to you," Rio repeated.

"You're high-handed." Martin shook his head. "What about the *Steeldeer*, now that you've seen me over the bumps?"

"You ain't over the bumps, and I don't want the *Steeldeer*. There's a boomer in next week, and no goo-goos in the messroom. I'll see then."

Martin tried to hide his embarrassment.

"Unaccustomed as I am—" he began.

"Stow it," interrupted Rio, jamming his cap on his head. "You got a job. I'll see you later."

"That's right," said Martin. He got out of bed and put on his coat. Then he stood looking solemnly at his friend. "I'll probably be back next week—or sooner——"

"You better go."

Martin kept looking at him. Then, without speaking further, he turned suddenly, went to the door and walked out.

When Rio could no longer hear his footsteps he sat down on the bed and lit a cigarette, but put it out immediately and carefully laid it on the washstand. For awhile he paced back and forth in his room. Then he went down to the desk and called out to the woman behind it.

"Where's the Brat, Rosie?" he asked.

Rio left the Brat and went to the waterfront. The salt air, the breeze and the innocuous drainage of people took away some of his disgust. The *Comber*, bound for Buenos Aires, was tied up at Pier V 9. A watchman stopped Rio at the gate.

"Hold off," he said roughly. "What's it from you?"

"Flowers for the shore gang," said Rio, in a high voice.

The watchman laughed.

"Oh. It's you, eh?" He passed his hand over the gray stubble on his chin. "I figured you'd be headin' south about this time."

"Who's the mate, Watch?" asked Rio, who was now grinning.

"The same baby they had last trip," answered the watchman, spitting abeam of the wind.

"Thanks, Cap," said Rio. He went through the warehouse to the pier and started up the gangplank. A mess-boy, flour covering his shoulders, cried "Gangway!" Rio twisted past him, indifferently brushing his sleeve where the boy had bumped into him. At the top of the plank Rio called to the quartermaster. "Where's the mate?"

"Up at No. 2."

Rio started forward, then turned and went aft to the last house 'midships. He opened the door of the sailors' messroom and walked in. A few men were sitting around the table which was covered with dirty oilcloth. They were drinking coffee. One of them got up.

"Hello, Rio. I ain't seen you since you broke your wrist over the Old Man's head in the Channel." The sailor laughed. "From bridge to brig in one trip." He rubbed his head with tattooed fingers while the crimson lady, dotted on his heavy forearm, danced. The printed line, ROTTERDAM GERTIE, under the figure, stretched as wide as the lady's hips.

"It wasn't a bad trip, Joe," answered Rio. "The brig's better'n the chainlocker." He looked suddenly interested. "How'd the Old Man make out?"

"I dunno. The last I seen him was when we tied up at Rotterdam. They was packin' him off down the Lekhaven."

"Down the Lekhaven, eh?" Rio looked grim. "His bones'd set of themselves on the Schiedamsche Dyk."

Joe waved the remark aside.

"What happened to you, Rio?"

"They broke me, and let it go at that."

"No more brass on your shoulders then."

"I'd rather polish it than wear it."

"Are you goin' to ship on this?"

"Don't know. Who's the bos'n?"

"I am. Seventy-five dollars, my own boy and radio."

"Company man, Joe?"

"Yeah. I never pass up this chicory." The bos'n poured more coffee. "Have some," he said.

Rio looked around the messroom. He saw the college boys staring at him, the flies on the wall and a cockroach settled under the percolator.

"Take it, Joe," he said. "And my compliments to B.A."

The bos'n followed him out of the messroom and walked beside him on the pier.

"They're all the same, Rio," he said, a little sadly. "The ships, the turnips and the crew. By God!—I won't rot on shore, though."

"I won't neither," said Rio. "I'll go back sometime."

They were passing a waterfront cafe. Its sign read: beer parlour. Joe pulled Rio inside and they sat down at a table.

"We shipped together for a long time," said the bos'n. "There's somethin' eatin' you. Drink up and get it off your chest."

Rio raised his glass and set it down empty. Joe followed and waved his red hand at the waitress.

"A head on two," he said.

Rio watched the girl pour the beer.

"I don't figure it myself, Joe."

"Drink up. Drink up and get it off your chest."

"Well, my shipmate, last trip, was a queer one. I don't mean there was funny business. I never knew nobody like him. He wasn't no sailor, and sometimes I thought he was a little off. I never felt like that before, and it was all jam. He didn't know how to take care of himself; so when he piled off in New York I knew he was in for it. I followed him and he was all over the town.

He met a fag who got him a job. Then he met a girl and fell in love with her. The fag had him fired, and he went off the deep end. He got drunk and the girl threw him over. I found him at the Doghouse. I got hold of the fag and fixed him up a little and went to the girl's place. And then—" Rio stopped and looked at the beer.

"Get it off your chest," said Joe, and the tattooed ring on his forefinger turned an evil blue in the dim light.

Rio took a deep draught before he spoke.

"You know I ain't cared for a woman since———"

"I know." Joe nodded.

"She's a swell girl," said Rio, leaning heavily on the table.

"Who?" Joe looked bewildered.

"Martin's girl. She's too good for him. I'd hate to see her hurt."

Joe thought a moment.

"What about you?" he asked.

"None of that," said Rio shortly.

Joe shoved his glass aside.

"Is that all of it?"

"No." Rio looked glum. "This Roberts—he's the fag—don't like the set-up. I think Martin and the girl'd make it but for him." Rio glanced up at Joe earnestly. "I got him bluffed, though, and as long as I hang around, he won't bother no one."

Joe made a disgusted sound.

"You can't wet nurse 'em the rest of your life."

"No, but I could make a short trip and look Roberts up afterwards."

Joe shook his head.

"And get thrown in jail? Listen!" Joe leaned closer to his friend. "Why don't you ship out, Rio? There ain't no use—" But something about Rio's appearance made him stop. "All right," Joe left the table. "If you change your mind, I'll be in No. 5."

"Good enough," said Rio, not looking up.

Joe walked back slowly to his ship and Rio drank coffee. When he left the restaurant he went straight down the waterfront to the South American Line. A small ship was sailing for Santa de Marina that evening, for bananas. Rio saw the first officer.

"I want to get out, Mister."

"We don't like pierhead jumps on the *Nancy II*" said the blunt little officer. Then he looked Rio over. "Have you seen the delegate? Is your gear handy?"

"Yeah."

"Bring it aboard. See the bos'n—Good Jesus, lad!" the mate yelled to an ordinary seaman who was scrubbing the whitework. "Soo-gee that bulkhead! Don't kiss it!"

Rio was forward when they cast off the lines. After the ship was made ready for sea he sat down on a bitt and watched the higher lights of Manhattan fade in the twilight.

CHAPTER XI

Martin left Rio's hotel and walked slowly along Fourteenth Street. His mind was blended with the darkness about him, for the street seemed to rest after the petty trading and rush of the day. He passed the cheap little shops and solitary stragglers, unconsciously accepting them in their place; nor did he turn his head to glance at the thin blue lights of a tiny cinema across the way. But a girl, in passing, brushed his shoulder lightly and asked him for a cigarette. He stopped, felt in his pockets and pulled out a package which he offered her.

"Mentholated, ain't they?" she said, pleased at her good luck. "Gee, I like mentholated." She took one of the cigarettes and handed back the package.

Martin looked at her and saw the rakish, ill-fitting dress, the tired expression in her eyes and the affected smile.

"Won't you keep them?" he asked.

"Thanks, Mister. That's swell," she said, stuffing them in her bag. "But d'you have any?" Here she hesitated. "You better have one," she said at last, carefully selecting a cigarette and handing it to him.

He accepted it and put it in his trousers pocket.

"Not there," she cautioned. "You'll smash it. Put it there." She pointed to the pocket of his coat.

Unthinkingly, he obeyed her.

"Say," she said, peering at him. "You look hungry."

"I'm not hungry," Martin smiled at her. "But now, I have to hurry." He smiled at her again, then walked on rapidly.

The girl kept at his side, looking at him, her mouth slightly open.

"You're a nice man," she said finally.

Martin stopped and looked directly at her.

"If you knew what I am, you'd run like a frightened cat. You'd run anywhere, and afterwards thank God for it." Then, seeing her eyes widen and her fingers clutch her bag, he continued more gently, "For you are a little cat, aren't you, Cat?" and he hastened on with long strides.

The girl stared after him, then turned, and with her head hanging down, walked slowly the other way.

As Martin approached Seventh Avenue he noticed a bright-eyed old woman on the corner. On the pavement in front of her was a basket of French marigolds. Martin hesitated and stared at the flowers for a second, then at the old woman.

"What do they mean?" he asked. "They look like wax."

"Oh, sir, they ain't. I grew 'em myself." The old woman watched him, her hands in her apron.

"Give me a bunch of the prettiest!" Martin pointed. "There!—in the center. They are for someone I love."

"Yes, sir. I'll give ye the bunch that's prettiest." She chose the freshest ones and carefully wrapped the stems in a piece of damp brown paper.

"Thanks, old lady," said Martin, dropping a coin in her hand. "And I'll give *you* a wish." For a moment she smiled, Martin thought rather shyly, regarding him with a strange, toothless understanding. He held the marigolds before him, sniffing occasionally as he hurried on.

When Deane saw him she wanted to cry; and taking the flowers, she fingered the little bouquet lovingly before laying it aside for a moment.

Martin sat down heavily on the divan.

"My God, I'm tired," he said. "Tired and hungry. Why, I'm just as tired as when I left here. That seems like a long time ago."

"Don't let's talk about it," said Deane, sitting down beside him. Martin could feel each pulse beating from her wrist in time with his own blood. He put his head against her arm, letting the faint sound ring into his temples. He rested against her naturally, faithfully, as though returning from a voyage of centuries or death.

Deane added to this dream-like state, this swift advance of years to year. She felt the soft wash of logic crumbling within her, loved him without exception, and remained quiescent. She heard Martin's breathing, felt an awakening, a weary happiness. A clear stream of words, unintelligible, fell through her hair....

Martin sat up.

"Did you sleep, too?" he asked.

"No," answered Deane, smiling. "But I was very happy. You slept like a baby. Don't you ever talk in your dreams?"

"I did have a dream," declared Martin, now thoroughly awake. "I dreamt that I met you at the point where the world meets itself. We decided instantly that we loved each other and——"

"What a lie!" interrupted Deane, laughing.

"I swear it!" said Martin, elaborately crossing his heart. "And I dreamt also that I was very hungry. Wasn't that strange?"

"Yes. A coincidence," said Deane, kissing him on the lips and starting to rise.

Martin caught the back of her hair and strained her to him.

"Deane!" he cried. But she pushed against his shoulders until he let her go.

"I'm going to cook some bacon and eggs, Martin," she said, panting. "Don't act that way now. You said you were hungry."

"For you," Martin argued, stretching out his body and holding out his arms.

Deane shook her head and went into the kitchen where she could hear Martin laughing.

"He is really a terrible person," she said to herself. But her lips trembled, and as she brushed the damp hair off her forehead the implication in her dark eyes was delightful.

When she brought in the feast Martin jumped up to help her with the tray. He could scarcely wait to taste the coffee.

"It's perfect," he said. "And how did you fix the eggs?"

"I beat them up with a little milk before putting them in the pan."

"They're wonderful," he repeated. "Let's make it a *real* feast. What do you say we wait up until dawn. There will be many colors and shapes in the clouds from this window." He pointed to where the late moon, a dull, inverted sickle, was shining in the east. "I can put my hand outside the window and almost touch Europe, Deane," he said.

"I don't want Europe," Deane said huskily. Her face seemed a little drawn as she watched him, her eyes half closing and unclosing.

Martin, noting the expression on her face, felt a kind of loving in his heart which he had never known before.

"Sweet little maniac," he said gently, and petted and caressed her. The sedative movement of his hands, which he worked most carefully, so as not to excite the blood or open the tiny nerves about her spine soon quieted Deane and she lay in his arms. "I'm going to tell you some stories," he said, rubbing his cool cheek against hers. "And later, we'll watch the dawn come up over Europe."

It was midnight. The last light had been extinguished in the giant buildings and only the raw sky and the face of the radio brought shadow into the room. Deane rested on the divan, her eyes on Martin who sat crosslegged on the floor in front of her. Suddenly, he leaned forward.

"This is a magical room, Deane, and this is a magical night. In older times, in an ancient time, there was a beautiful Princess—the loveliest in all the world. Arrogant Princes with long gleaming swords and many dragons to their credit wooed her. But she was unresponsive.

"Her father, the King, said, 'She is sick.'

"Her mother, the Queen, said, 'We shall see.'

"And so, one night, when the moon burned like a silver flame over the Kingdom, they stood at the wall of her room and peered through the chinks at their daughter. The Princess, a look of ecstasy upon her face, was in a chair, resting. In front of her was a little, old man—perched like a bird before her....

"'What does she see in the little man?' whispered the King.

"'What *does* she see?' demanded the Queen. Affection? A reflection of herself? Or some quality in the creature?'"

Martin stopped. Deane's hands braided and became sexed again. Once more, Martin leaned forward.

"Would you like to hear the sequel?... It happened in Paris, Deane. There was a gargoyle struck on the cornice of a gigantic cathedral. His stone eyes had been forced shut by the ages and his only tears were rain. His thick shoulders were bent by the centuries, and moss covered his throat.

"A beautiful woman, desired by all men, surfeited by leisure and adoration, saw this figure. And so, in secret, she took lodging across from the cathedral that she might watch the shadows move in the gargoyle's face by moonlight, by lightning-flash and in sun. Day by day she contemplated his patient, agonized expression; and day by day she became more contemptuous of the gracefulness and vanity of her suitors.

"One night, moonlit and vagaried with cloud, she was gazing at the asymmetrical face. Suddenly the head seemed to move. The woman's heart beat quickly and she grasped the sides of her chair. Deliberately, while she watched, the gargoyle's eyes opened and turned upon her, asking a question. The woman, protesting, held out her white hands. At this, the figure shuddered; then his stone arms pushed on the cornice and his shoulders broke from the wall.

"The woman ran to her mirror, regarding her pale, excited face. In her closet she touched her gowns—faster and faster her heart! Dressing herself in the loveliest gown of all, she returned in haste to her chair. There she waited, facing the empty cornice where a gargoyle had lain for centuries....

"There was a soft sound at her door. Now, through the opening, the woman could hear quick breathing. She pressed her hand against her throat, observing the figure as it entered.

"Slowly the gargoyle went to her, his movement quiet and purposeful. Laying his head upon his arms, he dropped down on his knees before her. Frightened, the woman looked away. Then her love, conquering fear, placed an infinite pity upon him. Her hands braced under his chin, lifting the agonized face until his eyes met hers. Lightly, her fingers caressed the deep cracks in his cheek, brushed the dry moss from his throat—and for one helpless, inarticulate moment, the gargoyle lived."

Martin felt the heavy wetness of his eyes. His twisted, passionate face looked up at Deane.

"She knew!" he cried. "And you know!"

Deane placed her hands upon his throat and drew him toward her.

"Yes," she said. While in an uneven, throaty voice she kept repeating, "She knew, and I know."

"Flower lips," Martin whispered, the taste of blood in his mouth, "squint your lovely eyes like old China—China eyes—" He moved her then, until she floated, insubstantial, upon the blue mosque of the couch. Once more, reality became a dream, and night pushed inward....

Martin watched the moon rise slowly and swing higher southward. Venus appeared, and then the Dipper, of such a calculating blue, such measured coldness that Martin shivered. He looked at Deane tenderly as she lay in his arms, trying to remember when such emotion had dominated him. Deane's face, a cameo in the steel-tinted light, was now upturned to him in a death-like stillness. He put his ear against her heart to reassure himself. Deftly, he disengaged his arm from her waist and slipped on one knee to the floor. Then he crept softly to the window and looked out over the vast eastern sky. He imagined that he could faintly see the first pale ravages of dawn, so he returned. Still kneeling on the floor, he blew upon Deane's hand and up her arm. He thought that she would never awaken, until suddenly he heard her say, "My, what a feeling you gave me! Did you enjoy the view from the window?"

"So you were awake all the time!" Martin laughed. "I thought as much."

"Then why did you blow so hard?" asked Deane. "And why did you sigh once?"

"Come on," said Martin, pulling her to her feet. "The sky's beginning to change." The sunrise was bleak, desolate and forbidding. "It just came out of the sea by way of Newfoundland," he added. "Everything is cold in that region—even the sun. Do you see those clouds streaking over the horizon? That's the point where all winds leave for a short visit with Mother Carey." Martin sniffed the air. "I thought so. Don't laugh, Deane, but I can smell icebergs."

"What do they smell like?" Deane asked curiously.

"Some sailors say the bergs smell like wet sea moss; others say it's like a pocket of cold salt. But to me they have no positive odor. It's more like a taste. It's like kissing an ammoniated mirror."

"That's strange," said Deane, looking at him queerly.

The wind outside was raging and whistling through the radio antennas as through the rigging of a ship.

Deane made fresh coffee. As Martin was finishing his cup, she asked him gravely, "Martin, how are you going to live? What will you do?"

He raised his head.

"I shouldn't worry about that, Deane; at least, not now. I know a typographer who, I think, will give me a job. It will probably be part time, but that's all the better, for I have some other work I'd like to do."

"What kind of work?" she asked.

"Along the same line," Martin answered. He pulled an oilskin envelope from his pocket and carefully took out some papers. "I'm building a type design that I've worked on quite awhile. As an avocation I find a good deal of pleasure in it. Some of the letters got a little wet, but I think you can see what I'm trying to do." He spread the papers out on a table and he and Deane bent over them. He pointed to one of the capital letters. "See, Deane?—The design is that of living forms—plant and animal. In the drawing, the bottom circles represent growth by cell structure in all life. By simply rolling up this series, beginning with the smallest cell, the face of the shell is seen, because that is the way shells grow—by rolling up themselves as they develop. Since the rate of development is normally the same, the flare of the sectors is constant.

"The black line of the drawing shows where the artist places the line for the letter stem, missing the center by half the radius. The blue line shows where the stem really should be placed. It looks much better that way. You will see that the straight line is intersected at an angle of about 100 degrees instead of the 90 degree angle.

"On the back of the drawing is seen how this measurement, 'the square of root 2' rule, is worked out for rectangular designs. The square root of 2 is 1.4141 etc.; its reciprocal, divided by 2, is .707 etc. That is, the strongest and most beautiful rectangle is 1.7 times as long as wide. Apply it to a book page. Width is determined mainly by size of type and number of columns per page. For a page 6 inches wide the length is 1.7 times 6 or 10.2 inches. This is the correct 'golden' or 'sacred' sector, used almost universally in the temples and sacred vessels. Textbooks give the page ratios 5 to 8 as the golden sector but it is not correct, neither is it so convenient or beautiful as the 6 to 10.2.

"The design is based on the soundest dimensional ratio known—'dynamic symmetry.' Many years were spent recovering this lost art, mainly in countries about the Eastern Mediterranean—Greece, Egypt, Persia, Arabia, and so on. The findings were published in a beautiful volume[1] and it was there I got my information and inspiration to design a type face.

"It is a humiliating fact that no original type face has ever been designed in America. Our type designers have been modifiers of European types, adding what Mark Twain called 'new and killing varieties.'"

Martin folded the papers and returned them to the oilskin envelope. He was absorbed by his subject and failed to notice Deane's expression, or her flushed cheeks.

"I'm ashamed of myself, Martin," she said quietly. "I didn't realize that you had such a definite structure running along with your life. Go on out now and try to get your job. And when you come back, I'll have fixed our dinner."

When she had tightly buttoned up his coat, he kissed her as a man would kiss his wife. She detained him for a second, ran into her bedroom and came out triumphantly waving a heavy muffler. After she had tied it properly around his throat, she threw her arms around him and sobbed quietly for just a moment. Then she shook the tears away in happiness, lifted her chin and gently pushed him through the door.

Martin, expressionless, with a steady tread, faced the sharp wind outside. He looked at the foot-prints on the thin film of snow that covered the sidewalks. He smiled. The passers-by could not tell whether his smile was that of a child, or of an idiot. He crossed the street.

CHAPTER XII

Once, while Deane was living with her aunt in a midwestern city, she had met a young man named Carol Stevens who was visiting there. Deane's aunt liked him—his little courtesies, the niceties of his behavior. But with Deane, he produced conflicting impressions. He loved a kitchen the way most men love a study or an office; and he moved among the pots and pans the way an artist walks before his canvas. His talent in bringing common food to life and giving it new meaning was no greater than his ability with a needle. He could take odds and ends of material and bring them together in an evening gown as fragile as a cloud. But more interesting than the things he created was his manner of creation; for he sewed with curving, meticulous gestures that were certain of each other. Sometimes Deane, watching him, would smile, and sometimes frown as though puzzled. After his visit, the young man returned to his home in Idaho and Deane forgot all about him.

She was having a quiet cup of tea one afternoon when he announced himself. When he came in he took her hands affectionately, as though they were long lost and newly reunited friends. He placed his topcoat carefully on a chair, sat down on the divan and pulled his trousers high above his ankles. In less than a minute he seemed quite at home.

"What a *dreadful* trip!" he said. "A simply dreadful trip, dear!—I'm exhausted. On a bus," he explained. "Gas fumes—oranges—babies! A man with a parachute on his back, or something," he ended wearily.

Deane laughed. She offered him tea, but he shook his head vigorously.

"Wine?" she asked.

"Wine," he repeated, and drew a line across his fingernail, adding, "—so much."

Deane went to a cabinet and poured a glassful of sherry.

Carol looked at the drink and stuck his tongue into it.

"Glorious!" he said, sipping like a kitten. Deane had the feeling he was going to take off his shoes.

To her relief Martin came in and she introduced the two men. Carol watched the newcomer suspiciously. He was shorter than Martin and chunky. He was broad in the belly; his waistband was spread with fat. His suit, which was more yellow than tan, accentuated his contour in spite of its good tailoring. His pale eyebrows lighted his pale eyes. His nose revolted at the tip and elevated itself, searching. His mouth was supposed to be prim and grim; but Martin wondered if he could catch it in a pot. His chin billowed out. His wrists were thick and his fingers perky. They touched things lightly. He took a cigarette holder from his pocket. Three of his fingers were around the stem and the fourth stuck out. Martin wondered how it would feel to bite this one off. It gave him a pleasant sensation to think of having the finger in his pocket, severed. He was so rapt in his thoughts that he smiled. This made Deane nervous. It was all right for Martin to act that way with her, but not with other people. When he smiled like that with other people it meant he was taking a trip. She tried to catch up with his thoughts before they became spectacular.

"Carol had a miserable time," she said. "It was on a bus; and there were detours—it's not pleasant."

"It's not pleasant," repeated Carol.

Martin frowned and looked at him. He looked at Carol and the more he looked, the more he disliked him. Carol was shocked at the way Martin was watching him. It made him uncomfortable and angry. He drew his mouth into a forced, straight line, tucked in his chin and spoke to Deane.

"It *was* wretched, dear. I bounced this way, and I bounced that way! And my traveling companions!" He rolled his eyes. "There was a salesman!" Carol snorted; a delicate snort, neither high nor loud. "The person had a case that he held on his lap all the way!" Carol's shoulders shook with mirth and the ashes from his cigarette fell on the rug. He stopped for a moment to nibble at his holder.

Martin felt something unhealthy—something that hung in the room like an infectious mist. But the young man squirmed comfortably and continued.

"There was an old lady. The proverbial old lady of all busses. The kind that has a basket of food and draws out apples and fried chicken and the right kind of sandwiches. She offered one of them to me." He had made himself laugh until he felt slightly sick. "And I bounced this way, and I bounced that way!"

Deane told Carol that it had been an amusing experience, but one not to be repeated; to which Carol replied as he raised one plump hand, the palm outward, "Heaven forbid!"

Deane tried to be pleasant, but she didn't feel well. The air was sticky, and she wanted to sit down with Martin and have him hold her tightly and listen to him swear for five minutes. Martin could swear so beautifully that it purified a room like rain.

Martin knew what Deane was thinking and he reached for her hand. Carol saw this and cleaned his cigarette holder with a clear, refined disapproval.

Then he meticulously cleaned his ear with the finger Martin wanted. He cleaned his ear thoroughly; but his movements were elegant. The expression on his face was Olympian.... He was alone in the room. Then he looked more cheerful. He was not alone. He was in New York, visiting.... He tried to yawn and couldn't; but he slapped his lips lightly and smiled at Martin.

"Deane has a lovely apartment—doesn't she?"

Martin nodded, but remained silent.

Carol's mouth became firm again and he tapped the floor petulantly with the toe of his shoe.

Martin arose, went to a table where there was whisky and poured himself a drink.

Carol watched him for a moment, then stood up and took Deane's hands.

"I have an appointment, my dear," he said gently. "It has been good to find you." He hesitated, lifting one eyebrow. "And I am happy to have met your friend."

Martin nodded again and took a drink.

Carol bit his lip and put on his coat, tenderly pressing a scarf of coral pink under his collar.

"Goodnight. I'll call you to-morrow, dear," he said to Deane as he left.

When the door closed behind him Martin put down his glass and went over to Deane.

"It's funny," he said, "how friendships like this spring up."

Deane looked away while she spoke.

"He hates you."

Martin squinted through the window at the colors in the dusk.

"Have your fun, Martin," she continued, "but not at his expense. Why were you so rude?"

"Because it's the easiest way."

"I know Carol's extravagances," she went on, "but I hate to see him hurt."

Martin wheeled around. "And I don't want you hurt," he answered. "Carol's bad luck. He's a fool and a parrot." Then, raising his voice a little, he repeated, "They're all damned bad luck."

All this time Carol was walking down the street. His walk was unusual but convincing. His hips had no vertical motion. They jerked horizontally, hesitated, and jerked to the other side. He knew that his hips did this. He liked it and did it on purpose, for he had always liked the abstract movement of a woman. So Carol went down the street, aware and proud of his unusual attraction. But he kept thinking of Deane and Martin. He shuddered. "They are like animals—they!" He looked swiftly at a man crossing the street. Then he shrugged his shoulders and thought again of Deane and Martin. "How carnal! How obvious! Why, even now they might be looking at each other—holding each other." The thought was too repugnant and he held a handkerchief to his lips. Yes; such things were—he waved his handkerchief almost imperceptibly—well, beyond endurance. Gently he picked up his cross and strapped it over his shoulders, basking in tribal strength. His friends had said: "Man and woman?—ah, yes,"—(with a yawn). Carol held the handkerchief closer.

He walked along the Avenue to Washington Square and sat down on a bench. A thin, blonde-haired woman with a pretty face passed him slowly. She thought rapidly, came back and sat down beside him.

Carol's mind was drifting pleasurably. He remembered a boy in Chicago who could quote poetry beautifully and whose blue eyes were oriental. The boy's hands were so strong that they could crack a walnut; and yet, they could be so gentle. Carol smiled, a sweet, remembering smile. The girl on the bench smiled, too. She thought he was affecting indifference and her interest increased. But he did not even know that she was there until she held a cigarette toward him.

"Pardon me. Do you have a match?" she asked.

Carol was taken from his dream. Not entirely. A moment, a memory, a little beauty remained. But this slender, light-haired creature had destroyed everything he felt most closely. He looked at her calmly. He knew women.

"I do not have a match. I do not smoke." He looked at her and she understood. Both had an expression of loathing. Each typified the thing in the world they disliked most. The girl stood up. She didn't know how to tell him what she felt, but an obscene, contemptuous movement of her hips sickened him. He looked in the other direction, praying that she would leave swiftly. It was humiliating.... The evening shadows hid her as she walked away and Carol tried to reminisce again. But it was no good. His dreams had gone.

Two boys strolled past him. They were students and they were talking about books. Their clothes were not well pressed and they were obviously thinking about technicalities. Another boy went by; thin, his hair uncut, looking straight before him. Several Italian sweethearts, laughing, holding hands, walked up and down. Carol watched them with indifference. Two more boys passed, close together. One of them was handsome. They laughed musically, and while Carol could hear only a fragment of their conversation, it made him lonely. Several young fellows with polo shirts under their coats approached him; but he was scornful. "Trade! Commercializing those wretches!"—He flicked it out of his mind with arrogance.

The moon undressed over the University. It was slender, strong and white. Carol had seen a boy like that one time—slim and white and very strong. Carol made his own standards when he had been hurt enough. The moon was a boy, dancing for him. Tears were in Carol's eyes and he wiped them away austerely. Still the moon danced before him. There was an animal cry in his throat, but he would not let it out. He arose and left the park, went to a telephone booth and called Deane. While he talked, he held the back of his neck tightly.

"Hello, Deane. Would it be imposing on you if I came over again for a few minutes?—just for a few minutes before I go to my hotel?"

Deane was a woman, too, and she felt the quality of hysteria in his voice.

"Of course you can. I'll be so glad to see you, Carol." "Right away," he said, and hung up. For a long time he stood there, staring blankly at the mouthpiece while his child-mind spun blankly round its core.

Deane returned to the living room, sat down beside Martin and lit a cigarette.

"Jesus Christ!" said Martin, looking at her.

The phone rang again.

"Jesus Christ!" he repeated.

This time it was Roberts. He asked Deane (rather pleadingly, she thought) if she would see him.

"Martin is here, Roberts," she replied.

"Please let me speak with him."

Deane beckoned to Martin, who flung himself out of the chair a bit impatiently and took the receiver from her hand.

"You think this is easy," said Roberts, when he heard his voice. "It isn't, Martin. You think I'm wrong, and I think you are. But that shouldn't be an issue. Right or wrong, there is something more important to which we owe our fidelity."

"What's that?"

"Ourselves, Martin. Listen! I've gone back and forth over our quarrel and God knows where the origin was, or worse yet, where the ends are now. Help me find them, dear boy. Everything is twisted. I can't sleep."

Martin rubbed his forehead. There was sincerity in Roberts' voice.

"Everything's all right, Roberts," he said at last. "Come along."

"Good boy! Good boy!"

Martin could hear a strange, sobbing chuckle.

"It's all right," he repeated. "And Deane wants you to come, too." Martin could see Deane incline her head gently. It was a gesture he loved and of which he was jealous. After he left the phone they sat for some minutes without speaking. Then Martin shook his head. "Jesus Christ!" he said once more.

He got up and went into the kitchen to mix the highballs. Before he had finished he heard Deane open the door and knew that it was Carol. The boy stepped across his brain—walked cozeningly, with his side-weave and his red, disarranged face. Then Martin heard Roberts. He felt the unreliable smile—saw the white, fanatical face. He felt the pressure of entering the room and held his fingers against the sides of his head. The two figures with Deane were waiting for him.... Carol, looking for a lost doll.... Roberts, handsome, leprous, searching for the impossible.... Martin waited until the introductions were over, then walked into the living room with the drinks. He placed the tray of highballs on a table.

Roberts got out of his chair at once and went to him, holding out his hand with an intense movement which Martin accepted quietly.

"You're looking well again, Martin," said the adviser. "And I'm glad to find it so." He turned halfway to Deane with a strained smile. "Isn't it splendid, Deane?"

She returned the smile, nodding her head and Martin broke in swiftly.

"I fell into a job, Roberts—free lance work that turned regular. Perhaps my relief shows in my appearance."

"Where is the job?" asked Roberts quickly, looking concerned.

"Downtown," said Martin, a vague expression in his eyes.

Roberts flushed and returned to his chair, while Martin sat down on the divan beside Deane. Carol, who had been watching the two men with fascination, leaned back sighing, a satisfied look softening his features as he drew out his cigarette holder.

"I knew New York would be this way—just this way. And I just *love* it!" He cocked his head at Martin and nodded wisely. "The swift pace of commerce," he added.

"Who said that?" asked Martin, amused.

Carol looked embarrassed.

"Why, I—why, I think the salesman did. But it was so apt—the salesman said—" He hesitated, and Martin raised his hand in agreement.

"It *is* apt, Carol," he replied. "I should know. It takes experience to make one understand 'the swift pace of commerce.' Mr. Roberts realizes this, too, though in a different way; for *he'll* never let commerce get at *his* heels."

"Indeed, I won't," said Roberts vehemently. "I'll follow it, trip it, mold it and make it carry me." He was about to continue when Deane spoke quietly, but with a certain implied request. Her beautiful eyes gleamed in the shaded light.

"Did you keep your appointment, Carol?" she asked, turning to him with mild interest.

"No, dear," he answered in a puzzled voice. "No, we must have been—well, mixed up," he went on more precisely. "So I went to the park—Washington Square, the policeman said it was. But oh!—I just felt so blue I *had* to call you up." He held a silken handkerchief daintily under his nose and let it flutter with his breath. "But there's a glorious moon," he continued, looking at Martin. "It really seems to be dancing. And speaking of dancing—I saw the *cutest* thing at a show the other night!" He became enthusiastic and stood up, still holding on to the handkerchief with one hand while he placed the other on his hip. Then he turned his head a little and looked coyly over one shoulder.

"What was it like?" asked Deane, a strange smile on her lips.

"I really can't say, dear. But," Carol's eyes brightened, "It *did* have—" he waved the handkerchief, "what do you call it?—'um-pah!'" Completely forgetful now of his surroundings, he pursed his lips into a curious form and began to sing in a rather wistful mood, "Ooh-ooh, woo-woo, me too," his hand on his hip, his handkerchief still fluttering. Then he circled his left foot back of the right, followed up, and continued until he was moving gracefully across the room in time with the weird intonation. At last he seemed to fade into the hallway as though it were the wings of a theater; and the three in the room could hear the words float in long after he had disappeared—"Ooh-ooh, woo-woo, me too."

Martin laughed without restraint and clapped his hands loudly. There was a gurgle of delight from the hall and Carol peeped around the doorway, his face aglow at such acclaim.

"Great!" continued Martin, as the young man came in beaming. "The best! The very best, Carol!" he went on, while the other, breathless, sat down and touched the handkerchief to his forehead. Deane's eyes still gleamed peculiarly; but Roberts had merely turned his face the other way.

Then suddenly, as though each wanted to convince the others that his own thoughts were spontaneous, they talked in animated sequence. They talked of music, and of tides, and of the government. Each word was a word—Roberts', like a dark sword in a silver lake; Carol's, like the hole in a fisherman's net; and Martin's and Deane's, like clouds over a river.

In a short while, Roberts stood up.

"I must go," he said gravely.

Carol got up also, and after a brief look at Martin, followed the adviser into another room to get his coat.

Outside there was a cool wind blowing. Carol led Roberts to Washington Square—an inexplicable impulse returning and behind the direction. The guards had raked the grass after the early snows. A pile of leaves burned slowly, and the soft flutter of pigeons beyond the firelight made the park seem homely and comfortable. On the icy concrete surrounding the fountain there were children with skates. Their flashing feet splintered the dark which lay under the moon, and around these romping figures the cool wind, blowing softly, held everything together.

Neither Carol nor Roberts noticed the pigeons or the children. They were watching their own hearts. Carol's beat slowly, with a regular, bovine thump. Roberts' beat quickly, irregularly, with acuity and despair. He was in such despair that he tried to find camaraderie within the boy beside him. His monologue pretended to be a conversation, but his bright words of indictment against Martin rolled across Carol's porcine cheek and were reflected, turning in to himself, weighting his bitterness more heavily.

"Yes, Carol," he said, "we must forget ourselves in this issue. We must save our friends from this domestic suicide. Clutching an insane illusion of love, they are bemused by carnal appetite. Lost on the horizon of flesh, their perspective becomes astigmatic. Drowned in beast's blood, they deliberately blind themselves to an obvious incompatibility. It is our duty to our strength, our lives, our God, to break this union." Roberts' mouth became loose and wet. "We must show them the truth.... Martin! Martin!" The adviser's eyes were like those of a sick horse. "Martin is so young—so fruitful. We must forgive him.... And that lovely woman—upset so terribly by him—we must give her our strength." Roberts dropped his head, unable to speak further.

Carol smiled vacuously.

"Yes," he replied.

And while Roberts cried into the vacant moon the boy beside him, uncomprehending, drooled on.

"Yes. We must give our strength. We must give ourselves. We must give—" Carol's voice became fainter and disappeared into the sound of leaves. He could feel Martin's arm around him, petting—forcing. Carol's face became curiously beautiful.... He was giving himself....

Roberts, taken from his sadness by this incoherent dribbling—Roberts, sensing the thought beside him, moved away. He looked at Carol, at the fat thighs, the fat cheeks, the desire; and he was suddenly sick. To have Martin touched, even in thought, was unbearable. Unsteadily he pushed himself off the bench and walked away without speaking. The moon was beautiful, but it was not for him. There was magic in the wind, but it made him feel more lonely.... For a long time he walked. The cornstalk he had left sitting on the bench was but a mild irritant now. It became less and less so until Roberts laughed.

Carol was not aware of the change. He knew only that Martin was closer— that his dream was real.

The bonfire had long been extinguished and the guards had left. There was no sound of skates; there was a hush of wings; and the moon looked down on the Italian lovers with their quick, dark hands.

CHAPTER XIII

Carol did not sleep well that night. He had dreams of strong and muscular things; but they felt good. Early in the morning his child-mind was tired. His fantasies and adult body had exhausted him. He awoke and turned over to be spanked. His father had always spanked him when he had been bad. But now he did not feel his father's calloused hand against him, nor could he see his father's frown and long, unshaven jaw. Carol turned over again, realizing vaguely where he was.... His father was dead. He was not being spanked. Something had been taken from him and his mouth trembled.... The strong nostalgia made him sick. He wanted to be bad, and then feel the hard hand and weep happily as his father struck him.

Carol was now fully awake. He got out of bed, rubbing his sticky eyes. Over the wash-basin there was a mirror in which he saw himself. He turned on the cold water, dipped his head in the bowl and rubbed his cheeks until they glowed. Then he bathed with a washcloth and afterwards, squirted toilet water under his arms. The hotel room was small and hot. He opened the window a little wider, returned to his bed and made it up carefully, patting the corners. At last, he put on a dressing gown with long, flowing sleeves, smiled at the reflection of his pink, clean face in the mirror and picked up the telephone.

"Give me outside," he said.

"What number do you want?" asked the operator, sucking her teeth.

Carol was startled. Then he gave the number.

Deane answered a little sleepily.

Carol lit a cigarette and blew the smoke in flat, blue layers.

"Did I get you out of bed, sweet?"

Deane smiled easily, the smooth skin at the corners of her eyes forming tiny lines.

"Of course not, Carol," she replied. "I'm glad you called. Did you enjoy your evening with Mr. Roberts?"

"Oh!" said Carol, "I had *such* a good time. Mr. Roberts is so interesting. And we talked about so many things. It was such a beautiful evening and so—" Carol's sibilant words came through the wire to Deane, awakening her thoroughly. "Let's have lunch together," he continued. "How about twelve, at the Astor?"

"I have some shopping to do," she answered, "but I'll be through by one. Suppose we make it then."

"All right, dear. I'll see you then," he said, stressing every other word. "I'll see you then. Good-by, dear."

Deane left the apartment in confusion, half amused and yet severe. Her tiny hat, which was like an autumn leaf, revoked the tailoring of her rust-colored velvet suit. On the street, old women smiled at her without knowing why; and newsboys became quiet for one starry-eyed, adolescent moment as she passed. But she kept thinking of Martin. She remembered him as he had been on the previous night. She loved him, but he was a problem. If his were artistry, it would be good to get back to solidity and minds that ran in clear, straight lines. She had thought this as she left the apartment. But in the shops she changed her mind. She saw strong, competent men and women and she liked them. But thoughts of Martin persisted—Martin with his hair sticking up—Martin, fumbling with design and people and dreams. He might find it! He *must* find it! Deane put her small, gloved hand to her throat. She wanted him suddenly, strongly. She wanted his incoherent sentences, his slippery body and his crazy, adoring heart. She laughed self-consciously in front of the pencilheads, typewriter-heads and blotting-paper faces, and made a few reckless purchases.

Carol met her at precisely one o'clock. His face was pink, natty and smiling. His belted coat showed his figure and he wore no hat. His astonishing scarf had been replaced by an ascot tie whose vivid background was accentuated by purple stripes. He took both of Deane's hands with sisterly affection, completely unconscious of the mild attention he had attracted in the lounge.

"A *dreadful* morning," he said wearily. "One can't eat in New York, can one?"

Deane was a little piqued.

"Well," she said, biting her scarlet underlip, "one's going to." More kindly she took his arm. "We're going to eat heartily, Carol. I'm hungry."

They went into the bar. The buttons on Carol's topcoat stuck out like feathers. He was conscious now of the atmosphere and of the woman with him. His exuberance spilled, porridge-like, over the barren years of his life and reached out toward the other patrons in the bar. Ostentatiously, he led Deane past a table where two elderly ladies were having whisky and soda. One of them wore three wedding rings. The other's plume on her tiny hat colored the dark fur over her shoulders. Carol's good nature manifested itself again and he nodded intimately to them. The old ladies looked at each other and went on drinking their whisky.

At last, Carol selected a table and held a chair for Deane. She wanted a glass of sherry, but tried to enjoy the drink he ordered. It was a fragile looking concoction of pale pink, with a lace of foam.

"At home, we call it a 'raspberry kiss,'" said Carol proudly.

Deane knew that he thought he was living. He sipped on, and sang on, hesitating briefly to glance at every man who walked into the bar. One or two of them looked at him in amused recognition, but most of them were absorbed in other matters and passed him, unnoticing. As the alcohol sifted through his mind, his sentences became more vapid, more pretentious, and louder. He began to simper—call attention to unimportant things. There was an angry moment with the waiter, who accepted his ridiculous complaints with thinly veiled contempt. It was difficult to embarrass Deane—the outside of Deane. But she refused a second drink, suggesting food instead, and together they went upstairs to the dining room.

The head waiter courteously guided them to a corner table. No one was close to them and Deane relaxed. Carol sighed, lit a cigarette and ordered the luncheon. Suddenly he leaned toward Deane.

"We have been friends too long, dear," he said, "for me to mince words. You don't mind my speaking?"

"Of course not," said Deane. "I don't mind at all."

"I have heard rumors," said Carol, shaking his head over his plate. "They have bothered me and I feel that you ought to know."

Deane looked amused.

"Rumors?" she repeated. "Honestly?"

"This," said Carol sternly, "is not a frivolous joke. It has no frivolity." He looked less stern now. Frivolity. He liked that word. He leaned back in his chair and tried, ineffectually, to blow a smoke ring. "This," he continued, "concerns your happiness. It will probably hurt you. But I know you will face it. I must forget myself in this issue."

"Issue?" asked Deane, frowning a little.

"Yes, Deane," went on Carol. "It's Martin and you. It is domestic suicide. I watch you clutch this insane illusion of love—bemused by carnal appetite. Lost on the horizon of flesh, your perspective becomes astigmatic. Drowned in beast's blood, you deliberately blind yourself to an obvious incompatibility. It is my duty to my strength, my life, my God, to break this union." He let his head rest against the wall for a moment, hypnotized by the magnificence of his words.

Deane was now frankly amazed. Where did these words come from? They were brilliant, hateful words. Carol was incapable of such expression. She hunted through her memory for the explanation. Then she recalled Martin's analogy of the parrot. Carol had heard the words and had remembered them.

Where had he heard them? No one knew Martin—ah! The good friend Roberts. That sounded like Roberts. That *was* Roberts.

She watched Carol—his eyes closed, three fingers on his holder. Retentiveness—that was it. Carol, the parrot. Retentiveness. Carol did not know what had broken from his memory. Deane knew that he believed it was himself speaking. She began to fear Roberts. Fear him so much that she forgot Carol was with her.

Carol squinted and nodded his head approvingly. That had done it. His great understanding had brought Deane to her senses. Her face showed it—pale, constricted. Carol cocked his flat, moist hands at her in sympathy.

"I know it's hard," he said, reaching womanishly toward her.

Deane did not move away from him, but she had an odd feeling. Once, she had had a dream that had given her the same sensation. She dreamed that in an adventurous moment she had descended to the bottom of the ocean, there to play with the mermaids, look at the starfish, and perhaps start a flirtation, harmless or otherwise, with friendly old Poseidon. She had dropped softly to the sands of the sea and it was more beautiful than she had expected. The water was the kind of blue pretty girls like in nightgowns. It was cool and restful and it felt good around her legs and her waist. She walked slowly and gracefully over the white sand and through the blue water. At last she saw a rock, half-embedded in moss; and there, holding it tightly, was her starfish. She knelt down to look at it. It was a large one of delicate yellow—not at all like those dried, smelly things she had studied at school. It was yellow, and it clung to the green moss. It seemed to be in love; but it was quiet. Deane knew it was asleep when she looked closer. Its crisp points were symmetrical and straight. Deane blushed, and through the twilight blue of the water the color of her cheeks was attractive to King Poseidon who had been peeking at her through a wall of seaweed. He was infatuated. She was different from Amphitrite. He loved Amphitrite—her long green hair, her white face and jeweled hips. Nevertheless, he wanted to kiss this strange woman. He wanted to kiss the color in her cheeks and touch her. But King Poseidon shook his head. Amphitrite could be very difficult if she became angry. Confound these appetites for rare and inedible dishes! Poseidon smiled though, a boyish, sheepish, proud smile. He had appetites. He was getting to be a little gray; and still, he had appetites. He looked at Deane once more, wistfully, and took his appetites to Amphitrite.

Amphitrite combed his beard. Poseidon looked at her and poked his finger at her and winked. She regarded him suspiciously, but when she saw the expression in his eyes something happened to her. Through the darkening blue her white cheeks softened, became pink and sent out threads of coral. Poseidon shook his head in wonderment and happiness. It was just what a man wanted. That was all. The memory of Deane faded from him as Amphitrite, her face still coral, gently removed his crown.

As the water became darker, Deane's dream became less happy. She couldn't compete with green hair, a white face and those commanding, jeweled hips. She was despondent. She didn't want King Poseidon. She wanted the earth again and stars and a warm, comfortable hand. It was the didactic part of her spoiling a beautiful dream.

Some dreams can't be shut off. As she drifted toward the surface of the water a white shadow crossed above her and twisted under her face. Its white was not a pure white, and there were dark objects fastened to its shoulders. Deane wasn't afraid. The creature didn't want her. It didn't have any sense; but it was close and revolting. In her dream she floated slowly upward. She was strong and disdainful, but that didn't push the creature from her. She rose slowly, grimly, with hate—motionless. Her hair caught the surface of the water. Stars poured into her eyes, the white shadow faded, and she awakened. She had gone into the bathroom and washed her teeth.

In the dining room Deane remembered this dream and her feeling for the snub-faced shadow. Carol leaned toward her. She did not fear him. She did not move from him, but she wanted clean air and a chance to brush her teeth.

"Carol," she said, "Martin and I are very good friends. I believe in him."

Carol lit another cigarette. He was bewildered. It was unfair. He had gone to Deane as a pal. He had tried to help her. His eloquent monologue still boomed within him. Then a friendly sorrow for himself killed some of the pain. He had done his duty although it had been unappreciated. He saw women—all womankind rotating under the phallic thumb of bestial domination. He shivered, reached for the check and stood up. Deane noticed that he left no tip for the waiter.

She hurried home and Carol returned to his hotel. He sat carefully on the edge of his bed and looked out at the moving cars and people. His face was serious. Deane needed him. His affection would win over this—this—he put his head down on the pillow and refused to think any more.

Deane glanced at the clock. Only an hour to wait. She was glad that Martin was coming at five. She was glad to get out of her tailored clothes and into the bath. It would be comfortable to feel her skin against the warm porcelain; to smell the soap and to watch the steam cover the glass. There was no aroma from the step-ins dropped upon the tile. Only the faint resonance of a discriminate healthiness from the underclothes was in the corner. Deane slipped into the tub, still wearing her brassiere and her wristwatch. Impatiently she took them off and now, she lay flat across the shoulders of the tub. Reaching around, with her eyes closed, she felt the cake of soap next her hips. She weighed it in her hands for an absent moment, thinking of Martin, and with a slow smile laid the bar upon one breast, which she had candidly lifted out of the water. The pride she held in her own body seemed an important thing to her and she constantly soaped the skin around her nipple in amusement—but laved it also, in possibilities too far to speak of, even to herself. At last the warmth of the bath claimed her more expressively than she had believed it could; and she remembered, with a shiver, the snows of childhood and buried herself again in the heat of the tub. One of her hands went gently, but shockingly to her knee; and again with a smile, not understandable, she lifted her body out of the water, which rang in constant drops of different colors from her naked throat.

While she dressed, she thought of her earrings. She chose a slender East Indian pair of beaten silver. They were long, nearly touching her bare shoulders, and of a deceptive quietness. She looked at her slippers—gold, vermilion, rust—at last selecting ones of purple from which she decided her gown. Its bodice, which she laced and tied, peasant fashion, closed tightly about her waist. The skirt swung slowly from her hips. She looked once more into the mirror and fastened her hair on one side behind her ear.

When Martin came, he put his arms around her, kissing her earrings and her throat, the scented smooth hollow under her arm, pressing her so close to him that she trembled.

"Tell me—what did you do to-day?" he whispered, holding her hand to his cheek.

"I went shopping," she said. "And later, I had lunch with Carol."

Martin spoke irritably.

"That one again? Why doesn't he go back to the Dust Bowl?"

"He isn't that bad, Martin." Deane tried to sound convincing.

"I should think," Martin said bitterly, "that you would be the last one to question my judgment where such people are concerned."

Deane lifted her delicate eyebrows.

"I'm glad I'm your sweetheart," she said. "That remark would sound curious to others."

"I suppose it would," replied Martin, a bit unhappily. "I'll admit, I'm prejudiced as the devil, but I can't help but see it. Carol's learning new tricks. The crust is breaking. He lives among his fantasies—dreams fired by sagebrush and loneliness. His desire is volatile and his friends right now may affect the nature of his entire life. I'm sorry Roberts is mixed up in it."

Deane was thoughtful for a moment. She cupped her chin in her hands and drew her small, slippered feet up under her.

"I believe you're right, Martin," she observed at last. "For the first time I see that it's a dangerous combination. I still believe, though, that Roberts is the one who, ultimately, will try to harm you. He's done it once and although you came out, he will try it again. He seems to know your vulnerable points."

Martin sounded a little angry.

"Why can't we just eliminate them?"

"It isn't quite so simple as that, Martin," answered Deane. "Roberts and I have mutual friends. I'd always be running into him. As for Carol—he has no one; and I couldn't bear to hurt him." Deane stared before her. "Besides," she added, "I'm wondering if elimination could bring about anything but superficial results. Roberts is ingenious." She turned to Martin impulsively and put her hand upon his arm. "Martin!—somehow, I don't know how—but somehow, Roberts will strike at us!"

In the city light, in the dusk, Deane's eyes were wide, as though some new and frightening thought had crossed her mind.

CHAPTER XIV

Rio left the bitt on which he had been sitting. He crossed the deck and walked down the ladder as the sea caught the ship and sent her rolling in long swells toward the Gulf Stream. He was going to his bunk when a man with a blue chin and hard, bloodshot eyes got up from the table where he had been drinking beer and went to him.

"Where's your book?" the man said abruptly, in a high, angry voice.

"That ain't no way to ask for it," Rio said slowly.

The sailors' delegate swore.

"Break out that god-damned union book!"

"You'll find it under this," said Rio, rubbing his fist.

"Oh! That's it!" said the delegate, coming closer, unconscious that his lips were still moving.

"Sure," continued Rio. "A chink in the Celebes told me wisdom came with lost teeth."

"Get wise then!" yelled the delegate, and swung hard.

Rio ducked, but the blow caught him across the jaw and a little blood ran down his neck. For an instant, his face was the outlawed Baptist's.

"Turn in," he said, almost in a whisper. "The next time you might fall."

The man swung again and Rio drove a wide fist straight into his face. Blood squirted out all over, covering both men. The delegate fell backwards; his head struck a stanchion. He rocked slowly and fell loosely sideways, his shoulder hitting the deck. Rio stepped over to the table and picked up the empty beer bottle.

"My God!" said one of the men. The rest of the crew turned the delegate's face over. They couldn't see the features. They talked among themselves quietly for a moment, then walked menacingly toward Rio. He jumped like a monkey into a corner, with the bottle in his left hand and his right fist cocked. He had pulled off his skivy-shirt and the men looked at his chest. It was brown and curiously bare. There was the mark of a slice bar and a dent across his ribs. They had never seen anything like it. They stopped and seemed to smell the blood. Suddenly they recognized the man—his style of fighting, the way animals do, without thought or compassion. Rio stood there, silent, massive, and the men went back to their bunks.

The able-bodied seamen carried the delegate into the washroom and started working on him. Rio put the bottle back on the table. Then he took his bucket and towel into the washroom. He didn't look at the huddle in the corner, or at the delegate crying softly on a bench, or hear an occasional curse from one of the sailors. He took his bath and returned to his bunk, turned in and stared at the overhead. He could feel the slow roll and sudden pitch of the ship. He loved it and felt at home again....

There were swift movements in the dark around him. Then the main light in the fo'c'sle came on and it was quiet for a moment. He could hear a man cough.

"Is he?"

Another voice.

"Yeah. He's dead."

And still another.

"Let's tell the mate on watch."

"And have your gear turned inside out, you fool?" said the first voice.

"You'd look funny in the commissioner's office, too," answered the third.

"For God's sake then, pipe down and let's drop him to Davy. I can't stand him in here. We'll say he got drunk ashore and when he came in he fell on his face. He said his head ached and went on deck. We looked for him an hour.... I go to the second mate. He'll soon be on watch. I tell him the story. Before he gets aft or calls the Old Man, you have the fo'c'sle cleaned and the beer hid. Stick by the story. That's all."

"What about the fellow who done it? He'll be on watch with the second."

"That guy ain't human. He won't show nothin'. O.K.?"

"O.K."

Rio heard the noise die down and went to sleep.

Rio felt his arm being shaken. He saw a figure bent over him, wearing oilskins which glistened from a flashlight.

"Seven bells," said the figure. "Coffee on the boatdeck. Watch it goin' 'midships. She's takin' a few seas."

Rio dressed silently, pulled on his sea boots and fastened his oilskins and sou'wester. On deck, he looked around the lee corner of the house and waited for a sea to break over. A small one came under the rail and hissed across the deck, winding up with a crash against the hatches. The white water ran into the scuppers. As she started to roll back, Rio ran as fast as he could to a ladder to the boatdeck. Then he went forward to a small house where a light was burning.

In there was a young man pouring coffee. His face was white and anxious. When he saw Rio he said, "They tell me you're my watch partner."

Rio smiled and nodded his head. He poured himself a cup of coffee and sat down to drink it.

The young man spoke again.

"I was told to report for lookout duty on the port side of the bridge. I don't know where that is."

"I'll show you."

"But what do I do as lookout?"

"Ask the man you relieve," said Rio. "And don't be upset if the mate yells a bit. It's hard for some of 'em to fasten a twelve-inch neck in a seventeen collar. Just lay low unless you see a ship comin' up. Then tell it to him as best you can and let him swear all he pleases. We better go up now," he added.

They went out into the wind and up the ladder to the bridge. The quartermaster, seeing Rio, left the wheel.

"One ninety-five," he said. "One ninety-five," he called to the third officer in the chartroom. The officer counted out the numbers and the quartermaster left.

The second mate entered the chartroom, relieving the third officer.

Rio saw the ship was on her course and looked out where his watch partner was walking hesitatingly toward the wheelhouse. He waved him back.

Soon, the second mate came in without speaking. He looked at the compass under the binnacle light. Then he stood up and silently regarded Rio, who gave the wheel a spoke or two. The mate became exasperated. He walked up and down, staring out of the glass. Suddenly he came over and looked at the compass again.

"You're off six degrees. Heading this way, we might make Jamaica."

"I had a wife there once," said Rio, his face impassive. "It's a good island."

"Wife! You said—'wife'?"

"Yeah. Up in the hills. She was a good worker, too."

The mate lit a cigarette. It was twelve-thirty and Rio struck one bell. Attentively, the officer waited for a few minutes.

"Where's that god-damned lookout?" He fastened his pea-jacket and went out on the bridge. Rio could hear voices through the wind and shrugged his shoulders. After awhile, the second mate came back puffing.

"A fine lot—a fine lot to work with!" he said.

A seaman stepped inside the wheelhouse and addressed the mate.

"There's a man missin', sir."

"A man missing—a man missing? What do you mean? What happened?"

"I dunno. The sailors' delegate got drunk ashore. He was a little foggy and fell on the deck. He didn't seem to mind and said he'd take a little air topside. When he didn't come down we went up and looked around."

"Mother of Christ!" cried the second mate. "Break out the crew—No!" He recalled the man. "I'll get the skipper." He ran out of the wheelhouse, his jacket open.

The man who had reported the accident looked at Rio. Rio's face was dark and kindly from the glow of the binnacle light.

Several nights later they passed the Gulf Stream and when Rio got up about eleven in the morning he saw the deep-purple waters of the Caribbean Sea. It was getting warmer. He put on clean dungarees and went to the sailors' mess for a plate of soup. He could tell little from the expression of the men around him, but rather, felt their sullen disapproval and was indifferent to it. He ate his soup, asked for another plateful, ate it and went up to the wheelhouse again. He had been steering for about five minutes with the second mate beside him when the latter went out of the house. Rio could hear him climb the ladder to the flying bridge to check the compass. When he came down, he walked in front of Rio and closed the door on the weather side, although it was hot already. He came back, looked at the compass and smiled a peculiar smile. Suddenly, there was a sharp noise and a saccharine odor and the second mate, still smiling, went out on the lee side of the bridge.

Rio held his nose.

"A virgin," he said to himself, leaving the wheel and throwing open the door.

The mate returned and brought the door to. A curious expression was on his face; but he still smiled as he left once more for the bridge.

"*That* fish was picked up in Nagasaki," said Rio aloud, and opened the door again.

The second mate slammed the door this time, standing by the wheel only a moment before wind cracked at his heels. Rio could see his tiny, blond mustache jump in the sunlight. But this time, Rio did not open the door. He followed the mate and stood beside him.

"For God's sake! Get back to that wheel, you damned fool!" yelled the officer.

"Not till both doors are open and the weather's cleared," said Rio in an even voice. He leaned on the rail, his fine eyes glistening.

The second mate rushed into the house where the wheel had turned until the ship was twenty degrees off her course. Nervously, but with a calculated deliberation, he gave her a few spokes at a time, trying to protect himself from the captain's eternal damnation. After awhile Rio walked past him, opened the weather door and took over. Neither man spoke until Rio was relieved.

The next day Rio was chipping spots on the deck when he felt a knee against his side. He pulled off his goggles and looked up. It was the second mate. Rio laid down his hammer and said, "I can hear."

"You can hear—what?"

"I can hear trouble if that's the way you wake me up again."

The mate grew excited.

"Listen! What's the matter with you? Don't you know discipline?"

Rio got up. He didn't say anything but his heavy brown face looked down with contempt.

The officer tried to retain his dignity.

"Why did you raise hell in the wheelhouse?" he asked.

Rio continued to look down at him.

"Because I'm a quiet-livin' man. I'm modest. And I don't like to be intimate."

The second mate's face turned red.

"Show me your union book," he said briefly.

Rio shook his head.

"That'd be too intimate. You don't carry your school-ship papers all the time, do you?"

"By God!" shouted the mate. "I'll have you thrown in the brig. It's hot in the forepeak."

Rio grinned, a slow, malicious grin.

"And there's dark nights and twenty-foot shark in the Gulf of Darien—a hell of a place for a snotty little mate to slip."

The officer walked away. His eyes seemed red in the sun and he seemed to be thinking.

Rio adjusted his goggles and went to work. He liked to see each rusted, brown flake disappear under the blows of his hammer and uncover the bright blue steel below. Suddenly, once more, he felt a knee against his side. The mate had come back. He ordered Rio to move over to the port side and chip rust near the fishplate. Rio crossed the deck, watching from the corner of his eye the vicious look of the officer who was crawling into No. 2 hatch. Rio grinned again.

"A good place for 'im if a freak wave shifts the cargo," he thought.

He had worked for an hour when he heard men shouting. The captain came down and ran aft, then back to the fore deck. Seeing Rio at work he hurried to him.

"Have you seen the second mate forward?" he asked.

"Yes, sir. About an hour ago. He told me to chip rust by the fishplate," answered Rio.

The captain looked puzzled.

"By the *fishplate*? Quick, man!—was that the last you saw him?"

"That's the last, sir."

"Put her about!" the captain shouted up at the bridge. "See that a boat's ready."

The ship had just swung round when the second mate's head appeared above the hatch. He blinked in the sunlight. His shirt was torn, his flashlight was crushed and he had a skinned right arm. He limped slowly toward the captain.

"I was just checking the cargo, sir," he said. He turned angrily toward Rio. "I know that man saw me go down."

The captain addressed his officer severely.

"Why aren't you on the bridge, Mr. Birch? Do you check cargo on your own watch?—And with a beam sea like this running?"

"I'm sorry, sir," answered the mate, looking away.

"Go and clean yourself up, Mr. Birch." The captain turned to speak to Rio, but the steady blows of the chipping hammer were sounding by the fishplate.

Rio was standing outside the galley on the *Nancy II* when she steamed along the South American coast into the harbor of Santa de Marina. Once before, when he had entered the bay, it had been night; and there, tucked at the feet of the Andes, the town was obliterated by the proximity of the moon. This time, by day, he knew that nature had sustained a lasting brilliance to endure around the many-colored houses—beyond, the olive shade of mountain; and before, the whitest line of sand between the elbows of the cliff that closed upon a canvas of blue harbor. Lesser energies surrendered in an atmosphere of light that dominated cooler tones.

It was late morning and Rio saw the ancient, Spanish town suspended. Soon it would be siesta time—a quiet drink and heavy sleep while native children watched the ship and languorously ate their fruit. Rio did not know he had the same pure look of indolence. The shore's breath and the sound of hidden insects were leeward to the ship; but Rio recognized them all. This was a town so close to him with heat and spiced, familiar odors, its bright mantle turned away the thoughts of other things. New York—its equidistant problems that changed with unexpectedness—was left behind, or so he felt; and just before him was a point of tropics with a sweet demand he understood.

As the *Nancy II* came alongside the banana docks she pulled up aft of another ship of about the same tonnage. The letters on her stern spelled *Swamp Rat.*

Rio ran forward to help with the lines. The gangplank was lowered and he went back to the fo'c'sle to wash up. Later, he saw the first mate, spoke with him and went down the gangplank into the heavy glare of the sun. Longshoremen were already unloading No. 4 hatch and the banana machine was being set up. A large gang of peons waited patiently to go to work. A sad-faced one with a skin of pure black saw Rio looking at them. He smiled suddenly, and from his squatting position jumped six feet in the air, clicking his bare heels together rapidly and coming down on one foot, his ragged trousers flapping. The rest of the peons clapped and laughed, shoving each other. But the black was watching Rio; and when Rio smiled, the black clapped louder than all the rest. Then quickly, as though he had just thought of it, he ran to a stack of freshly-cut bananas of a lizard-green. Seizing a huge bunch from the pile, he tossed it in the air and Rio, moving nearer, could see the hard muscles of the man strain as he caught it in both hands before it hit the ground. Some of the peons were chanting now, and some were slapping the boards of the warehouse with a native rhythm. But the black still watched for Rio's approval and this time, when Rio clapped, the peon squatted down again, rolling his big eyes and making a clucking sound.

Amused, yet abiding by an adolescent impulse to exhibit, Rio walked to the bunch of bananas which the black had returned to the pile and took firm hold of the large stem with one hand. He threw himself forward, then backward and down, till the tip of the bunch was pointing upward and the stem was braced against his neck. Slowly he came up, the veins pulsing in his forehead and sweat trickling into his eyes. For a second he stood at full height. Then the white heat, the black men and the misty, green bananas began to turn. He staggered; but pulling himself together, lowered the bananas to the pile again. The peons laughed loudly and the big black jumped up and down. Easing closer, he examined Rio's arm. At last, he called out to the others.

"*Dos músculos en un brazo!*" he shouted triumphantly.

A young oiler from the *Swamp Rat* nudged Rio.

"What did he say?" he asked.

"He said I have two muscles in one arm." Rio turned to the black and shook his head. "*Fué un engaño*—it was a trick!"

The peon grinned and his fellow-workers yelled, "*Engaño! Engaño!*—Trick! Trick!"

They were still noisy when Rio started for town. Off the edge of the wharf he heard children laughing happily. He noticed that a group of five was huddled around a bunch of bananas which had fallen from a truck. One of the children, a boy, dressed in a clean cotton shirt and ankle-length trousers, had his back to him and was flicking a little whip at the fruit. As Rio walked that way there was a shrill, warning whistle and the boy with the whip turned as though he had been pinched. When he saw Rio however, he straightened up and for a moment surveyed him carefully. Then he modestly lowered his eyes.

"A penny, sir mate?" begged the child.

Rio stared at the boy and struggled to think clearly. The face was that of Martin—the same chin, the same forehead. He had the same way of standing. Yes, he was a dark replica of Martin, much younger and with a more beautiful face—but still the face of his friend. One thing further startled Rio. On each cheekbone of the child was a clearly defined disk of rouge, the size of a dollar.

Rio felt a little angry and spoke roughly.

"What have you done to earn a penny?" he asked.

The boy seemed quietly mischievous and a flush appeared above the rouge. Rio thought he posed against the sunlight.

"If I trap my enemy, sir tarantula, sir," he said, "then will I earn a penny?"

The rest of the children laughed.

"How will you catch him?" asked Rio, bending over the bananas for a possible sight of the creature.

The boy cracked his whip and pointed to the edge of the wharf. At his command several children ran and brought back an old piece of tarpaulin. This they held silently over the bananas, making sure that no light could filter in. Then the boy drew a line in the sand and spoke softly in a jargon unfamiliar to Rio. Whereupon with a shout the others threw back the canvas and a large, hairy spider which had crawled out into the darkness was revealed. The boy flicked his little whip—and the tarantula was divided. For a second, the halves quivered. The beauty of the boy's eyes sharpened and the other children shrieked with glee. When the quivering ceased the lad stooped, and picking up one broken part of the spider, fastened it to the end of his whip. Rio dropped a penny, studying the little fellow, who looked down admiringly at his kill and at the coin.

Rio was suddenly thirsty and headed down a road by the sea for the town. It was a hot patch to cross that day and he stopped often to look at the harbor which somehow gave him the illusion of coolness. Once, as he stood, he noticed the boy with the little whip silently following. Rio put his hands on his hips and waited for him.

The child was excited, but restrained. He had been running and was breathing rapidly. His shirt was open and the damp cotton fabric was plastered to his slender body. Ringlets of dark copper hung to the small beads of perspiration on his forehead or curled away from his brow. His intense brown eyes looked directly at Rio and he stood most straight as though expectant and afraid. Rio was struck by the attitude and by the sudden unnatural impression of maturity. He had never seen a lad so full of fever—and knew this picture was as colorful as any wild and distant fragment of his own. The boy stepped nearer and pointed toward the town.

"May I walk through you, sir mate?" he asked.

Rio nodded his head and when the boy came alongside he dropped his hand on his shoulder. The lad was shaking. Rio took his hand away and the boy quieted. Rio started sweating. This wasn't sense. He walked on more rapidly, the boy keeping pace with him.

"The Cafe El Americano stays open long, sir mate. Will you not see my sister first? She comes from the sea." The child took long strides, matching those of Rio. He was nearly breathless. "Always ... out of the sea ... come our sisters and daughters.... Even to your big hefty."

The sidewalks were narrow and Rio sat down on the curb and rocked and laughed and rocked till the charming old ladies crossed both themselves and the street for the rum this sailor must have taken. In solemn condemnation, they shook their fingers behind black fans with each other—but hastened away where they could laugh delightedly in their loneliness. At last, Rio stood up and wiped his eyes. He gave the boy ten cents in silver, looked at the drying tarantula still fastened to the little whip, and entered the Cafe El Americano. The lad's face was wistful. He shook the spider violently, flinging up one delicate, brown hand.

Instead of standing at the bar, a group of seamen had grabbed some chairs and were sitting around while the proprietor brought drinks. Rio pulled up a chair and asked for a rum punch. The seamen were from the other ship and he did not know any of them. They were teasing a young sailor who was apparently making his first trip. The boy looked sullen. One good-natured seaman with the face of a German butcher whom the others called "Dutch," was particularly amused. He turned to Rio, who was near him, and said, "The kid did like all of us, first time out—struck bells for stars, thinkin' they was ships' lights. The pay-off came after the mate gave him the devil and told him not to miss a god-damned ship, but to skip the stars; for we met the whole Pacific Fleet doin' maneuvers, and the kid hit so many bells the Old Man came down and asked where in hell the fire was."

The sailors roared and Rio smiled; but the harassed young seaman said, "Aw, shut up. God! You've told that fifteen times." His face was as red as the German's.

Dutch was still laughing.

"Wait till I tell it the thirtieth, lad—wait till I tell it to your mutter."

"Wait till you tell it to my 'mutter'!—God!" The kid threw himself at Dutch, both arms flailing. The sailors laughed and scrambled for him, holding him from Dutch who had his head in his lap and was howling louder than ever. Finally the kid was exhausted and the sailors set him up in his chair. Dutch got up, went over to him and gave him a pat on the back.

"I'll tell you the last one I picked up," he said. "I was in Iran when I got this yarn out of a peddler who had brought it down from Baghdad. He sold it to me for coffee."

The kid grinned and the sailors settled down.

"This peddler," continued Dutch, "said there was a couple up there soon to be married when the Sultan spotted the woman. He takes her into his harem and bein' a cruel son-of-a-bitch, orders his Chief Barber to castrate the man. Then he plans to bring the poor bastard into the Royal Household as Chief Eunuch so he can watch the guy suffer every time he sees his old girl. The fellow asks one favor—that his father, who is also a barber, be the one to do the trick.

"The Sultan says yes, but that he'll take a look afterwards to see there's no funny business. Well, the father's a sport and gives his son a stroke with his blade 'midships, and fastens him up with a few stitches. The man takes it like a good egg, only he fans himself a bit and takes a bottle of spirits in one swig. He lays around for several days, and finally gets up, a little pale, but whole in body except for his watch pocket. Then he goes to the Palace and the Sultan takes a few sights at the evacuated area and is satisfied.

"Now the Sultan has led a hell of a life, and the girl tips off her sweetheart that in spite of turtle eggs, snake wine, pampas beetles and blended herbs from Crete, the old boy can't get it up. So the Chief Eunuch tells her he has a little surprise for her; and they go down to the lily pond to observe the constellations. Then he returns to his post and she to her couch to sleep sweetly. A few months later the Sultan gets suspicious.

"The Favorite says, 'You did it in your dreams, Celestial Master.'

"'O.K., my little sugared rose leaf,' says the Sultan.

"And when the brat is born the Sultan slices off the heads of twenty prisoners to celebrate.

"Well, it wasn't no time before the Favorite sidles up to him again.

"'You had another dream, Celestial Master.'

"But this time he's wise. He hides behind the reeds of the lily pond one night, and sees the Eunuch and his old girl come down the trail. In a few minutes the Sultan's eyes pop out of his head. He hears the rustle of the grass and the next thing he knows, a tight mainstay and a tall foremast is reflected in the water of the pond beside the lily pads.

"Of course, both heads was thrown into the Tigris. But the Sultan, thinkin' maybe the first time was a dream, handed over ten concubines and the Great Emerald of Phallis to his son."

Dutch stopped talking. The seamen's faces were blank.

"I don't get it," said one of the sailors. "How could Balled Billy swing it?"

"That's what I paid coffee to find out," said Dutch, solemnly. "There was a god-damned testicle under his vest. It didn't come down when he was born. It was hangin' high—but it worked."

There was a moment of silence.

"God!" said the kid.

Rio went to the bar, had a small rum straight and left the Cafe El Americano.

The boy who looked like Martin sat, half sleeping, on the sidewalk where there was shade. He still clutched his little whip and Rio noticed that the dried portion of the spider was still fastened to it. When the child saw Rio he jumped up.

"At last, sir mate, are you ready to go to the house of my sister?"

It was mid-afternoon and as hot as a volcano. Rio wanted to find the coolest place he could and take a nap; but he looked at the youngster and said yes.

The boy piloted him through a small market. The siesta hour was over and the stalls were being reopened. The air was heavy with the odor of pawpaw and fish; heavier still with the heat. The cloying scent of khus-khus arose from one section of the market as an ageless woman, more Indian than Spanish, smiled between her shoulders and bobbed in front of Rio, one arm around a bundle of the grass. Rio, enjoying its fragrance, handed her a coin. In the stalls much of the fruit was so thickly covered with flies it was impossible to tell its original colors. The vendors, mostly Spanish, seemed indifferent to sales and followed Rio apathetically. Once, he stopped to admire a woven mat, then walked on laughing at the obscene pattern.

Alongside him the child waved his whip at the flies. At the next corner he stole a piece of dried fish. They passed the square gray box which was the solitary bank, the stucco houses with their virulent colors well moderated by the prodigality of vines, went on to the outskirts of town and into the Street of Curtains.

There was no sidewalk. They walked unhurriedly along the dusty road. Everywhere, the heat fell like individual hammers. It lay in a transparent film between the rows of houses and gathered in blue puddles across their path. It was too early for the girls to work and everything was quiet except for a wind from the harbor which disturbed the curtains that formed the entire front wall of each house. Once a small brown arm reached out languidly, and once they heard a giggle and a soft whistle.

"I like this Street, sir mate," said the boy. "Everyone gets happy here by ten o'clock every night. Believe me, sir, they get fine and drunk here. Last night a girl smoked weeds and ran nakedly down the Street. She screamed beautifully and nakedly. And a seaman from the *Swamp Rat* wouldn't pay El Gaucho." The boy laughed.

"Who's El Gaucho?" asked Rio.

"She is the biggest woman on the Street, and has four Snakes working for her. When the seaman didn't pay for one of her girls, we all knew what. Yes, he was fine and bloody when she finished whipping him with her garbage can. Some of the girls, sir mate, call her 'Mister.' And that might be truth, for I saw her give money for just a feel to a woman. But sir, we are home." He took Rio by the hand, pushed aside the curtains and they went into the house.

A girl was sitting in the corner, reading a book by the dim light of a lamp. The boy ran to the table upon which the lamp was burning and turned up the flame, although it was blazing outside beyond the tightly drawn curtains.

The girl closed her book and looked at Rio steadily for a moment; and Rio felt that he had entered a different country. There was a wild perfume, sharp as a chemical. In the angle of light and cut of the draperies the girl's skin became darker. Rio tried desperately to find her eyes which were vague under the heavy lashes. She was not so beautiful as her little brother; but some mystical quality outlined her charm more severely.

"Hello," she said.

The boy went to her and caught her about the waist, holding on until the girl bent over and kissed him on the forehead.

"Hello," said Rio, feeling awkward, and yet wanting savagely to hold them both in his arms. That might be his salvation. He desired them both with such a horrible necessity that for a second he was paralyzed. They moved apart and Rio felt that one moment of fruition had been blasted into Hell. He took off his cap.

"My sister isn't from here," said the boy to him jubilantly. "I love her, and I like it here. But I wouldn't want her from here." He turned to the girl. "I'm going to make a cool green drink for sir mate, and bring him a cool towel, sister. For he's had that bad rum at the Americano."

The girl's expression did not change when the boy had gone; but she motioned Rio into a chair.

"Where did you find him?" she asked. "Where did you find my little brother? Marius is a strange child. He drifts around, but he seems safe from everybody—" her voice rose passionately, "—everybody."

Rio replied absently, fascinated by the girl's frail dignity, so contrary to her enterprise.

"I found him playin' in the sand by the banana docks," he said. "He kind of reminded me of my best friend. Somehow, he made me think of Martin."

The girl spoke frankly.

"It only happens so. Our father loved our mother and lived here many years with her. One day he was caught in a storm. He was fishing—" She hesitated. "And after that, our mother could not remember things. It was well she died.... He was an educated man—a gentleman who came this way.... That is why the boy speaks as he does. He remembers the lessons of our father."

Marius returned to the room with a chilled lime drink for Rio, and rubbed Rio's face with a moist towel.

"Where did you get the ice?" asked his sister, smiling. "Did you steal it?"

"No," answered the child. "I bought two pennies' worth from the ugly red man in the ugly red cart." He picked up a box of rouge and went to a wide mirror. Then he carefully repainted his cheeks. The deep color, though applied in indiscriminate and garish quantities, served still further the willful abandonment of his features.

"You use too much," said his sister. "Why do you use so much?"

"Because it makes me look like an old girl. Just like an old girl I know," replied the boy.

"That isn't true, Marius," answered his sister scornfully. "You think it makes you pretty. You're too pretty already. The Snakes have told you it was pretty, and you let them play with you. I won't let them play with you." The girl's cheeks were flushed.

"A damned poor women are the Snakes," said the boy. "Before that happened, I'd talk sassily. Besides, I don't like women." He threw the rouge back on the dresser and left.

Rio walked over to the girl.

"This is a queer place, sis, and he's a queer boy, and you're a queer girl. I don't get it. I feel almost like one of the family, and yet—" he put his arms under the girl's shoulders and lifted her to her feet, "—and yet, I feel funny. Like I been doped. I'm crazy about you and the kid and the story you told me. Aw, hell! Why talk about it." Almost angrily he took a twenty dollar bill from his pocket and laid it on the dresser.

The girl didn't smile. She looked curiously at the money for a moment and then covered it with a book.

Rio held her tightly and then stepped away, his eyes closed. When he opened them she was quietly undressing. He tried to help her. But his fingers were clumsy.

The girl threw back the curtain around the bed and lay down, her eyes staring upward as though searching for something. Rio looked up too, and saw a tapestry hung like a canopy over them.

"The Madonna!" he cried. "Good God! Not here!—where She can see!"

The girl lifted herself. On her face lay the shadow of pain. She spread her thick hair on the pillow with swift fingers, except for one dark strand which cut across her breast like a wound.

"Why do you mind Her?" she asked. "She is kind.... She is forgiving.... She is there, where one can pray to Her—afterwards."

There was no hesitation in the girl's voice—no quality of naïveté or assumed virginity. There was a cold knowledge of fatality and an inflexible acceptance. There was even the protective shroud of fanaticism; and Rio saw her, gentle, but receptively immune.

He thought of Martin. Martin would turn the picture of the Madonna upside down and go ahead.... Yes, he thought, Martin would take her and her sisters—and even old Agnes in the unplowed field. But he wasn't Martin, thank God!... And for a second or two he repeated to himself, "Thank God! Thank God!"

"No," he said. He knelt down and held the girl as though she were a child. He whispered something to her and she smiled at him. After a bit, he stood up and searched through all his pockets for coins. He found that it amounted to about ten dollars. He laid this with the other money.

The girl had put on her light dress and they stood for a second by the curtain. They stood looking at each other. Then Rio went out into the early twilight.

That evening the girl did not light the tiny kerosene lamp outside her curtained doorway.

As Rio started up the Street of Curtains Marius ran to him. The boy was chewing vigorously on a sandwich and in the hand in which he held the whip was a package. He gave it to Rio who found a similar sandwich within the package.

"Try it, sir mate," he said. "It's good, if you're on the gamey-flavor side of things."

Rio bit into the sandwich, found it tough and certainly on the gamey side, but made palatable with some lettuce and pepper sauce. It was refreshing to him; and he was glad to see the boy again; gladder still to leave, for awhile, the world of frangipani—a world which called and yet rebelled inevitably against him.

By this time lights were beginning to be seen along the Street, and a few brown girls began to call to Rio. One unusually persistent one followed them for several paces.

Marius stopped, turned round and said in Spanish, "Bah! How many times would you have a man break his back!"

The woman replied in a high voice.

"Shut up, little pimp!"

To which the boy shouted, "How will your favorite cat look when I eat him to-morrow night?"

The woman screamed and ran back to her stall.

Rio looked at his sandwich suspiciously, then dropped it guardedly where the child could not see.

They went back to the ship the same way they had come. On the edge of the town by the road to the sea, the boy tugged at Rio. Nearby, an hibiscus bush was in full bloom. Marius pointed to it. The red disks on his cheeks glowed in the twilight. Fastening his trousers about his slim, bare ankles, he leaped into the air and caught one blossom. Then he gave Rio a shy, sweet glance and gravely hung the flower behind his ear....

Rio was carrying the little whip when they walked onto the docks. He looked down at the child beside him.

"Sir," he said to the boy, "do you think I could catch sir tarantula, sir?"

He didn't know whether Marius was crying, for his own eyes were wet. But he did know that a child of untranslatable beauty, with a mouth like a bow and a heart which he knew was indisputedly his, was standing quite still before him. He lifted the boy—kissed him on the mouth, and headed for his ship, half stumbling.

CHAPTER XV

When Deane opened the door Rio was standing there. He bent his head a little as the light from the room beyond fell upon him. He looked at the back of his wrist where an ugly scab, ripped by a loose strand of cable, seemed an offensive sight in front of this woman. He tried to cover up the wound with his cap. It was such a painful moment as he stared at his great crude hands that Deane moved instinctively toward him. She saw the hurt, shamed child in him, but more than that, within the tense breach she saw the man. Rio's arms, which now hung by his side as though he were disgraced, fascinated her, then became repellent by her very daintiness. Yet she ventured still further. What a wide cloth across his wrist! And why the heavy jaw and painted muscles of his neck—dark by one edge and golden by his collar!... What a tie!—so hideous, that clarified the purpose in his eyes! For now he was looking down at her.

"Close," he said in a low voice. "Very close," he repeated, remembering the urge, the fomenting inspiration when he had left her before. In his eyes Deane had the appearance of a small, dark seal. It was more than the shimmering under her dress—more than a watery sea movement of her hips that led him on until he touched her. As he held her by the arm her black velvet gown fell sharply away from her throat, and he looked for the first time at her breasts. The maturity, the obvious, sleek movement contained within her resembled his own feeling now. He lowered his head. Deane closed the door and clasped her hands behind his neck. His lips were burning her unbearably. She tried weakly to brush them off.

"I can't help it," she almost cried. "I can't."

Rio took his face away from her throat and laid his hands upon her thighs. Without effort he lifted her high above him. He was calm. There was no note of hysteria in his voice, only a slight tension of his muscles. Then he said, "Spit!" turning his face sideways so that he could feel it better. "Two dogs," he repeated intensely. "Spit!"

Held like a doll above him—understanding his meaning, accepting the fact of her treachery, Deane turned as wild as the awakened animal beneath her. She knew that she was floating, knew that she was full of hatred for Martin and not Rio. She opened her little red mouth and spat against Rio's cheek— once, twice, three times!—until she was breathless. And Rio, grim, lost again from his friend, lowered her and shook her by the hair until they came together squarely and the dull sound of illicit kisses moaned through the empty corridor.

When Rio released her they stood apart, looking at each other with only Deane's breath and the metallic drops upon his cheek as a memory. Then Rio sighed and wiped his face with the cuff of his sleeve.

"Whatever kind of God there is," he said, "I'm damned! *Now* I've showed Martin the kind I am!" he continued as if to himself. "He's crazy—he'll know…. And as for you," Rio turned to the woman once more and whispered fiercely, "you're a black witch."

Deane was leaning against the wall, still breathing heavily. She made no attempt to answer and Rio continued.

"We better go in now and face him," he said. "It's the first time in my life I been ashamed like this."

"I've kissed a fool," replied Deane in a soft voice, "and I don't want to stand here any longer with him!" She bit her lips. "Mr. Roberts will be glad to see you. Come on in." She opened the door.

"I'll come," said Rio, following her.

Martin heard his voice and stood up.

"Hello, Rio," he called. "That was a short trip."

Without speaking, Rio went to him. Then he looked around, frowning, saw Roberts, saw the young man he had met in the hall and another, a stranger. Martin watched him with a puzzled expression.

"What the devil?" he asked.

Deane interrupted.

"I believe you know Mr. Roberts, Rio," she said.

Rio turned in the adviser's direction, shrugged his shoulders and nodded.

"I know him, Mrs. Idara."

Roberts was sitting at the far end of the room. The north light from the window was so severe that it formed a blue overshadow on his dark hair and outlined his proud face in a series of sharp angles, unnoticed by any but Deane. He arose and bowed stiffly, his lips set.

Carol had been watching the newcomer intently all the while and now at this cue from Roberts, he skirted two chairs and smilingly eager, held out his hand to Rio who looked amused.

"My name is Stevens," he said. "Carol Stevens." Rio pulled his hand away but Carol continued. "I know why you boys look like sailors." He glanced at

Martin, then back at Rio. "You both do, you know. You get so nice and tan. My goodness!—but you travel so! It's simply romantic, isn't it, Deane?" he added, still staring at Rio.

"Yes," Deane answered, preoccupied, her hand to her hair. "It is romantic, Carol." She turned to Drew who was standing patiently by his chair, a rather vacant expression on his face.

Rio looked at the immaculate, slender fellow sourly when he was introduced. Drew, however, gestured in mild acknowledgment, maintaining his appearance of abstraction. Then deliberately he stepped forward and reached for a short, thick cigarette on the small end-table where Rio, partly leaning, had placed his hand. The cigarette glowed unnaturally as Drew touched a match to it, and he looked straight into the eyes of the sailor which were now even with his own. Then, as the two men stood there face to face, Drew's lips parted slightly and the smoke curled in a heavy roll from his mouth. When the dense vapor disappeared, he smiled unevenly, and with eyes lowered, returned to his chair where he leaned upon it gracefully, one slim hand upon its back.

Martin watched the fantastic play in a stolid, philosophic mood, coldly regarding Rio's frightened look.

Deane became uneasy.... "What was Drew's secret action that had accomplished such an unthinkable expression upon Rio's face. Was it," she reminded herself, "the smoke?—or Drew's protective anger based on his uncanny knowledge of her own affair beyond the door?—or was his melancholy fury a safekeeping just for Martin!"

Roberts had begun to cough violently. With each paroxysm he held a handkerchief closely to his lips. Deane went to him but he waved at her with petulance.

"I'm all right," he answered in reply to her question of concern. "It's this strangulation! Damn such an affair!" he said irritably and sat down. "I don't understand it, and I don't want to," he added, and immediately went off into another seizure of coughing. The others stood around him anxiously, not knowing what to do.

"Oh, please sit down," said Deane, throwing herself on the divan and waving her pretty arms in little, indecisive movements.

Rio and Carol obeyed her, but Martin hurried into the kitchen and Drew, still pensive, continued to lean upon the back of his chair, watching Roberts as though but vaguely aware of his predicament. Martin returned with a glass of water and putting his arm around the adviser's shoulders, held the glass to his lips, trying to get him to swallow between spasms. Gradually the spell quieted and Roberts looked up at his friend. Then he took the glass from the other's hand and gulped the rest of the water.

"I'd like another," he said, wiping his eyes.

Martin nodded, took the glass and returned to the kitchen. When he came back Roberts accepted the drink more slowly.

"Will you please hold your arm the way it supported me before?" he asked, looking again at Martin, this time with a rather contemptuous smile.

Martin put his hands in his pockets and stared out of the window, his eyes the color of the gray, low-sweeping clouds.

The adviser watched him for a moment, then put down the tumbler of water almost untouched. With a half suspicious expression he now looked around at the others.

"No," he said distinctly, "I'm not afflicted. And Drew, this isn't hysteria, so stop thinking of that."

"I know," agreed Drew, nodding his head.

"Let me make some tea," suggested Deane, as spiritedly as she could.

For a moment the adviser was gentle.

"No, Deane," he said. "You shouldn't bother. You see," he smiled somewhat wanly, "everything is stimulated enough."

"Of course," said Drew. "It's getting too late anyway."

Across from them, Carol's head seemed to pivot around the side of his chair like the brass plate of a revolving door.

"Of course, dear," he repeated. "It's getting too late." Then with a slithering movement, his head spun slowly round again and he could be heard faintly whispering, "It will soon be cocktail time ... cocktail time."

Roberts shuddered.

"That should settle it," said Martin. He lit a cigarette and looked at Rio. "But it won't. Do you have anything to add about tea, sailor?"

"No, by heaven!" exclaimed Rio. "What I have to say ain't about tea. Of all the people and talk I ever seen—" He had started to rise when Deane stopped him.

"Tell us about your trip, Rio," she said. "Where did you go?"

He hesitated, but finally sat down on the edge of his chair, looking sullen.

"A little banana town. In South America," he answered at last.

"Santa de Marina?" asked Martin, looking interested.

"Yeah," said Rio.

Martin turned to the others and spoke proudly.

"Rio took his own ship into that harbor once."

"So Rio was a master!" observed Roberts. Then, staring at the floor, he said with a cruel abstractness, "Yes, the sea is relentless. Many derelicts seek my aid on land when they find deep water too deep."

"That's true," declared Martin instantly. "And many landlubbers are drowned because *they* can't step a mudpuddle. But they are not even derelicts. They're just old bags. Of course," he said, turning round, "you're a derelict, Rio. But Mr. Roberts wasn't thinking of you. I'm sure of that."

Rio was watching Roberts with such dreadful intensity that when Martin finished, the adviser's head snapped back like that of a toy.

Carol shifted about in his chair and stretched his legs. He felt the confused streams in the room, and it made him restless.

"That's right," said Rio, still watching Roberts intently. "He didn't mean me. Once he made a mistake and I saved him from a derelict. Maybe the fellow let him go just so he could try it again some time. That thing you said about the mudpuddle is right, too, Martin. I'd think Mr. Roberts would be afraid. But he ain't, Martin."

Roberts did not hear all of this. He remembered those bitter eyes and hands too clearly.

Carol broke in.

"I wish I could talk like *you* talk," he said, addressing Martin. "I think you have the most—well, the most *exciting* things to say." His face was pink and moist.

Rio grinned wickedly.

"He's an exciting man, Carol. That's why he says exciting things," he declared, emphasizing his words with a sly nod of approval.

Roberts looked distastefully about him. "My God! This!—all over again!" he thought.

But Carol continued, beaming, "I knew a boy in Chicago that was almost the same way as you, Martin. Every one of us boys said it must have been a trick. He could just turn everything into the best time. And my!—he was handsome! I think he was a bouncer at some cafe. And strong—Oooooh!" Carol adjusted his yellow tie and his eyelids fluttered.

Martin felt increasing annoyance at Rio's persistent grin.

Still Carol went on blindly. "I'd like to work the way you do, Martin, and get oil and things on me from those machines. And that linotype you operate!" he continued. "I'd just *love* that!" He put his hands flat on his trousers. "Imagine," he said, turning to Deane at last, "having one of those big things to play with!"

Rio laughed openly, and Roberts turned away in disgust; but Martin said, "That's right, Carol. We'll have a talk one day, all by ourselves." He went over to Rio. He didn't say anything. He didn't need to say anything. But he cursed him with his eyes, and with a vagrant motion of his lips.

"What is it?" Rio asked him.

Martin replied coldly, "You're a fundamentalist. I can tell it from the expression on your face." Then he went to the door. Before he closed it behind him he looked back. "It's taken me nearly thirty years to get this picture," he said, and he was gone.

Rio stared at the door where Martin had left.

"There goes a clever lad," he said. "He knows us well." He turned to Roberts and glared at him. "He knows you well, indeed. I'd hate to be you. I can see the black days. And," he added, laughing, "he knows me, all right—but, he don't know himself. He'll whip himself to death." At the word "whip," Rio had hesitated. Although the room was cool, he started sweating. Without even saying good-by to Deane, he put on his cap, quickly went outside and slammed the door so hard that the floor shook.

"Thank heaven," said Roberts quietly. "Humanity is maintained—the anthropoids have gone—civilization stands. Let them yell into space and beat their knuckles on drums made of their own skins. But pray God, they yell in the forest and not here. Thank heaven for Society!—even if it is covered by a fool's cap," he continued, watching Carol. Turning his eyes to the ceiling and then to Deane, he added incoherently, "We have been shown our destiny. Our portraits, painted by savages, hang on Olympus.... I hope, Deane, that you are not disturbed by the painting, or," he said, bowing, "by your destiny." He breathed deeply, painfully. His shoulders were bowed, his face whiter. "You must excuse me," he said. He walked to the door, opened it, walked out and closed it gently.

Drew also went to Deane and spoke so that Carol could not hear.

"A strange afternoon, little sister," he said, bending over her affectionately. Then he turned around. "I'm holding a drag to-morrow night, Carol. I'd like to have you come."

Carol's eyes sparkled.

"Oh, Drew, I'd love it! To think!—I can come in drag!"

Drew restrained an impulse to pet the boy who was regarding him delightedly, as in some glorious enchantment.

"There is a sort of radiance about him," he thought, half smiling at himself for thinking it. But as he left, Drew took Deane's hand once more. "Don't see Roberts until I talk with you," he whispered. Deane nodded her head and Drew went into the hall.

Carol twisted his cigarette holder, put in a cigarette and lit it grandly.

"Isn't he sweet?" he said. "Martin's sweeter, though.... But the others!" he added with disdain. "Of course, you have your own life, Deane, so I won't ask you why you tolerate such people about." He sighed gratefully. "But isn't it nice, dear, to be alone? I never could stand vulgarness. I'm really quite surprised at Mr. Roberts to let himself be upset by—" Carol thought hard, but couldn't quite understand what he was talking about. He smiled gently though, and continued, "—to be upset by—well—just everything." He leaned back against his chair and put his feet up on another. That was well said. He could tell from the way Deane looked that it had affected her.

Deane regarded the smiling, piggish face.

"Sometimes, Carol," she said, thoughtfully, "I don't understand, either."

The night became darker and the lamps inside softened Carol's features. Deane tried to rest. It was good to be away from men for awhile. Even Drew was difficult at times. She unfastened one of her stockings. Carol smoked and smiled and nodded his head at the wall. This was as it should be.

Suddenly, to Deane, came the sickening realization that both Carol and herself were thinking of the same man.

CHAPTER XVI

After the maids had cleaned the apartment and had left, Drew went to the dressing room, removed his white shirt and collar, handed them to a small Chinese boy and seated himself before the vanity, observing the strain on his features which had come so suddenly.

"Your father was a wise man, little Tai," he said to the child. "Place your hand on my shoulder. Do you find it hot?"

The child bowed and went to Drew, acting as he had been bidden. He avoided Drew's eyes in the mirror and his voice trembled.

"Yes, Master," he said, but he could not keep back his tears; so cupping his tiny hand, the little, hot gems were caught before they fell upon Drew's head, which now rested upon the edge of the vanity.

"We will go away very soon, Tai," Drew said at last.

The Chinese boy did not answer, still fearful of betraying his emotion; but for an instant he hovered over Drew with the same patient love of his own distant gods.

"Master," he whispered finally, "I have some secret petals from my father. He told—he told me—" Little Tai burst into open tears and kneeling, placed his head upon the floor.

Drew turned around in surprise and seeing the lad prostrated before him, bent his own shoulders lower, the Orient in his eyes. Then, scorning in his tenderness all laws of blood and caste, he picked up the boy and laid him upon the ottoman. Still weeping, Tai lay in a tiny curl, his golden tunic tight against his back. Drew quickly knelt down and whispered to him.

"Were the petals for my bath, little one?" he asked.

"Yes," sobbed the child.

"Tai," said Drew gently, his soft fingers brushing the tears away, "they were given to you for a time when I should be very sick. Is that not so?"

"It is so, Master," whispered the child. He sat up with a cat-like movement. "I have a little golden whip, Master. Will you strike me?"

Drew looked at him strangely. Rio had mentioned that word in a curious fashion only the day before. Could it be that by coincidence?—Drew stopped the course of his reflections and arose. The symbol of the whip was ridiculous!

"Bring me the scourge!" he said.

Tai ran to a wall-cabinet, and from the vase which held his father's ashes he pulled, coil by coil, a gilded whip and handed it to Drew who took it by its handle looking with intensity at the cruel barbs at the end, and wondering if they were poisonous.

"I shall not beat you, Tai," he said finally. He looked now at the handle and thong which held his wrist. "Tai," he said, "are the petals a secret, really?"

"Yes, Master," said the boy, smiling shyly.

Drew held out his delicate fingers.

Blushing, and timidly approaching, Tai bowed over his master's hand; and in his moment of adoration murmured a little prayer his mother had taught him. Then taking a small, scented package from the breast of his tunic, he ran toward the bathroom, turning once in the doorway to bow his devotion.

When he had gone, Drew replaced the whip and laid his arms across his face. And as he heard the sound of small feet on the tile and the water running for his bath, he looked again into the vanity and cried out in a high, soft voice an unintelligible name....

Tai twisted a white satin robe about Drew's slender form as Floyd, the hairdresser, was announced.

"Is everything in readiness for Madame's coiffure?" asked the expert, mincing forward.

"Yes, Florabelle," said Drew, standing once more before the vanity.

Tai withdrew with backward steps.

"Florabelle" took a small silk handkerchief from his pocket and gently dusted the bench upon which he suggested that "Madame" rest her slender form. With much bowing and curtsying, Floyd was now ready to proceed with his masterful art of transforming this man into a charming hostess.

The beautician was slight, with tiny features. Although he was well on in years, he looked no more than fifty. "A half century plant," he had once called himself. He wore his hair long and dyed it periodically, according to the fashion. On his feet were patent leather pumps of shining black, with medium heels. With his frock coat of gray he wore dark trousers. While engaged in his profession, he affected a long white smock with a lavender lace handkerchief in the pocket over his heart. His cheeks, having been recently paraffined, were now symmetrical and would remain that way for weeks to come, when their contour would again have to be remodeled.

He fingered Drew's hair, combing it straight back from the head. The short locks fell gracefully between his fingers as they discussed the different styles—dismissing this, then that one until the matter was decided. Then quickly Floyd began his craft.

"Madame," he said, "as a privileged acquaintance of long standing, do I know any of your guests of this evening?"

"Yes, Florabelle," said Drew, in a soft and gracious tone. "You recall Beulah. She has been suffering lately with acute indigestion and general complications. But she's coming."

"My *dear* Madame!" The artist raised his eyes to the ceiling. "*That* one! *She* should have retired from society years ago! She is very well fixed financially, you know, but oh!—she is so tight! I'll wager she's home now dressing her own hair! Imagine! The ends will all be burned, and there'll probably be some burns on her neck. It simply makes me shiver! And she'll wait until she gets here to-night to use *your* powder! It's not that I care—but I could transform her into a beautiful person. Her taste is vile—simply vile! And dearie, with *that* face!—I'd have to work for hours and hours! As I've said before, I don't care what she does, but she *could* be made ravishing!"

Florabelle's dainty white fingers had been busy at work—shampooing and rinsing—and were now in the act of combing the hair and turning the soft ends under.

"What gown has Madame selected to enhance her singular beauty, if I may ask?" questioned the little hairdresser.

"White velvet, 'Belle. I feel nostalgic this evening," answered Drew.

"Ah!" cried Florabelle in delight. "Then indeed I have a gorgeous surprise for you! I have an amazing lotion, greaseless, odorless, which tints the hair an incredibly lovely white. I used it on Monsieur—" he bent down and whispered a name into Drew's ear. "She insisted upon it. Madame was *very gay* that evening. It was the first time I had tried the preparation on any of my exclusive clientele. Madame was wearing a short velvet jacquette of green over her white velvet gown; and she wore green rouge on her cheeks and lips in the current Parisian fashion. Dearie," the hairdresser put one finger to his lips and took a step backward, "would you like to be the first to use these tints in America?"

"I should love white hair with the dress," said Drew thoughtfully. "But not the green. I prefer to wear a small jacquette of black velvet lined with red. Make my lips the same shade as the lining."

"Oh!" cried Florabelle. "You shall be a dream!" And he set to work.

Drew sat quietly, continually admiring himself in the mirror—an occasional turn of the lip or a raised eyebrow showing approval—amazed with each glance at the artistry of the man who was transforming him.

Florabelle talked incessantly, constantly gesturing until Madame's coiffure was finished.

"Ah, Drewena!" now cried the little hairdresser. "You are complete—so perfect!" he exclaimed delightedly, finishing off with a touch of perfume upon the eyebrows and behind the lobes of Drew's ears.

Drewena walked slowly through the drawing room and critically observed the fold of the draperies. It was just before twilight and through a high, oval window crested with stained glass, she idly watched the towers below her. There were tears in her eyes. The light became softer, barely touching now the throats of the doves which nested in the eaveless pinnacles, subduing the irregular flash against their wings. Their silent, ever-changing motion somehow caused her to think of Martin; and the recollection of the mannerisms of her friend—that isolate, strange night in the cocktail lounge—his actions there, sometimes gentle, but more times cruel, made Drewena close her eyes. Why these tears?—like those of a younger passion—full of the same anxiety, the same dull anger at enslavement and desire to escape! She looked into the east, formed her lips into a smile and turned away. Tying her white satin robe more closely about her waist, Drewena sat down at the piano, one slim, white leg against the casing of deep ivory. On each end of the piano was a tall cathedral taper, lighted. The irradiance was vague under her hands as she improvised. The melody was reminiscent of Chopin, and again of Debussy. Drewena consciously built a theme upon their lovely chords, and smiled to herself as she thought of the semblance of originality attained by other contemporary plagiarists. As she continued to improvise, Patsy, known as "Pat" on more sober days, entered the drawing room.

An "English" butler, whose father had been Irish, Patsy was carrying a small bouquet of black lilies brought from the Malay peninsula at great trouble by Drew's florist. Devoid of her usual attire, Patsy was somewhat ridiculous. Her concave nose and forehead where the toupee failed to hide the round, bald skull, gave her a strange type of "swish." Her upper teeth sagged in the back when she talked, and her bulbous lips had the appearance of an aging tomato. She wore a little "how-de-do!" of white lace upon her wig which had become entwined in it. A single wart of considerable size pushed through the tiny cap which fell at intervals over her nose for lack of better support. Her black silk skirt was short, showing the bony protuberance of her knee where once, in a moment of folly, she had mounted a horse and was promptly unseated, bruised and flattened. Her blouse was full, barely concealing two lemons she had taken from the icebox. Altogether, with her wide grin and unhappy form she was seemingly the most pathetic of creatures. But when Drewena languidly motioned for silence while she played on, there was an amused understanding between the servant and mistress as Patsy adjusted the flowers on one corner of a table where they would catch the reflection of their darkness in a tall mirror whose frame was a wreath of golden doves in flight.

In Deane's living room, Martin stood by the divan examining a long-trained evening gown of canary yellow. Its pale satin sheen in the lamplight was unusually luminous against the blur of the couch. Martin spoke earnestly.

"But I don't understand, Deane. A guest can't be just an observer at one of these private affairs. I'd be clumsy. I wouldn't fit in and I don't see why you want me to go."

There was a perverse light in Deane's eyes. She was thinking strangely. She wondered: *Is he sure, really sure he won't fit in?* But aloud she said, "Drew invited you and that is sufficient reason."

Martin looked at the dress again.

"Am I supposed to wear that fantastic rig just to satisfy a whim of yours and Drew's? I tell you, Deane, the entire situation is repellant to me."

Again Deane thought in the same odd manner: *It isn't like him to shy away from anything. He knows himself so well—is it that he's afraid?*—she stopped these thoughts. "It only seems repellant, Martin," she observed. "Drew will make things easy." She bit her lip. "And Carol and Roberts will be there, too. Why don't you take it as a joke?" She tried to laugh, but the effect was so hollow and unusual that Martin turned and put his arms around her.

"What is really behind this, Deane?" he asked her gently. "Is Drew attempting a new type of drama, and are you in on it? If it's a game, I'll go along with you."

"It isn't a game," said Deane insistently. "There isn't anything dark or mysterious about it. It's just a costume party—a stag affair, that's all." She avoided his searching gaze.

Martin laughed brutally, the hurt and sickness inside him manifested. Then he sobered, looked at her steadily for a moment, a faint shine in his eyes.

"All right," he said quietly. "What do I do first?..."

After he had taken a bath, he shaved as closely as possible and rubbed his glowing body with a scent not unpleasant, although he imagined that he detected the impossible effluvium of man-oil as its base. Next he pulled on long stockings of a light sun-tan, his lip curling. But the curious feel of silken underwear and all the intricacies of the garter belt intrigued him, and he laughed aloud as he fastened his stockings to it. The artificial breasts were made of soft rubber fiber, of medium size and cup-shaped in appearance. It was with considerable trouble that he hooked these objects on, the elastic and stays acting contrary. The dress went over his head with difficulty, also; but he twisted and pulled it until it came into place. After he had smoothed out the wrinkles with his hands and set it square with a few quick jerks he felt more comfortable—the gown was even cool and good against his belly. So he sat down with relief and put on the pale yellow satin slippers set aside for him. When he stood up, however, one ankle bent under the strain of the high heel. After that he moved more cautiously, trying to remember the principles of navigation on an icy, rolling deck, and although he lacked a certain naturalness, he soon walked easily enough.

Deane laughed and clapped her hands when she saw him and seemed herself again; but in a moment she returned to the grim abstruseness of her former attitude. She narrowed her eyes, put on an apron, then draped a towel around his neck to keep from spilling the make-up on his shoulders. Martin leaned back, closing his eyes in silent despair; while Deane, testing each shade of lipstick on her hand until she found the right one, realized that she had never tried so hard with herself. She gave his lips, which seemed carved, a brilliant color for the artificial light.

"Damn it," he said.

Deane did not reply. It was unlikely that she heard him, for the same antagonistic attitude surrounded her; and, too, she was absorbed by her painstaking job. The blue line of underbeard around the jaw and chin had to be blocked out; for this, she used a flesh-colored paste, rubbing it in gently. The rice powder was rachel in shade, made almost the color of Martin's skin by the addition of a pinch of ocher. This was carefully smoothed away. She used no rouge. And so she continued, blending and examining, until she stepped aside to view her finished handiwork and exclaimed rather sharply, "Sit up!"

Which Martin did, looking at her with a kind of agitated wonder. But Deane, seeing only his face—with his gray eyes now turned to green, and his somewhat melancholy expression softened by women's devices, ran to him, fell on her knees and began to weep deeply. At this, Martin lifted her to him, holding her, trying to kiss her cheeks. But she slipped away and dried her tears and blew her nose, saying, "It would spoil your looks and I've worked too hard for that."

He started to put his hand to his head but Deane cried out, "Oh, no!" For his hair, parted in the middle, had been combed back of the ears to a point at the base of his neck, where a braid, similar in shade and texture, had been cleverly attached, wrapped and pinned. His hair was now the same wheat-like color as his skin; and the cold, precise line from his head to his shoulders had the essence of that deliberate, calculated passion which so often appeals to the sensitized, yet physical individual. When at last he stood up and lit a cigarette, leaning with a conscious gracefulness upon the piano, Deane went to him and looked up at him uncertainly. Seeing him stand there in such elegance and strength, she bitterly regretted the perversity which had driven her to push him toward this mad adventure. And though her pride rebelled at calling it off at this late moment, she said rather timidly, "Of course, Martin, you don't have to go if you really dislike it so much."

"What?" he almost shouted, looking at her incredulously. "Well, I'll be damned!"

"Oh, hush!" said Deane nervously. "Of course you're going! I was just teasing." But she looked at this man in woman's clothing and she realized she had never been so attracted. She watched the long muscles flex in his arm as he moved his cigarette. A furious desire struck her.

"You must hurry," she whispered, gritting her teeth. "You will be late." Again Martin looked at her steadily, the green glaze covering his eyes.

"I'll return immediately after the party," he said, picking up the wrap she had chosen for him. "Read this—" and he pressed a letter into her hands and left, unsmiling.

When he had gone, Deane opened the letter with feverish haste and read it swiftly. Still standing, she threw it across the room, removed her hairpins and mussed her hair until it was wild. With a sob she flung herself face down on the divan and worked her body on the pillows until she screamed. Then she wept until she fell asleep.

Carol arrived at the drag wearing a leopard cape with a high, stiff collar. There was a single stone in his triple-peaked tiara, filigree work coiling around the gem. Patsy helped him off with his wrap, glanced slyly at his rather buxom figure, and announced him in the drawing room in a falsetto voice.

"Miss Stevens," cried Patsy, in her unusual pitch.

Drewena hurried forward and put her arms around her guest.

"Carrie!" she exclaimed. "You look simply gorgeous!"

Carrie's cheeks deepened with pleasure. Her saucer-like eyes gave out a wet, blue happiness.

"I'm *so* glad you like me," she said. "I didn't want to look tacky."

"'Tacky,' indeed!" said Drewena, for the beauty of Carrie's gown astonished her. "*That*," she continued, looking at the dress, "*is* a creation! Where did you find it?"

Carrie's eyes shone with pride, though at the same time there was delicacy in the way she modeled the skirt with her hands.

"I didn't find it, Drewena. I designed it. I made it for next spring, thinking perhaps I *might* be a June bride. I planned to do it in white if the style was attractive." Carrie looked a little anxious. "Is the severe line too much for my hips?—they are rather large."

"Of course not, dear," answered Drewena. "It is very becoming."

"Then," said Carrie, "you *do* prefer the material to taffeta or crepe. I'm *so* glad," she continued. "Those flouncy things always make me feel like a middle-aged matron." She pushed the blonde hair of her transformation more firmly behind her ears and touched the roll at the back of her neck.

Drewena marveled at the change in her young friend. How awkward and lonely Carol had appeared in the stilted, formalized trousers styled for men! And how charming was this lovely Carrie, away from the stiff tailoring of masculine attire!

Drewena studied the gown. As she saw it, the waist-line—the Grecian fashion in which the garment fell into the imperceptible folds of the long train, had the artless symmetry of certain sculpture. The dress was without sleeves, close-fitting, with high, pointed breasts, and with its back cut low, to the waist. Its color was a gentle pink of shaded salmon that blended into Carrie's smooth bare arms. There were two golden bracelets on her wrists and two small bells on the ring-finger of her left hand. Following the soft curve of her throat was an exquisite, golden necklace. As she stood and turned in such a manner that her white back, with a tiny mole on the shoulder could be seen, Drewena put her arm around her waist, and pulled her aside, where they could talk alone.

Out in the hall, Carrie grasped the arm of her hostess.

"Will Martin be here to-night?" she asked almost shyly.

Drewena frowned.

"I don't know, my dear," she said at last, noting the child-like look of disappointment which appeared on Carrie's face.

Inside the dressing room, which had been transformed into a powder room for the guests, a pompous creature was seated at the vanity. "Beulah" was a retired manufacturer with a great deal of money in the bank, but no penchant for spending it. In fact, she was known to drive the sharpest bargain for "trade" of any of her sisters, never carrying more than a quarter in her pocket when she cruised. Nor did her pick-up have to be presentable, for she worked the doughnut shift. "They're all the same," she used to say sententiously. "Just throw a sack over it, and shoo it out before dawn.... And never give them breakfast," she would caution, if permitted. "It spoils them." Whenever the fleet was in, she would go into retirement. She would lock all her doors and keep her butler on a kind of sentry duty, not even admitting a hallboy who might have an idle moment. As far as the fleet was concerned, no one quite understood Beulah's strange reaction. But it was established fact that once, avoiding her usual care, she had sneaked away to the drugstore for a soda. Intent upon her guzzling, she had failed to notice a sailor who had sat down close beside her. But upon turning her head and seeing the man in uniform, Beulah had let out a shriek, her eyeballs had rolled upward and she had fainted dead away. Some said that doubtless it had been some frightful experience which had given her this strange allergy. "It must *simply* have put her in stitches!" one of her friends had observed.... As for the hallboys, it was true, she never paid them well; but there were always things to be picked up, and Beulah's eyes were failing. The hallboys loved her for this little infirmity, and never took anything more than they felt was honestly due. Altogether, Beulah was regarded as a rather queer, but decidedly powerful person in her set; and no young debutante could expect a successful coming out unless Beulah was behind her—which she usually was.

Thus Drewena realized the value of this social contact for Carrie if the young girl was to spend much time in New York.

"You look awfully nice this evening, Beulah," she said. "What are you doing out here all alone?"

"Powdering my face like *mad*," Beulah answered, daintily packing the rich powder into the sore jaw and chin where she had shaved too closely. "Those faggots outside are dishing me to death. Just wait till I go in, though. They'll stop their cackling!"

Drewena led Carrie to her by the hand.

"Beulah," she said, "I want you to take Carrie under your wing to-night. She may not be in New York long and I want her to have a grand evening. I'll want her part of the time, when I'm not going the rounds."

Beulah lifted her sagging, experienced face to Carrie, who stood there, fluttering slightly. Then the dowager graciously held out both her hands.

"I'll show you the *best* people, dearie," she said. "Just hold on to your old auntie's arm and we'll see if there isn't some trade in sheep's clothing. And by the way," she added, smiling shrewdly in the sunless room, "is that little bitch, Kate, going to be here? I've made a vow to do that one! She can't fool these old professional eyes—tired though they may be."

Drewena laughed.

"Yes, Beulah, she's here. And quite beautiful too, in green. She just got back from Chili—some kind of an electrical engineering project."

"'Project,' my grandmother!—rest her bones." Beulah sniffed. "Doing the Indians again—what she sees in *them* is beyond me! But the hussy *is* interesting." Beulah swished the bow at her back, spread the wide skirts of her lavender gown and opened a long black ostrich feather fan. Breathing deeply, so that her large bust swelled out, she followed Drewena out of the room, taking Carrie on her arm.

"There she is," she whispered hoarsely, and the old lady stopped to glance covetously at Kate.

Kate was dressed in a green velvet gown of a deep jade cast. Her necklace was of intercircled loops of jade as was her linked green bracelet. The earrings were slender pendants of the same hue and stone. With this ensemble she was bound to use a cautious make-up—her skin, tanned by the flat sun of the Andes, being almost enough. Only a dark red splash across her lips, as though she had been recklessly eating cherries, seemed a necessary cosmetic. Her black hair was curled bewitchingly, up from the forehead and sides. When she saw Beulah, she beckoned wildly and the green purse which hung from her arm banged against a punchbowl which was near the tiny bar.

"Common!" someone said in a stage whisper, but Kate only laughed and crooked her finger at Beulah again, who strode forward with aggressive, formidable steps, half dragging Carrie.

"Have a drink, darlin'?" asked Kate, looking up at the dowager.

"Thank you, my dear," said Beulah, in an affected voice. "It's *so* sweet of you to ask me."

Kate ladled out two drinks. As she handed one to Carrie, she said, "That's a lovely gown, honey. Drewena told me you made it yourself. Why don't you drop around at my place some time next week and show me how you do it?"

Beulah coughed slightly and pinched Carrie's arm.

Kate turned to her with another glassful of punch.

"Here you are, dear," she said. "It will be good for you." But she was thinking, "I'll bet it's the first free drink she's had in months!" Aloud, Kate spoke again. "And now, darlin', *do* have another."

Beulah nodded graciously, her eyes a little brighter.

Kate thought once more, "You old bitch! I hope you choke on it and get as blue as blue can be!"

"Kate, dearie," said Beulah, after her fourth, "there's just the right touch of bitters to the bottle—it makes one have a feeling of heavenly bliss!"

Kate smiled and thought, "You don't know a good drink from a bad one. You just take all you can get, and that's all you know. You might have been pretty in your day—but your blooming days are past forever."

At this moment, a splendid creature bore down upon them, all sails set. She was a broad-shouldered fellow, whose snappy skirts and impudent coiffure failed to cover her intention.

"Mercy!" she exclaimed. "Just dishing it!"

Kate took a whisky straight and smiled at the "debbie" in a tantalizing fashion.

"To think," said Kate, "a moment ago there wasn't a piece of trade in sight! I was just hoping."

The big girl turned around and looked back over her shoulder.

"Oh!" she cried in an obligato, "you New Yorkers *can* be so bitchy!" Then she sailed on and rounded the turn to the powder-room.

"Dirt!" said Beulah.

"Tawdry!" exclaimed Carrie.

"From Boston?" asked Beulah.

"No, Baltimore," answered Kate. "Working up from the bottom in her father's steel mill, I believe. That's where she got the muscles. The thick head came naturally though." Kate opened her purse and took out a small bottle of perfume from which she removed the stopper. Shaking a few drops of the scent on her fingers, she touched them to her ears and throat, patting the remaining moisture on the imperceptible beard around her chin.

Just then, Patsy's familiar voice announced "Miss Roberts."

Drewena was standing by the door as the newcomer, somber of face even through her high, natural coloring, and as Drewena thought, all the more beautiful because of her stone-like gravity, entered the drawing room; for, dressed in a cunningly fashioned gown of silver cloth, she looked more like an impassioned Joan of Arc in mailed armor than a modern executive of lives. Around her throat lay her mother's string of black pearls, and her hands were encased in an unusual muff of blue fox.

"I'm so glad you came after all, Roberta," said the hostess quietly. "You have been keeping too much to yourself, and I'm sure that you'll have a little fun to-night. Carrie is here—she's the most amusing camp! And Kate, and Beulah, and Docky——"

"Damn them all!" interrupted Roberta. "Take me to that corner over there where no one is standing."

Drewena saw the painful expression on her face and nodded agreement, sitting down with her for a moment.

"Is Martin coming to-night?" asked Roberta nervously.

"Why, yes," said Drewena. "That is, I think so. I sent him a note, urging him to be here. I have such a pretty name for him."

"Yes, yes, of course," answered Roberta, a little absently, tapping her silver slipper against the side of her chair. "Is Rio coming?"

"Indeed not," said Drewena, amazed at the question. "Ask that man up?—I should say not!"

"'Man'—my petticoat!" observed Roberta. "What's the matter with you, Drewena? *That* one is dashed for fair! Her hard-boiled act doesn't fool me a bit. She's a damned *poseur* and as full of bitchery as——"

"Stop shaking," broke in Drewena. "For heaven's sake! All the cats are beginning to gossip about the way you're acting. See old Docky talking with her hand over her mouth? She knows perfectly well that I can read lips. If she hadn't been a splendid surgeon in her day and attended my father years ago, I should never have invited her."

And Docky was saying to the more elderly group clustered around her at this moment, "It's shameful the way Roberta monopolizes Drewena's time. In a way though, one can't blame her. For dearies, Roberta hasn't long to be a queen at the rate *she's* going!" Docky pulled her shawl more tightly about her neck.

"What *is* wrong with her, Docky?" asked one rather vapid, sweet-faced auntie. "Is she sick?"

At this, Docky raised her lorgnette and looked at the speaker, a quiver of amusement lacing her cheeks back and forth until it seemed they would have met if her nose hadn't kept them apart.

"Precious!" She lifted her hand. Enormous jewels sparkled and flickered on every finger. "*I* wouldn't know. I haven't been out with her since she was a child—ah!" Docky breathed. "Those halcyon days!"

Back in the corner Drewena sighed.

"If you won't, you won't, Roberta; but it looks like intrigue, and I hate intrigue. You're positive you won't give even a short number? I wish you'd read one of your own lovely poems. You did, last year, and they'll expect it. Of course, if you won't, I'll send Carrie over to keep you company during the program."

"Not unless you want a murder at your drag," said Roberta in such a menacing voice that Drewena started, then watched her guest for a moment until the fire was out of Roberta's eyes, and some of the hatred expressed on her face had dissipated.

"Roberta," she said at last, "if you are ill, you should go home. It would be doing both of us a kindness."

"I'm not sick," said Roberta evenly.

"Why do you hate Carrie so much?" persisted Drewena.

"Don't talk like that," said Roberta, in despair. "It's just that she *thinks* of Martin. She thinks of him in a terrible way. Please don't question me further." Roberta opened her compact, studied herself in the tiny mirror and powdered her face lightly, smoothing away the lines from her forehead and looking with detachment at the shadows under her eyes. Drewena took her hand for an instant and held it tightly before she left. But as she walked toward the punchbowl with its merry company, there was an intimate, definite foreboding and a striking glance of prescience from her heavy-lidded eyes. Her appearance was so exotic, so provocative, that when Kate offered her a drink, she wanted to offer her a kiss as well.

The widows around Docky, however, were still discussing Roberta.

"Look at her," said Daisy, the pretty one. "Holding her jaws down at the side in that manner. If I were half so pretty as she, I wouldn't hide in the corner like that."

"I'll *bet* you wouldn't," yawned Docky, grasping her upper plate, as she had a horror of swallowing it.

Again Patsy's high voice rang out, this time against the music of the orchestra.

"Miss Devaud," she bawled.

Drewena's face grew whiter as she went gracefully but swiftly to the arch-like entrance to greet the new arrival, whose perfect casting—the unusual make-up against the wheat-colored hair, against the long, pale yellow dress, against the turquoise of her eyes, and the strong, uneven modeling of her features brought the hostess to a stop before she reached her guest.

"Beautiful Miriam," she whispered.

Miriam contemplated Drewena without expression, though enjoying her beauty far more than she liked to admit. While Drewena was thinking in confusion how and where to get her friend alone—away from the others who would spoil her with their eyes—yes, with their thoughts, as Roberta had said. If she, Drewena, could only touch her once—could only hold her.... So taking her guest by the hand, she quickly pulled her back into the hall.

"Come upstairs for a moment, Miriam," she whispered hoarsely. "You must have earrings to make you perfect. I have some of jet that will make you lovelier than ever!" They ascended the wide spiral staircase.

Carrie ran after them. On the bottom step she paused. As they disappeared around a bend in the stairs, Carrie clung tightly to the newel post. Then turning, her eyes wide, she stepped down and hurried to Beulah.

Roberta, sitting in her corner, saw all this, and the rapidity with which she changed coloring caused old Docky to chuckle something about adrenalin. But Roberta was really acting strangely. She seemed ready to leave her chair, then at intervals would pull something halfway out of her muff. Docky could not quite see, for Roberta covered the object cleverly. Each movement, however, was hesitant, until finally, with a certain air of fatalism, Roberta settled down in a rigid posture which she maintained for some time.

Upstairs, Drewena opened a door beyond the staircase, and led Miriam out on the terrace. Saturn was in conjunction with the frozen moon. Midway between the zenith and the horizon, the moon, as if by some prearrangement lightened Drewena's white face until her beauty would have been nebulous had she not been pressed so closely to her friend. Miriam's face, however, had caught the amber tone of the planet, and her cheeks seemed flushed as though by moonburn. Drewena pulled her inside again and sat beside her on the bed. She turned out the indirect lights and lay down, her head on Miriam's lap. The moon shone upon them brightly.

"Miriam," she said, "is that a halo around your head, dearest?"

"It's the moon in the fuzz of my wig," answered Miriam seriously.

Drewena sighed. "How I wish," she said, "that we could have stayed out on the terrace!—Perhaps we can come up here after the guests have gone.... This bed is so deep and wide, we'll cool off quickly.... And to-morrow we can go to a little cottage I have up on the coast near Cape Cod.... We'll listen to the wind—and there'll be snow, and the surf breaking on the rocks under our doorstep.... You'll carry a lamp to help me to my bed. I want to be dependent on you—oh! you understand!" Drewena put her gentle hands on Miriam's cheeks. "They're hot, Miriam. Perhaps you are excited, too—perhaps I won't have to go away as I told Tai! He's my little protegé! I'll send him to France with his tutor.... My dearest, tell me that I needn't go!"

Miriam petted her gently and explained quite simply that of course she didn't have to leave; but when that was said, she kept repeating, "Go!—go!—go!—" continuing to blend the words until they became untranslatable.

Drewena looked at her in astonishment.

"What do you mean?" she asked. "Those words—they have a cadence that makes me feel insane—Please don't talk like that!... Dear God!—All I ask is that you bear with me. I'd never cheat Deane. It's on a different plane. Quite different. Kiss my lips, Miriam—I'm tired—so tired."

"Aye," said Miriam gently, "that I *can* do! For you're as sweet a little maiden as I've ever seen, lying so in the moonlight." And bending over, she pressed her lips upon Drewena's. The white-tinted hair fell over her shoulders and Drewena shuddered as Deane had shuddered. There was no distaste, for Drewena lay quietly now in Miriam's arms, only a slight, convulsive movement betraying her passion. Then Miriam sat up and leaned away as though into the moon; for a feeling had come over her during that kiss that she could not interpret. It was a half sick, half desirous mood of great intensity. And so, unaccustomed to tempering her emotions, she threw Drewena back upon the bed and held her tightly, her mouth pressing on her throat. Drewena did not resist until the desire had grown and Miriam groped blindly. Then quickly Drewena struggled away and as quickly turned on the lamps.

"Not now," she laughed, a splendid light in her eyes. "Later—after the party. Oh," she exclaimed, bending toward her friend, "it's the heaven I thought I'd never find—the soul, the mind, the body.... But now, we must hurry and touch ourselves up." And she hung the long, jet pendants from Miriam's ears. So the gowns were smoothed out, the hair recombed and pinned, the make-up applied anew.

When at last they entered the drawing room there was only the faintest buzzing of interest among the more intrepid of the gossipers. Even this ceased as Drewena, her arm linked closely in Miriam's, stopped at various groups to introduce her friend. Docky stopped chattering just long enough to size up Miriam's figure.

"Miriam, my dear," she said at once, "if I'd known *you* were coming, I'd have worn my new gown of cardinal red. To think!—you see me in the faded splendor of this musty blue! You must come and chat with us this evening." She looked at Miriam intently and pulled her shawl even tighter. Then she smiled, a good deal of understanding and more than that, compassion, expressed in her face. When Drewena took Miriam with her to the punchbowl, Beulah turned on Docky in a fury.

"Only past sixty, and you're back to childhood! I could scratch your eyes out! Miriam is simply lovely, and now you've driven her away!"

"There, there," Docky said, in her best professional tone. "It's just as well—Drewena loves him."

"'Him'?" screeched Daisy, fascinated.

"Don't get so excited, Daisy. Remember your blood pressure," said Docky calmly. "Of course, 'him'! The boy's as jam as the preserves you used to steal off your mother's shelf!"

"Absurd!" said Beulah. "She has a *grand* dash!"

"On the edge, dearie, but he's never fallen off, and I doubt if he ever will. The habit pattern has unfortunately fixated him for women. Ah!—if I could have had him to mold some years ago!"

"*Jam'!*" cried Daisy once more, her hands to her ears.

Docky pushed back the wisps of gray hair from her forehead and took out her left eye, wiping it carefully.

"Mercy!" said Beulah. "*Must* you do that in company?" She tossed her head angrily. "And don't tell us how you lost your real one at Ypres! There!" She pointed swiftly toward the punchbowl. "I *knew* it! Kate is trying to snitch Miriam from Drewena!"

"Common!" said the same sepulchral voice that had uttered this word before.

Everyone turned around to see who had repeated it, but there was no one in sight. Docky chuckled.

Kate was speaking vivaciously to Miriam until she caught Drewena's eye, whereupon she merely shrugged her strong bare shoulders and turned petulantly away. The moment of ensuing silence was broken by Patsy's high-pitched tremulo, which seemed to be growing weaker.

"Miss Murphy!" she shouted feebly.

Miss Murphy did not wait for Drewena's welcome. She flew into the room in a state of deshabille, her black lace dress torn slightly on the shoulder, her corsage of gardenias darkening around the edges as though they had been crushed in a heavy fist.

"Oh, my God!" she said, breathing heavily as Drewena comforted her.

Kate stole a glance at Miriam and whispered, "Doing the taxis again!" Then she took a glass to the newcomer.

"Drink this, Sophie," she began, when the other turned on her, stamping her foot and pulling the torn lace back over her shoulder.

"Don't you *dare* offer me any of that sickening, frothy slop!" she cried. "I want a straight one, or I'll just *die*!"

Kate lifted the glass and drained it.

"'It was good enough for mother, and it's good enough for me,'" she quoted sweetly. But Drewena called for a glassful of whisky and handed it to Sophie who began to drink it greedily.

Docky had her hand over her mouth again and was leaning toward Beulah.

"Don't look now," she said. "Sophie's watching us like *mad*. I'll bet she thinks we're dishing her."

"Well, dearie," said Beulah, her hand covering her lips also, "she's right. But I won't smile, and don't you *dare* look now."

But Docky went on, the rest of the group straining toward her, for no one could dish like Docky.

"My God, Beulah," she said, "they speak of *courage* in history. But she has a *nerve* to come here in *that* lace!"

"'Lace'!" Beulah appeared shocked. "She bought that netting at the ten cent store to cover her trade with, when she gets that Cleopatrine feeling! No *wonder* all the cab drivers around Pennsylvania Station are looking tired these days!"

"Shish!" said Docky. "Look now, dearie. She's terrible from the front. Do you notice her fallen chest?... And what do you think of the back? And oh!—

what ugly hands! I'm sure those hands have snitched many pieces of silver in *her* time!"

"I don't care how much silver she has snitched," said Beulah, "but I *do* hope she'll keep her dirty mitts off Miriam. Really, Docky, you don't honestly believe that Miriam might be jam, now do you?"

Docky leaned over and spoke into Beulah's ear.

"Don't tell anyone, but I'm really sure. I really shouldn't have told you, but since you have thrown so much my way in the past———"

"Christ!" said Daisy, fidgeting with her lavaliere. "Sophie really makes me ill. She always looks as though she's straight from the washtub."

"True," said Docky, "from the shanty on the other side of the tracks. It's a shame for her to have money, with me dodging creditors like *mad*! Look at her trying to be elegant, wiping her nose with her soft, raggy wrist—and dearie, her nose isn't running from a cold. *That* one's been broken down for years and years. Old saddley ass! She looks as though she had three pillows in her rear!"

"It *is* indecent," agreed Beulah. "And she doesn't have fallen arches for nothing. She's been cruising *most* of her life."

"That she has!" said Docky. "My God!" Docky leaned forward excitedly. "She's picking up her skirts! Do you see those varicose veins on her leg? They stand out like the knots on a pinetree!"

Drewena was now urging Sophie to give the first "number" of the evening. But Sophie, partly drunk from her brief, but thrilling escapade with the cab driver, kept showing a bruise on her shoulder.

"It hit me! The person really hit me! It was all over that cage I brought for my number. Will you have Patsy bring me the cage I left with her? I'll be in the powder room."

When she had gone, Drewena explained to Miriam that each guest always gave a little act.

Miriam was thunderstruck.

"I don't know anything to do. It's impossible for me."

"Just anything," said Drewena, with composure. "It doesn't have to be much."

Miriam thought a moment, observing the heavy beam above her, the high ceiling and the shadows.

"Was that Tai whom I saw peeping out into the hall a moment ago? The child looked Indo-Chinese. If you'd lend him to me...."

"I can't risk the child," said Drewena slowly. "His father nursed me. And next to you, Miriam, I love him better than anyone but Deane." Drewena gave a queer smile. "*She* has a portion of the roundtable of my mind that no one, not even you, my dearest, can fathom."

"I won't hurt the child," said Miriam earnestly. "He'll think it's a lot of fun. You can see what I'll do!"

"It isn't that," said Drewena, flushing. Then, "All right. Tai is yours for the trick. What else do you need?"

"A man with powerful shoulders, and a rope," said Miriam. "And have the orchestra play loudly while I work."

Suddenly Drewena laughed.

"Oh, you are really good!—I see it now. You've always just pretended to be an impossible person. I believe you'd cry easily."

"Yes, I cry very easily," Miriam agreed.

"Have you seen Roberta?" asked Drewena suddenly. "She was asking about you."

"You mean Roberts? No, I haven't."

"Well, she's in a corner, pouting about something. It's either you, or Carrie—perhaps even myself. She is in a terrible mood to-night. Please don't have a scene with her. And please, Miriam, remember, this *is* a drag. I don't care how masculine they may seem to you,—call them by their feminine names, or address them impersonally as 'she.' Do you see Beulah over there in her lavender gown?... He was thirty-nine and three times married before he recognized himself for what he was. Being a flexible character, he slipped quite naturally into his present rôle—that of a tight-fisted, gossipy old dowager, but behind the intermittent lechery of his old and experienced eyes he is a strong man and a gentleman. No one in the everyday world even suspects. They've marked him down, in fact, as a devil with the ladies. Kate is a harsher type. He married one of the most beautiful women I have ever seen. She bore him a lovely boy. Then one day, Kate became irritated over a trifle and threw his wife across the room. Fortunately, she was not injured; but he went into a 'break' or nervous explosion. From that, into a depressive state and out of it in a wild hysteria. Then came his first love—his consulting psychiatrist.... The pattern was woven swiftly enough—and Kate, too, slipped into her niche, not so pleasant a one as Beulah's, who takes them as she finds them. Kate is now searching desperately. You will not?—" Drewena hesitated. "Forgive me, Miriam. And now, let us visit Roberta. Please give her a smile and I know she will feel better. We must hurry. Sophie will soon be ready for her act, and you must prepare your magic."

They walked across the floor, both sated—one by boredom, the other by necessity. When they approached Roberta, she stood up, one hand touching the pearls at her throat, the other holding her muff.

"Drewena," she said quietly, with slow sarcasm, "it would be a pleasure to meet your friend. She is very pretty in yellow. Did Carrie make the dress?" Roberta's lip curled. Once more her hand moved convulsively in her muff.

Without a word Miriam stepped up close and running her fingers down Roberta's arm, slipped her own hand well inside the tiny fur. Roberta shook her off; but Miriam, now looking at her friend as though intrigued, said slowly, "Perhaps you'd like another cocktail, Roberta. It will warm you. Your hands are like ice."

Drewena looked on, but finding the scene too difficult to interpret, shook her head sadly, murmured something about the program and led Miriam away.

Roberta, still brooding, was left alone in her corner.

Standing by the piano, Drewena clapped her hands and the crowd grew quiet.

"First," she said, "since Sophie is not ready, I'll ask Daisy, who has come in her perennial form of the 'Prairie Flower' to sing for us."

Docky sniffed and whispered to Beulah, "Look at her! She doesn't even have to make up for the part! My dear, do I *have* to listen to that miserable dentist do her wild flower act again? It's just been repeated and repeated till I could simply scream! Imagine, trying to carry on at *her* age when we *all* know she's well into the menopause!"

Daisy, however, tripped across the floor, her black taffeta dress flouncing around her wide hips. After bowing to the somewhat bored and suffering crowd, she put her hands to her shoulders and bent her knees. In a stringy voice she sang—

> "I'm a little Prairie Flower
>
> Growing wilder every hour!
>
> No one here to care about me—
>
> I'm as wild as wild can be!"

Then she put one hand on the top of her head, and the other on her hip. Jigging up and down to the music of the piano, she began to rotate on her toes. The frayed voice continued—

"I'm a little patchwork quilt

All my edges trimmed in gilt!

No one here to cuddle with me—

I'm as cuddly as can be!"

There was loud, determined clapping, and Daisy ran off the floor, her face suffused with blushes.

"Perfectly grand, dear," said one of the guests. "So much sweeter than the *first* time you gave it."

"*That* won't last," said Beulah, looking at Daisy who had returned to the room and was holding someone's hand, obviously searching the face of her friend for signs of approval. "It won't last—I've been all through it."

In the alcove, six musicians wearing short red skirts, white blouses, white silk stockings and red sandals, were holding their instruments in readiness. They were camping among themselves, though the one with the clarinet looked just a trifle uncomfortable. Drewena asked them to play a slow drag and they began "Mood Indigo," the harpsichordist tapping her red sandal on the side of her chair, each musician looking oddly like his instrument. Drewena favored a tempered arrangement of popular music in the modern idiom. For a simplified expression of this type of instrumentation she had chosen the curious grouping of harpsichord, vibraphone, harp, bassoon, clarinet and drums. She felt that any brass, even muted, would destroy the exotic, passionate tenor of the music achieved by the combination of strings and reeds (the drums having been modulated by casings) and affected also by the arranger, who had found the predominant oriental theme from listening to Drewena herself at the piano.

Some of the dancers walked idly, in as slow a tempo as possible. Others, however, flew around the floor in a febrile reaction to the sometimes sweet, sometimes wild expression of the orchestra. Carrie's popularity was noticeable. She flew from partner to partner. But her dancing was a little heavy, and her large, moist eyes followed Miriam.

Drewena held on to Miriam tightly, preferring to be led.

"Your arm is like a rock, Miriam," she whispered.

This winter idyll was drenched in an arbor of delicate flowers that grew from the basketball scents of the dancers. A cloth seemed to cover Miriam's eyes; but as she opened them, it was Drewena's white-tinted hair that confused her. The soft waves and ringlets covered Miriam's arm and the paths that had intrigued her so long were now undivided. Nevertheless, as she breathed of Drewena's cheek, that which had been unrevealed before came swiftly in an explicable panic. She stopped in the middle of the floor. Her mouth was dry.

"I'd better prepare for my act," she said quite suddenly.

Without a word Drewena broke from her, and Miriam followed her quick steps through the archway.

"How irresponsible you are to-night, my Miriam," she breathed, a grave smile darkening her eyes. Then she called Tai.

The child ran into the powder room and bowed reverently before her.

"You will obey my friend for a trick," she said. "It will not take long." She placed her hand for a second on his shoulder before she left.

"It will be fun, Tai," said Miriam, noting the child's frightened look.

Tai bowed again.

"I shall do as you bid, mistress," he whispered, his piquant face quite solemn.

Just then a footman entered with a good hemp rope. Miriam rapidly explained the routine of the act, asked the man if his shoulders were strong, gave a simple instruction to Tai, finishing just as the orchestra ceased. The second number was being announced as she returned to the drawing room.

Someone screamed very faintly and Docky looked at Beulah; for, radiant with smiles and dressed in long white tights, Sophie posed in the doorway, a wild-looking pigeon in her hand. She began to pivot slowly.

Docky raised her scented handkerchief to her nose.

"*Pee-yoo!*" she said softly. "Here comes the pigeon-woman! She's gone pervert on us!"

"Yes," agreed Beulah, and began to hum. "'*We're camping to-night on the old campground.*'"

A person near them who was dressed in a hoopskirt made in the shape of a bell, stood up, the bell chiming once, twice, before she adjusted her bodice.

"Your clapper rings indiscriminately," said Beulah, in a mild tone.

"It is rusty from lack of use, my sweet," replied Angela, who was an undertaker.

"It is atrophied," said Docky. "But let's watch the dance."

Sophie, who had waited until all attention was centered upon her, now leaped from the doorway, flinging out the pigeon which was tied to her wrist by a string. Upon alighting, one of her thin legs bent under her, then she began to dance. She pirouetted and waved her flabby hips while the bird tried desperately to escape. Once it descended upon her head and lifted the transformation. The guests had a fleeting glimpse of a pink, bald dome. Occasionally Sophie's joints cracked. The effect was macabre.

"Mercy!" said Beulah. "If *my* bones were in that condition, I'd have brought my little can of lubricating oil. She positively drowns out the orchestra!"

"'Little' can, did you say?" timidly questioned Daisy, who had rejoined the group.

Beulah did not turn her head. Only the bulges on her neck seemed to stiffen and bulge out further.

But Sophie was now in difficulty. The pigeon had become terrified and was jerking at the string. All pretense of dancing stopped and Sophie stood there, feebly waving her arms. Pitying her, Drewena stepped to her side, closed one hand gently around the panicky bird and slipped the noose from its leg. Out in the dim corridor she opened a window, touched her cheek to the bird's soft, rumpled feathers and, with a sigh, tossed it into the darkness.

Miriam had returned to the powder room when Sophie came in, near to hysteria, weeping.

"Oh, heavens!" she cried, while the mascara streamed down her cheeks. "It stooled on me!" And she wiped the top of her bare head with a handkerchief.

"That's nothing—a seagull once did the same for me," said Miriam. "You can't get it off that way. Why don't you stick your head under the shower?"

"You're insulting," said Sophie, drying her eyes.

Miriam left the room in disgust.

Another number was on. Carrie, her fingers fan-shaped over her heart, was singing "*Mother Macree*" in a soft voice, high and clear. The strange tonal quality was like that of a contralto.

Drewena was accompanying her. And along the rows of gossips there was now complete silence. Miriam noticed that both Beulah and Docky were holding handkerchiefs to their eyes, and when the last words—"God keep you and bless you, Mother Macree" trailed off, Miriam watched a solid, tremulous emotion sweep the crowd. Only Kate, openly defiant to any sentiment, poured a drink down her throat and looked at the others with disdain.

This time, as they danced, Miriam sneaked the footman in through the back, and hoisted him to the long beam, one end of which lay in shadow. Once more, she whispered instructions to her assistant, then went for Tai. The music ceased and she could hear Drewena quieting the crowd.

Then Miriam entered the room. She did not walk with the air of one experienced in drag, but her stalking, feline movements seemed even more proper. Several paces behind her came Tai, a rope over one tiny shoulder, his eyes lowered. He still wore the golden tunic and it gleamed against his little body as he held out the rope to Miriam. She took it, coiling it sailor-fashion on the floor, then hurled one end to the ceiling where it held, in a rim of shadow. Immediately Tai grabbed it and climbed upward to the beam, apparently on a rope which was in no way supported. Only the magician could see the tensed form of the footman holding the slight weight of the child. Then Tai disappeared. Miriam lifted her arms and the rope fell in waves over her shoulders. She dropped it, turned to the crowd and solemnly picked up her train. Tai, smiling and bowing, ran forth from its folds, and held out his arms to Drewena.

The crowd was charmed; but Drewena, furious, caught up the child and hurrying with him through the corridor, took him into his own room and laid him upon his own bed.

For a moment her hot cheek rested against the child who petted her, saying nothing. Then she swept into the powder room where she knew she would find Miriam. Still furious, she faced her friend.

"Miriam," she cried, "that was a coarse trick." Her eyes were narrowed and a drop of blood was welling out of the corner of her lip where she had bitten herself. "What made you do it?"

Miriam inhaled the smoke of her cigarette.

"We don't think alike, Drewena," she said reflectively at last. "There was nothing coarse in the act. It is a good trick."

"Under your skirts, Miriam!" said Drewena, her deep blue eyes watching her friend intensely.

Miriam shrugged.

"You and I have a different attitude toward such things, I fear. I hope the child feels the way I do about it. He is quite innocent—as apparently am I." Then for an instant Miriam's eyes became colder than Drewena's. "Of course, I cannot help, nor can I control your interpretations." A dark, ugly vein showed vertically now in the center of Miriam's forehead. Drewena's white velvet gown seemed to turn blood-red before her.

Even in her own anger, Drewena was amazed. Surely these could not be the features of her friend! She watched Miriam as she turned and walked to the ottoman where she sat down, breathing heavily. A tremor passed through her body and she sat, looking straight ahead. Fascinated, Drewena saw the vein in Miriam's forehead diminish at last and her features become natural again. A little frightened, she went over and put her hand on the shoulder of her friend.

"It's just that I love both of you so much, Miriam," she said. "I was jealous of you both. Please, forgive me." Her hand was trembling. "And now," she added, trying to compose herself, "I must announce Kate's dance. Won't you come out?—she dances divinely."

"Later, Drewena," Miriam said in a despondent voice. And when Drewena had gone, still looking disturbed, Miriam lay down on her back on the couch and stared at the ceiling with both eyes open wide. Her thoughts were jumbled and confused in this strange atmosphere. She had felt singular reactions. Desires that were new to her had come upon her without warning. Were her concepts changing? Or had they lain dormant, awaiting only the right moment to make her aware of another facet in her individuality?... And did this constitute a shame to God? Should the mind reject what the spirit had planted?... Was this not a possibility for every man, as well as the necessity for the cultivated group outside?... It was obscure to Miriam, lying there. Her mind was tired from these perplexing questions. Such problems as these charged without apparent reason. She stood up, held the sides of her head which now ached violently. Slowly she went to the doorway in time to hear Drewena announce Kate's dance.

The crowd applauded vigorously and Miriam could feel again the mass excitement.

"As usual," continued Drewena, "Kate has adapted a native dance-ritual to her own choreography. To-night she will interpret the fire dance of a tribe of Andean people."

Drewena stepped back as Patsy came from the corridor with a smoldering, perfumed brazier which she placed upon the floor, now cleared for a space in the center. The music began, the muted drums became more prominent, and Kate walked from the shadows of the alcove to the brazier, standing quietly beside it, her eyes lifted upward, watching the smoke, her hands palm outward before her. There was a leather strap around her forehead and a leather wristlet above the left hand. On her upper arm was a metal band which had the dull gleam of copper.

The high knee movement as she circled the brazier showed the control and discipline of her deeply tanned legs, and the supple flexibility of a professional dancer. Her bare feet slapped stiffly against the wooden floor as she continued to circle the smoke which was now rising like a slender blue pillar. As she went round the coals, her body rotated while circling, so that at times she faced the low flames and at others had her back to them, her body always arched, her circled head often coming close to the flickering brazier. A soft, faun-colored wrap that looked like chamois swung from Kate's waist; but on one side it had been cut in from the hips where the fine webbing of her dark jockstrap covered her.

Among the excited watchers, none was more affected than Beulah. She kept wiping her mouth and whispering, "My God!" to Docky. Docky, however, for once, was too fascinated to reply.

Intoxicated by the wild music and by the incense which now pervaded the room, even more by the dance itself, Kate continued her steps with more abandon, her copper body whirling with such rapidity that she seemed to be weaving amid the smoke, making it catch her enthusiasm as it leaned toward her at every angle until it spiraled upward as though part of the dance. A bolo knife with a polished bone handle rested against the nearby wall and Kate leaped toward it, picked it up swiftly and fastened the looped thong around her wrist. Then as the song of the Firebird[2] grew wilder, she swung the heavy, shining blade as though cutting her way through vines and wet, tall grass, until the knife sang in the air and Kate's slim, powerful body weaved from side to side in her savage desire to get once more to the flames. Her teeth were drawn back as though fighting with intangible yet formidable spirits, and her handsome face was set in a perfect mask of determination to get to her own beckoning god—the crimson soul of the flame—life-giving and protecting. At last she reached the genie of the fire-bowl, her face, arms and belly streaming with sweat, the bolo knife held rigidly over her head and her left hand supporting the sinews of the wrist which held it.

This time, instead of circling the brazier, she leaped over it, held herself suspended one fraction of a second before she dropped lightly on the other side, wheeled instantly and repeated the floating movement until the blur of her body became one with the smoke. Suddenly, to the horror of the guests, there was a soft whisper, like fire through damp reeds, and the odor of burning hair mixed with the scent of the pitch. As the crowd held its breath sharply, Kate let out a fierce, sensuous shout of triumph, and whirled in eccentric half-turns into the shadows of the alcove....

There was no applause. The crowd was stunned by this amazing, painful exhibition into deep silence. Docky abstractedly removed and wiped her glass eye again, and Beulah dabbed futilely at her aging face. But their attention was now quickly drawn to the corner where Roberta had been sitting. She was standing in such an imperious manner that everyone turned toward her in astonishment. The broken rays from a chandelier nearby revealed her beautiful, tragic face as she said with the elegance of contempt, "And now—let *me* speak!" Her resonate voice filled the deep silence, and she crossed the floor to a place where she could face the crowd more fully.

Rather nervously, Drewena hurried to her and whispered something; but Roberta's desperate expression stopped her from speaking further and she drew back, more than ever perplexed. At this, Miriam, watching the blue fox muff attentively, walked quietly to Roberta until her eyes said, "Stop!" which Miriam did, a few paces away.

Then, in level voice and without gesture, never taking her eyes from Miriam's face, Roberta said—

> There on the sheets, my lad,
>
> With small gold arms and hair tossed back
>
> Most carelessly,
>
> She bears the quality we lack.
>
> And older, perhaps weary, I'm some sad.
>
> Here in my arms, my lad,
>
> With strong gold wrists and hair tossed back
>
> In liberty,
>
> You bear the quality I lack.
>
> And older, perhaps weary, I'm some sad.
>
> But in my glass, sweet lad,
>
> I see thy dreams, thy lady's,
>
> And thy profligacy.
>
> And *know* the quality you lack....
>
> Yet still I'm older, perhaps weary, and some sad.

There was a buzz of disapproval as Roberta finished. "Well," said Beulah, "we may have *lived* in our time, but we *never* carried on like *that*! In those pastel days," and she tapped Docky's arm with her fan, parting her lips with a snap, "we *did* carry on a bit—but this is *too* much! I feel like entering the philanthropies. They're so much quieter."

"Yes, yes," said Docky, "I tried it once. But it's too expensive, Beulah. And don't expect, dear, too much of your personality. We're getting wrinkles. Soon the lovelies won't *look* at us for less than a dollar! How your quarter has worked as long as it has, is beyond me!"

Roberta had returned to the solitude of her corner when there was a terrified screech from Patsy, and Rio, completely drunken, in servant's skirts held high above his knees, lurched into the drawing room. He stood there just inside the doorway, swaying and looking around at the gathering.

"Whores!" he shouted stridently, raising one heavy brown arm in his anger. "You lousy, campy sons-of-bitches!" He forced his risqué Robin Hood hat down to his ears, his shoulders nearly popping out of his dress, and his great legs encased in red football stockings which were rolled just beneath his hairy knees. Then he saw Miriam looking at him without amusement as she leaned against the piano. Rio walked slowly to her, his arms hanging like lead. As he approached, Miriam did not stir and there was a contemptuous look upon her face. Rio moved his lips in an obscene gesture and pretended to whimper.

"Could a old 'ooman show 'ee the sights o' Cooney Island? I'll do no traffic with 'ee."

Miriam smiled, for in his hatred Rio had mimicked his character with perfection. Even the crowd began to think it was a camp when suddenly, without warning, Rio struck Miriam who fell slowly to the floor. Drewena noticed that she looked like Tai, the way she was curled. With a low scream, Drewena ran swiftly from the room while Rio looked on with contempt. But his expression changed as he saw his friend still lying open-mouthed, a little absent, upon the floor, one slippered foot thrust out from the folds of the yellow dress.

Drewena now returned silently. She was carrying a long, gilded whip. She held it firmly in her delicate hands, the barbs away from her, ready to be snapped. As Rio bent over his friend, he started to kneel. But before his knee was completely bent, Drewena brought the thorned end of the gold scourge straight down across his shoulders, the faint swish modified by Rio's cry of pain and surprise; for as the flesh was ripped from his back there was the sound of crushed bubbles. In his agony, he rushed at the white-gowned hostess, but Drewena, as though in a fantastic ballet, dodged him and pivoted so swiftly that when Rio passed, the wrench and throb of his sickening pain as he was struck again, brought forth a groan from everyone in the room. Drewena stood poised for the next thrust, and her expression brought Rio on once more, his great hands searching for her through his agony. Again she avoided him and turned to lay the hooked rods into his lacerated flesh. Rio, in all his bravery could stand no more and fell upon his face, his arms reaching out like claws. Cool and mindful of her action, Drewena struck him again until the blood formed in small pools by his side.

Roberta still stood silently in the shadow of her corner. Docky, who had been watching her, had seen with her one alert, keen eye, a single movement and a flash of steel as Roberta withdrew her hand from her muff, then returned it stoically when Rio fell.

This time, as Drewena lifted her arm, Miriam sat up. There was no movement, no shudder from the prone figure on the floor.

"Wait, Drew!" called Miriam. "Leave the man alone!"

Drewena looked at her incredulously.

"This beast knocked you down," she said, "and without reason."

She turned again to strike, but Miriam arose unsteadily and held Drewena's arm.

Drewena dropped the whip.

"Do you, then, consider *this* more important?" she asked nodding toward Rio who was still lying quietly, his blouse in shreds upon his blood-soaked back.

"He is my friend," said Miriam. "We are going home."

"Our rendezvous?" breathed Drewena.

"Will wait," said Miriam.

Then, kneeling down by the stricken man whose face showed no expression as she turned it toward her, Miriam repeated, "It's Martin, Rio, ... Martin ... we are going home." Half lifting, half imploring, Martin got Rio to his feet, and as the man leaned heavily against him, they crossed the floor amid the horrified silence of the crowd.

Then "Boor!" ... "Common!" ... "Stiff!" ... came to Martin's ears as he bore the weight of his friend onward to the doorway. At last, he could stand no more of it.

"You!" he cried, turning. "You! Leave us alone!—my friend and me!"

In the hall, Martin looked at Rio's thrashed back.

"We'd better go to my room," he said. "Call a cab for us, Patsy." And he threw Deane's coat over Rio.... As they left, they could hear the sound of music and dancing.

Carrie had gone into hysterics. Her high heel had caught in her train and ripped it open. She was rushing to the powder room when Drewena saw her. The hostess followed her guest through the groups of dancers and found Carrie on the ottoman, crying brokenly. Drewena closed and locked the door. Her lips were bitter—to have revealed herself and lost her caste over a graceless Polynesian was unbearable! She went through a hidden paneled doorway into Tai's room and lightly kissed his fingers, listening to the sweet sound of his even breathing. Then opening the door into the corridor, she called the footman who brought Patsy to her at once.

"We are leaving, Patsy," she said. "Arrange for an early departure. We will go to Paris. Cable Jacques to meet us."

Patsy bowed.

"May I say 'thank God,' Madame? I speak reverently."

Drewena laughed, and for a moment looked into Patsy's faithful eyes.

"Arrange things quickly," she repeated as the attendant left.

Again Drewena tiptoed past the sleeping, tired baby and entered the powder room, closing the panel behind her and ignoring the pounding on the door.

Carrie still cried, her tears dampening the golden pillows of the couch.

"Miriam left without asking me to dance," she kept on sobbing.

Drewena picked her up bodily and making a cradle out of her own slender arms, held the unhappy girl. Singing a soft, melodic lullaby, she rocked Carrie, thinking, "It is time once more, for me to go. Ah, Martin!—indiscriminate man!—you see beauty only through your prostitution.... How I envy you!... How I ..." Drewena's thick tears clung to her lashes and did not fall on Carrie who, now rocked asleep, held tightly to Drewena's comforting breast.

CHAPTER XVII

On the low coffee table in front of Deane was a bowl of yellow roses. She had broken off one of the blossoms and was slowly, abstractedly pulling it to pieces. Listlessly she allowed the golden petals to fall to the floor.

"Why didn't you tell me of Drew's love letter earlier, Martin?" she asked.

"It was an invitation," he answered. "I shouldn't have shown it at all."

Deane lit a cigarette nervously.

"But what did you do?—I mean—oh!" she cried out, hiding her face in her hands.

Martin shook his head but did not speak.

"And now," continued Deane, "you insist on meeting him in the Bowery."

"Yes," Martin nodded.

"But it isn't like Drew to go to such a terrible place. Why did you agree to such a rendezvous?"

"I don't know, except that he sounded sincere and almost desperate over the phone."

"How *did* he sound?" asked Deane. "Remember, I know him."

"Cool on the surface, but determined," answered Martin, "and worried—no, not worried; just rather desperate."

"You *can't* go!" cried Deane. "I've been driven through the place at night. It's terrifying; a street of yellow lanterns, and figures huddled in shadow like fallen bric-a-brac."

"I must go," said Martin.

"Won't you stay, for me?"

Martin pressed his hand against his temple.

"Yes, Deane," he answered at last.

"Thank God!" she said. "There is something cruel in the air to-night." Then, relieved, she asked, "What happened to Rio?"

Martin regarded her so long and steadily that she flushed, looking a little frightened. At last he answered, "The driver helped me get him into the cab and he slept all the way to my place. When I got him on the bed with his shirt off, he awoke in great pain and I smelt a curious odor that came from his back. I'm sure the thorns of the whip held some kind of drug. Rio said they felt like fishhooks and that he was dizzy a moment before he fell on the floor. It's odd the way Drew is able to handle him. They fought like two dancers."

Deane's face was white and she spoke quietly, as though faint.

"I believe you enjoyed it. How can you be so impersonal?"

Martin put his chin in his hands. How could two people, close in passion, united in mind, lapse into these subtle quarrels? There was no basis. The quarrel was an excuse for something deeper.

Analyzing himself, Martin tried to find the fault within him. Coldly, impersonally, he reviewed the scene, not sparing himself in any way. It was impossible. Deane had subtly forced the argument. Deeply, actually, she had been the aggressor. Martin accepted this with no pleasure. Deane would not intentionally wound him. *Not intentionally.* The phrase gathered meaning. Unconsciously she had created the picture. Why? Nothing on the surface. Nothing of which she was conscious. Rather, some deep-seated demand for pain. Pain for herself and for him. A hunger to wound and be wounded. Martin shook his head helplessly. From his chair he could see Deane sitting quietly serene, apparently indifferent. No. It was a simulated indifference. A strange play with no tenable motive. She must be as aware of the chasm between them as he. Out of this isolation she was drawing something. Something that fed her. It was inexplicable to Martin, for Deane was not a tyrant. She was, however, feminine. And now, the roots of all womanhood shone grimly through. Martin wondered, hesitated, and spoke.

"Deane, are you well? I mean," he continued, "is it the time of the moon, you know?"

Deane was casual.

"Yes, Martin." Her voice was tolerant.

"Well, then," he said, "I should have been more considerate."

"Don't be impossible," Deane exclaimed. "My condition has nothing at all to do with our discussion."

"I'm inclined to believe, Deane, that it has everything to do with it."

"That is ridiculous," she answered, flushing. "It isn't nice."

Martin looked at her closely. Deane's eyes were implacable. Cold, glassed-in, the poisonous shell moved around her. He could not reach her. He thought quickly, fantastically, in his unhappiness. The period. The time of the moon. The time eggs swell and burst into a live stream. In his vision he watched a flood of red, elliptical objects swing in a gigantic arch from heaven to earth. Rolling and whispering through the dark air, they poured in a fast tide past his aching eyes. Redolent of life, acrid with blood, they cried from the great sky-womb into the whirling land. Symbolic of woman's supremacy, the scarlet bank lightened, faded and died, that it might live again.

"Deane!" cried Martin. "I have seen the secret."

"What secret, Martin?"

"The secret that you have a secret. That you have a secret that I will never know. That no man will ever know. It is your earth-quality, your heritage as a woman. A glory and a pride, and I have confused it."

Deane turned her dark, lovely eyes toward him.

"What do you mean?" she asked, and a tiny nerve close to her mouth quivered.

Martin laughed. He had the key. He had turned the key and the glass had broken. Gone was the poisonous mist and doubt from Deane's eyes.

"I mean that there is a completeness in woman that man will never have," he said, with quiet conviction. "A secret that man will never fully understand. A secret that women are not aware of—consciously. A pact of woman in the woman that is not revealed until the life-flow moves from their bodies. A pact so complete, so magnificent, that man takes on his true perspective—an interloper."

Deane turned and hugged him to her. Her hair fell over his shoulder—burned him.

"You're crazy," she said. But there was warmth in her voice, and love, and some belief.

"I'm not crazy," said Martin, kissing her. He held her proudly, and looked at her and kissed her again. He was arrogant of his weakness and proud of her strength. He was that way, whether he was wrong, or right. And there was the man, and there was the woman.

It was quite dark and raining when Martin left Deane's. The wind, cold and full of smoke, sifted into his nostrils. Halfway down the block he pressed against the wall, partly out of the storm, and lit a cigarette. The glare of the match showed his calm features. Shielding his cigarette from the downpour with his hand, he walked slowly toward the Bowery.

As he turned into Third Avenue he became, once more, aware of a madman's world. Little dwarfs with sour, twisted faces uplifted in the rain implored with mocking smiles a cigarette; and when he gave it he could feel the jeers carried after him by the wind. Soon he went into Bowery Lane and a blind man stumbled into him.

"You're not real," said Martin. "Don't ever believe that you're real."

"What?" cried the man, tapping the street with his stick. "You scoundrel," he went on, "let me go! I'll call the damned police, curse them!" And he walked on swiftly, tapping his cane through the mist.

Martin continued along the Bowery until he saw a saloon. He crossed the street and went inside wondering if he had time for a drink. Looking at his watch he saw that he was far too early for his appointment with Drew.

"Step up, Mac," called out a fat, red-faced gentleman at the bar. "Name it, and I'll buy it."

"Thanks," said Martin. "I'll have a Bass Ale."

"To my little lady I left in the west!" said the florid man, a few tears trickling down the side of his pudgy nose. "Ain't that right, Allie?" he continued, turning to a slab-headed man next to him.

"Yeah," replied Allie, looking Martin over.

The three men lifted their glasses. Allie belched and took a package of baking soda from his pocket. He dumped a teaspoonful into the remainder of his beer and stirred it. Swallowing this concoction with some effort, he turned to Martin.

"It takes a goddam acid out," he said earnestly. "It don't give a gas like a plain goddam beer—" he stopped to belch again.

Martin nodded in agreement.

"I must be going now," he said, "but before I do, kindly have a drink on me."

Allie insisted on a third which Martin thanked him for, but put down untouched after seeing the fellow cleverly add an astonishing portion of "mickey" to it.

The men were sullen as he said goodnight, and a little way down the street Martin knew he was being followed by them. He ducked around a corner and into a doorway for a moment, but they were even closer behind him as he started on. Ahead of him four men were huddled on a stoop out of the rain, the light from a yellow lamp streaking their greasy features. Martin thought momentarily of Deane's weird description, then looking back and seeing Allie and his friend closing in upon him, he went directly to the little group on the doorstep and addressed them earnestly.

"It's cold," he said. "A smoke for the soul's sake," he continued, handing some cigarettes around, one at a time, to the greedy, shaking fingers. One cigarette was now left in the case, and one man was left out. "I just came down from Heaven, sir," Martin said to the man quite solemnly. "They told me that worldly goods were without blessing unless freely given." He handed the cigarette to the man, who backed slightly away, but who accepted it nevertheless. All the men lit up and formed a thinly protective group against Martin, who heard one of them whisper, "The kid's cracked. Hope he ain't got no 'shiv.' Religion guys go fast wit' a knife."

Another, a giant in a white shirt and dark coat said, "Don't squawk. Lookit a kid's face in a lamp. God!—a smoke is sweet! Lookit a kid." They all studied Martin whose uplifted face and exalted eyes seemed far away from them. They talked on quietly among themselves as the rain streaked down Martin's cheeks unnoticed.

By this time Allie and his companion had reached the little group.

"Hello, Pal," said Allie, addressing Martin.

Martin did not answer, but turned to his new friends.

"These men are evil," he said in a deep, resonant tone. "The very lips of the Devil are among us!" Martin lifted his voice into an hysterical pitch as he noticed with curiosity the strange effect of his words upon the men about him.

The giant with the coat carefully hung the dripping garment on a railing, and the dirty shirt and muscular reach of his arms showed in the yellow, muckish light.

"Amen!" he cried, and advanced slowly toward Allie.

"Amen, amen!" echoed through the group behind him. The little fat man ran crying into the heavy rain; but it was with singular detachment that Martin watched the giant he had converted, strike tirelessly the broken form of Allie until the body was dumped, face down, in the swirling length of gutter.

Martin strode to the hard-breathing giant, placed his hand on the fellow's damp shoulder and said softly, "It was a message! It has been answered." And he went silently into the rain again.

A square away he paused and looked at a large clock. Once more he saw that in his impatience he was ahead of time. The cold rain had now penetrated the shoulders of his coat and Martin felt the steam rising from his hot body. What did Drew want in this undesirable section? Accustomed as Martin was to certain ways of life, he could not help but feel the disease of this unnatural quarter. He stood on the corner of Bowery and Pell—the Chinese street—a mimeographed edition of its former tong retreat and underground silence. It was true, a small group of thin-lipped, older men with their discreet smoke-houses and their hatchet-men survived. But the list was growing smaller so swiftly that the aroma of opium now had a death-like stench. The neon lights of New America had quickly dispelled the shadows and the soft lanterns of oriental intrigue. Martin looked across the street toward the little theater on the corner. It was half hidden by rain, but he could faintly see the line of trade in front of it. As the fog deepened, sailing lower under Brooklyn Bridge, Martin could hear the tangled music of a victrola somewhere nearby. The singsong lady of Shanghai was mute behind the stalls. But her Tiao-wu chords brought about by twangy, cut-off strings and yellow pipes as high as reeds can go, caused him to reflect upon the ancient wailing destined to wail forever....

Suddenly he felt his arm seized and the hard mouth of a gun pressed into his back.

"Don't make a mistake," said a harsh, low voice.

Martin dropped swiftly on his hands and brought his heels upward, barely missing the other's chin. The fellow chuckled.

"Still good with your feet, eh, Martin," he said. "Damn your French foot! It nearly got me!"

Martin squatted by the gutter as he rinsed his stinging hands in the pure flow of rainwater. Getting up, he rubbed his sore shoulders.

"You've gone to hell, Duke," he said. "You weren't this bad when I left Panama. You should have stuck to reefers. What is it now?"

"The Duke" drew his fingers slowly under his nose, then brought up his coat collar to hide his face, pretending to shake.

Martin smiled, shook hands with his friend whose uproarious laughter followed this act, and pulled him along to a tea-shop on Pell Street. Inside, he ordered coffee while the Duke took Chow Mein with tea.

Martin leaned on the table.

"It's good to see you," he said. "Heroin can't hurt you, apparently."

"Yes, it can," said the Duke, nervously pressing a small blue butterfly which was tattooed on his wrist. "Sometimes it hits me like dynamite, and I'll go on a mad rob for a dollar. But it's worse when I get cop-fever. Then I go back to my room—Christ!" he said, wiping his face. "Sometimes I crawl back of the dresser. Say—maybe I get peddled the wrong junk?" He looked at Martin hopefully.

"No," said Martin, "the stuff is all right. You know your contact." But he was beginning to see certain signs in The Duke's eyes even now. "Get the tea down," he continued, "and we'll move out. Where's your room?"

With a grotesque, frightening look, the Duke sat up.

"I'm cut short," he said, the sweat breaking out on his face. "God, Mart!—get me back to my room! Jesus!—it's the snow!... Cut off the cold wind, Mart!—it's down on my head!" The Duke's white face seemed blue in the yellow light. "God, Mart!... Mate!—ah!" he cried, the perspiration running from his forehead in streams.

Martin snapped his fingers at the Chinese waiter who was watching The Duke with placid, averted eyes, took a bill from his pocket and laid it on the table.

"Quickly—where does my friend live?" he asked.

"I do not know, sir," the waiter smiled.

Martin added another bill to his account.

"Where might he live?" he asked soberly, adding, "when the man is sick, we are all brothers."

"I would not live against that proverb," said the waiter. "The hotel is directly across the street—there—" The Chinaman pointed to a large bulb, glowing, but marked with age. "His room may be ascertained at the desk," he added, bowing low.

"Thanks," said Martin, as The Duke got to his feet, the horrified turmoil within pressing out through his eyes. He clung to the arm of his friend, but once inside the hotel, tried to dash to the stairs. He was stopped, however, by a quiet little gray-headed Chinese clerk.

"Let me get him up," Martin said to the man. "I'll see about his rent later."

"We do not want Mr. Duke," said the clerk mildly. He was wearing octagonal glasses which were useless but for their dignity.

"Then I must ask you for his room for only a few minutes," continued Martin.

"A woman waits for him also," said the Chinaman.

Martin became cold, as though he were facing a crisis of his own.

"Please show me his room," he insisted, and perhaps it was his unequivocal stare that made the Chinese submit graciously to his demand.

The cranky elevator stopped and Martin helped The Duke into the hall.

As they approached his room a slim woman—a beautiful Eurasian, so Martin judged by the hall's dim light, stepped from the door and ran at him.

"Fag!" she cried, as she tried to strike his face.

Martin wrapped her long hair around his wrist, and holding his friend and the woman, entered the room.

The Duke ran to the window, looking out.

"I'll jump!" he said. "This rat-hole's too crowded. It'll call the police." He stood, bending down to the sill.

"Go ahead," said Martin, watching him closely, his hand still wrapped in the beautiful long blue hair of the squirming girl.

"No, I'll hide from them," cried the Duke, and he began to crawl under the carpet.

The Eurasian, slant-eyed, watched him. Then quickly she turned to Martin.

"Babee!" she said, in a Dutch accent, her yellow eyes lifted to his. "Come with me. Let my hair go."

Martin saw that The Duke, now flat under the carpet was quiet, and he loosened his own wrist from the woman's soft hair.

"What is your name?" he asked.

"It is Siedred!"

"A mongrel boy," he said, his teeth closing and unclosing. "Where do you wish me to go?"

"To my room."

"In this hall?"

"It is so."

Martin looked once more at the shaking body under the carpet and took the girl by the waist.

"Come," he said.

The Eurasian led him from the room, across the hall and to another door which she unlocked silently. Once inside, she turned the lock again and laid the key upon a table.

Breathing without restraint, she slipped her blouse over her head and snapped the buttons from her skirt. As she looked at Martin, her breast filled, then fell, then rose again until Martin, impatient, lifted her and tossed her on the bed, laughing.

"I love you," cried the native girl as she felt his pointed tongue.

"You are so hot," replied Martin. "This is not love."

"It is, it is!" the woman insisted. "Touch me again!"

"Siedred," said Martin.

"What?"

"Siedred." He pulled the long cord of the lamp which hung above them. There was a frantic sound of broken clothes, of sighs too distressing, of a single, smothered scream.

"Oh, oh!" Siedred cried.

And out in the corridor, besieged by following tears and moans, Martin crept down the stairs into the street. Unquestioning, he waited before the tiny theater for Drew's arrival.

As Martin watched, a limousine drew up before the theater and stopped. Drew, his friend, stepped out. He made no sign, but pulled down his hat and turned up the collar of his coat, bringing it under his chin. Then he observed the trade, beckoning at last to a roughly dressed youngster with golden skin and frightened eyes. As he helped the lad into his car, he closed the door upon him, and turning to Martin who stood so quietly in the rain, Drew removed his hat, keeping it off until the water spilled over his blond, pinned hair. His lips spelled "Night." He bowed slightly and entered the car, closing the door as Martin started toward him. As the limousine passed, Martin could see his mocking, tired face.

CHAPTER XVIII

In his room Martin laid his head upon his desk. He wondered about Roberts, his magnificence at the drag, the mad poem intended for himself. Confused by these thoughts, he fell asleep. He dreamed that he was in the bow of a shining canoe, spinning down a great white length of rapids. In the stern of the boat two men were fighting. Rio, and the giant with the white, rain-soaked shirt were striking each other fiercely. Above them hovered the spirit of Freud, smiling at both of them and holding a battered text in one hand and a setscrew in the other which were apparently to be awarded to the victor. Roberts, however, in the form of mist, obstructed the blows of the fighters until the two gladiators became entangled and suddenly dissolved. The spirit of Freud withdrew hastily, while the adviser, with a faint smile at Martin, sat down in the boat as it rotated toward destruction.

Martin awakened from the dream with a somber expression. Then he shook his head and laughed.

"What a symbol!" he exclaimed to himself.

The deep whistles of a ship ready to sail seemed to agitate him and he lowered his head upon the desk again. He thought of Paris, where Drew was going, of Tai with him, and of Deane seeing him off. Once more Martin fell asleep, this time in a world uninhabited by dreams.

This was true for the most part, for Tai was playing in Drew's suite, while Pat attended him as though he were a little saint.

In the great lounge of the liner Drew was talking seriously with Deane.

"I can't understand Martin," he said. "And I must confess that it is impossible for me to live within his orbit."

"You dislike him so?" Deane raised her dark eyes.

Drew shook his head.

"I can't connect that term with him," he answered. "I loved him very deeply at one time. Now, I hate him, or rather, am frightfully jealous of him."

"Of his sins?" asked Deane.

"No," replied Drew irritably. "He has no sins. He has none because he does not believe the things he does are wrong." Drew touched a handkerchief to his head. "Martin," he continued, "could destroy the world and it would not be sinful. He is selfish, but because he knows it, there is no feeling of blame. He's like a ghost, and all of the people around him are like ghosts. Even I came to feel like one. There is no reality about him. Yes," Drew sighed, "he is the most physical creature in the world, and the most untouchable. Oh— I know what you're thinking, Deane! And I know I'm just putting on." Suddenly Drew stopped and lit a cigarette for Deane and one for himself.

"I like him the way he is," said Deane. "I like his unreality. And he isn't the way you think he is."

"Oh, *no*," said Drew, arching his eyebrows. "Oh, dear no!"

"Just the same," went on Deane quietly, "although I've seen him pretend to have the quality you say he has, I'm a woman, and I would know. I would rebel." She tapped out her cigarette. "Surely, Drew, you can see that he speculates about himself in order to enjoy his own pursuits."

"That may be so," agreed Drew, somewhat sardonically. "But I have something of more immediate importance, Deane. Roberts is not well. I don't know what the trouble is, but he has changed terribly in the past few months. His reaction to Martin is instantaneous and violent. This may affect you. Please see as little as you can of him."

"I know," said Deane with a charming, puzzled frown. "I've felt it too, and sometimes it frightens me."

"Please come to Paris," suggested Drew impulsively, leaning forward and taking both her hands in his.

"Sweet Drew," whispered Deane, "how good you are! But I love Martin and I need to be with him, I want to go right away to him. Now. Even now," She stood up and held Drew's arm as they strolled to the promenade.

"Let's say good-by right here," she said, her full, red lips trembling. "I'm about to cry."

"It isn't good-by at all, dearest," said Drew, smiling gravely. "You know that in spite of anything, we'll always be together. Go to Martin now, but remember that *we* have the phone, the cable, the secret bond and love in understanding." He kissed her on both cheeks and as Deane turned, she saw that his eyes were misty.

After she had gone, Drew went into Tai's little room. The ship was slipping out of the pier and the child clapped his hands at the movement. Drew lay down on the couch and laid his arms over his eyes. This!—to happen for the second time in his life! It was too severe. There could not be a third. Little Tai approached softly and kissed the tears away. It was all he knew, and suddenly Drew smiled.

Before he went on the promenade he looked out through the darkness and saw the black, rolling water. He gazed at himself in the mirror and drew a warm scarf under his dark overcoat. Then he pulled his dark hat over his forehead, looked steadily at himself once more and went on deck.

He hesitated for a moment by a large ventilator as he saw a young man leaning on the rail, studying the ocean. The boy's profile was quaint in the dim overhead lights. Drew pulled his own hat lower, turned up the collar of his coat and approached the stranger with unhurried, gentle steps.

CHAPTER XIX

The concert hall quieted. Conversation hushed.

The White Peacock,[3] sorrowful and majestic, appeared in the faint light. Winding through deep white reeds, brushing through ghostly ferns, he approached. Wading the moon-puddles, breaking the mist with silver feathers, he looked at Deane. Holding his white throat into the stars, moving the fallen petals, he sang to her—sang a clear, demanding song of his remote, pale island. Deane shivered under the soft notes, loosening her gown. The White Peacock, his snowy tail drifting over the moon-flowers, lifted his scarlet eyes—lifted his eyes through clouds and placed each strong tone against her.... The music changed tempo. The white bird screamed shrilly, his bright whistle falling through glissandi of sound. The exquisite melody rose into the wind, hesitated, and dropped murmuring into the white sea.... The White Peacock faded in the fluid light, became distant—Deane, following with her arms the receding shadow.

The music died. People moved in their chairs and the subdued whispers grew into applause. The mood was broken and Deane touched her eyes. She put on a coat of soft gray fur, adjusted her little tight-fitting blue toque and carelessly pinned back on her collar a small bunch of violets which had fallen to her lap during the concert. As she was rising someone addressed her.

"Then you, too, are fond of modern music?"

Surprised, Deane looked up. Roberts stood before her.

"It was beautiful," she answered. "Beautiful, and intimate."

Roberts smiled in appreciation, acutely aware of the faint and lovely perfume of her violets.

"Did you come alone, Deane?" he asked.

"Yes."

"Then," said the adviser, his voice curiously naive and youthful, "let me drive you home. I have my car."

She stepped into the aisle by his side and as they walked out together the distinguished grace of his movements and the coloring in his cheeks, still flushed by the spell of the music, made Deane conscious of the beauty of a sex that shocked her heart but held her mind; and in this acceptance every light in her hair and eyes acquired luminance until she was betrayed—and Roberts looked, turned blind, and never looked again.

The early darkness of winter had descended and the streets were brightly lit with red and green lights. Snow, falling gently, coated the buildings and walks.

The holiday atmosphere—the thought of Christmas, gave them a feeling of friendliness. They drove over to Fifth Avenue.

All down the broad expanse of the great boulevard swept the Yuletide spirit. The thick streams of people, carrying boxes and parcels wrapped in colored paper, seemed compact—a constant mass instead of one of gigantic fluctuation. At the corners they bumped and jostled each other, frantically trying to retrieve dropped packages, laughing all the while. There they were, pouring their laughter and hustle and gay concern over the Avenue—a huge, comforting block of the world, this infinite throng.

As Deane and Roberts passed St. Patrick's Cathedral they noticed that the doors of the church had been thrown open—a silent welcome to the holiday crowds. There was an impression of austere immensity; and over the kneeling figures which had sought tranquillity within the sacred vault there shone a great soft radiance, whether from electric lights or candles on the altar, Deane and Roberts did not know.

Farther down the Avenue they could hear the muffled sound of chimes; and as they drew near one of the department stores the sound became more brilliant until they noticed that behind the glass of the one window which ran its entire front length there was nothing but an illusion of depth in a green-blue sky and two large gold bells, swinging slowly back and forth.

Deane turned to Roberts and was astonished to find that he was looking at her instead of the lovely window.

"It is as glorious as that other vault we passed," she said quietly, amazed at his attitude.

"Yes," he answered, still regarding her gravely, "and although beauty, to me, is but a dream gone by—a vagrant moment—a motion lost before it's held—oddly, I find it stationary for one evening." He paused and added, looking at her fixedly, "Even within a superb commercial painting."

The chiming now covered the air with invisible shadows. There was an icy wind; and as Deane sensing its fury within the well-heated car, pulled her coat more tightly around her shoulders, Roberts again caught the perfume of the flowers she was wearing, and their fragrance seemed to him to become as audible—to have a resonance and vibration quite as definite as the chimes.

They spoke no more but continued down the Avenue until they came upon a children's shop with such a pretty charm about it that Roberts stopped the car. For the shop's display there was a miniature snowstorm—a tiny replica of the one outside which was increasing in density each moment. Amidst the artificial snow within the window were artificial children posed in different attitudes. One small boy had his hand raised against a snowman as though building him. A little girl stood by, just watching. And still another boy was stooped as though gathering more snow. The scene was such a dainty one that Roberts looked at it wistfully, with a reserved hunger that seemed to demand release; and Deane, fascinated, clasped her hands together. On the street a ragged boy, walking beside a hulk of a man, stopped for a moment to look quietly, but in silent despair at these happy children who played in the snow and wore such pretty clothes. He stared particularly at the little girl, with her long, blond curls and piquant face and her little dress and coat that were like a dream. But the man, resentful, cuffed the boy's cheek roughly, pulling him along. The lad cringed. Deane thought she heard him cry out once and turned her face away; while Roberts, who had also witnessed the episode, started the car and drove on swiftly through the storm.

Near the lower part of the Avenue, just before they turned off on Deane's street, they came upon a Christmas tree which had been set up in the courtyard of a large apartment hotel. The branches of the pine were straight and proud; and instead of the usual strings of many-colored lights which had dressed the other trees along the boulevard, on this, there were dull points of red under the boughs, or brilliant ones of green that stood far out, so awkwardly, that by their very misplacement the tree appeared to be native and uncut. It was without tinsel. There was only the snow. The wind and the shadows did the rest. The unusual reflections dwelt upon Deane's face and Roberts turned to her impulsively.

"You are beautiful this evening, Deane," he said.

She looked at him once more and smiled, although she was a bit perplexed. For some time she continued to gaze at him, watching the man, as vivid as the tree itself against the snow. Then abruptly, the notion came to her that his temperament might be flexible, and she lifted her head higher, as though challenging him. Her eyes were sparkling.

Roberts seemed frightened at first at her audacity and turned away in embarrassment. Then, looking back to meet her dancing eyes, he broke into a choppy laugh of singular amusement which Deane echoed. During the rest of the drive they were silent; but there was a tenuous bond of understanding between them; and when they reached Deane's apartment, Roberts stopped the engine and placed his hand lightly on hers.

"Yes, you are a beautiful and an intricate woman," he said quietly.

Deane quickly withdrew her hand. She was surprised at the instantaneous feeling of revulsion which came over her. There had been no possessiveness in Roberts' action—no suggestion of desire or intimacy. It had been the movement of a child. But the contact had chilled her. What was the quality about him that disturbed her now? Could it be a strong jealousy of his interest in Martin? She could see Roberts stiffen in the semi-darkness.

"I beg your pardon," he said, with hauteur. "My remark was entirely impersonal."

"I know," she said gently. Then, annoyed with herself, she added, "I was thinking of Drew. To-night he arrives in France. I wonder if it is snowing there."

The adviser dropped his shoulders.

"It is snowing everywhere," he said gravely. And as he assisted Deane out of the car, he repeated, "—everywhere."

Feeling his wild and plaintive loneliness and his sorrow, Deane stepped quite close to him, resting her gloved hand on his sleeve.

"William!" she murmured softly.

For one moment, their antipodal forces swung into parallel; and, so going, Deane and Roberts smiled together.

When Martin came that evening, Deane said to him at once, "I saw Roberts at the concert and he brought me home in his car. I liked him better than ever before."

"Well," Martin was thoughtful, "I can't say that I like it—oh, you needn't explain his charm! I'm quite aware of it. But I'm afraid of his mind. I'm afraid of the way it works, and I wish to God he'd get out of the picture. It's getting a little too uncanny—the way he checks on me." Martin pulled his chair closer to Deane's. "I found out that he tried to block my part-time job. Still, with all of it," he continued, "my attitude toward him remains variable; for underneath his mask lies a real and secret protest. This protest is limitless— and if I'm right, rather beautiful." Martin laughed shortly. "Odd as it may be, I'm certain that I'm responsible for many of his appearances. His sickness, if he *is* sick, is now abiding in a perfect culture."

"And what is that?" asked Deane, looking at him with her large eyes.

"A medium of vicious love engendered by myself."

Deane laughed without restraint.

"Darling," she said, taking Martin's face in her hands, "you want to be so awfully bad, don't you?"

Martin smiled with her and she was satisfied, promptly forgetting the adviser.

"Drew looked very sad when he left, Martin," she said. "Tell me—did he go just because of you?"

"Deane," Martin said quite seriously, "we mustn't keep on thinking that all these forces are created by me." Martin was pale in the shadows. "That would be a timeless, horrible thought—a possible eternity. Can anything be more terrible than eternity? All this action is separate from myself. It *must* be. It's not possible that my demand has been too much!" He was speaking hoarsely when Deane put her arms around him.

"Darling," she whispered, "I understand. Won't you love me a little?" By instinct she had given him that temporary haven where the mind of man retreats after being frightened by its own infinite possibilities. Deane's gentle whisper and her fascinating implication of certain physical contacts quieted his nerves abruptly and he felt as though a sweet fire were crossing his spine. He closed his eyes, and allowing Deane to lead him into the gray-paneled bedroom, he lay back on the sheets, feeling her soft hands stroke his skin until he shivered.

"Delightful boy—delicious boy," she said, her voice trembling and growing fainter.

Martin tried to speak to her, but his mouth was dry. He lifted his arms and held on to the rail of the bed, trying to pull away from the searing. Then it overcame him. He rolled and pretended to fight, but in his brain there was only an exultant shouting.

As Deane knelt at the foot of the bed she looked down at Martin and thought of the White Peacock; of the Gargoyle; and of their relation to this man; and she felt the lustful brooding of this trilogy which was dominant in her life. Her breasts rubbed against the fine hair of his knees and each touch made her wilder. Pulling at him, she crawled up beside him, her fingernails scratching the sheets. Then, from her throat came a strange cry, a small cry, like the wail of a new-born child.

The snow kept piling against the windshield. Once, Roberts had to get out and wipe it off from the outside. As he stepped back into the car his foot slipped on something. Deane's violets! He flung them into the snow. In his imagination he saw Martin and Deane together—saw her laughingly repeat their conversation of the afternoon. He visualized Martin's shrug, and contemptuous remarks. Roberts' cheeks burned in the dark and he drove more recklessly. At this very moment the woman was probably in Martin's arms.... Martin, with his sultry gray eyes and tanned face. Martin, outlined like a flame before him.... Roberts breathed the cold wind and spoke aloud. "He deserves nothing but my hatred. If I could make him suffer as he has made me suffer! His picture before me always!—superior, contemptuous and desirable! The night he sat with me in my apartment, fresh from the sea—wind and salt in his eyes and hair, I thought I had found life. My happiness stretched into the horizon of his understanding. Solemn and patient, he spoke to me and laughed with me. Now, he speaks of me, and laughs *at* me—with her! I can hear him laughing—" Roberts voice rose more fiercely. "He is saying, 'What?—tried to hold your hand? What the devil would he want with that?'" The irritating, superior tones rang in Roberts' imagination. "Yes, I can hear them: 'Poor old Roberts—what a pity—chap must lead an awful life—imagine going around with that handicap—not that there's any moral application, just a matter of convenience—continually frustrated.'" Roberts pounded the steering wheel with his fist. "The cattle!" he whispered hoarsely. "As if they could understand—as if *anyone* could understand. Damn them—their laughter and their insufferable attitude! Damn their happiness.... Drink it, Roberts!—That I should measure my life in terms of one night! One night with Martin, with his young face and old eyes. With his laughter and his understanding. What agony to be born one night and die the same! Better not to be born at all.... Why, Martin, did you swagger through the door with your flapping dungarees and proud head?... Angels dancing in the eyes that hold only devils now. Such insolence! A bright, beautiful distillation of evil. Martin—the god of selfishness, salt to the desire. A blinding picture that grows with absence. A dust that burns the eyes and chokes the appetite.... Delete the image!—step upon it, crush it only to see it rise anew, more beautiful and vicious than before." Hot tears distorted Roberts' vision. He drew his hand across his face angrily. In a flashing, intolerable whiteness, he saw himself swinging on the tapestry of his heritage. "God!" he cried into the night. "Predestination—crucified in the womb!" The image grew more hateful in his mind. The cold wind dried his tears. Slowly his mouth narrowed into a fanatical line. "He has made me suffer. Moving relentlessly, superficially, over people and life—eating life and dripping its tantalizing crumbs from an overstuffed mouth—ruthless and immaculate, he has made me suffer." Roberts' face was white in the light from the windshield. White, unsmiling and purposeful.

CHAPTER XX

Martin met few people; but there was an atmosphere of tension everywhere he walked. It didn't make any difference what color their eyes were—blue or brown or clay, there was action. Mostly it was antipathy engendered by something the fulcrum of this hate could not understand. Sometimes, however, it was love—a piercing, shrill movement that fell, ageless and sexless, over his shoulders.

He did well with his work at the printing plant and was finally transferred to a night shift where he found, to his relief, that the hours were shorter, thus giving him precious moments that he could spend with Deane or devote to the perfecting of his type design. He liked also the quality of concentrated activity during these working hours at the plant, occasioned in part by the darkness which enveloped the building and grounds. He had no contact with the men around him except at coffeetime; and they, in turn, sensed an indivisible chasm where their thoughts and his whirled in confusion above them.

Once, during the evening, a machine squirted. The operator, swearing loudly, kicked back his chair and was picking the lead from his trousers when Martin glanced up, a phrase from the copy still in his mind. He went to the man at once to help him; but the molten metal, already hardened into splinters, had entered the fleshy part of the operator's leg, and the man, in considerable discomfort, nodded his thanks to Martin and still swearing, softly now to himself, limped out of the room and down the hall.

It was two o'clock in the morning and time for the men to knock off. In the awkward blue light Martin wiped a smear of oil from his cheek. The mirror was so distorted and the light so penetrating that his face seemed one sided and all the lines about his mouth and eyes were pulling in the wrong directions. He washed his hands and face, glanced again into the crazy mirror, buttoned his pea-jacket and headed for his room in Greenwich Village.

His street was in a dimly lighted section made up of rooming houses occupied chiefly by small tradesmen. He had walked several blocks before he stopped to light a cigarette. It was very quiet and through the shabby elms the night seemed beautiful and lonely. As he started on he heard someone behind him. From the sound of the step, it was a woman. Vaguely, he wondered about her; but he walked on briskly, enjoying this brief, cold freedom, then stopped again, looking with interest straight overhead at the same stars he had watched move in different latitudes and from different ships. For the second time he heard the steps behind him and turned round. At this, they broke off sharply, but not before Martin had caught a distinctive note in them. They had a giddy pitch that was not purely feminine. His curiosity was aroused. He started down the street once more, walking slowly now, with a precise, even stride. Then he stopped abruptly. The feet behind him tapped on for a second, fluttered, hesitated and stopped again. Suddenly, in Martin's mind, the unmusical gait gathered motif, meaning and form. He remembered a repulsively ardent smile.... "Carol!" he shouted. There was no answer. Again he tried. "Hi! Carol!" This time his follower ran quickly toward him.

"How did you know it was me, Martin?" asked the boy excitedly, all smiles.

Martin, chameleon-like, studied the dregs of his memory for similar situations or, he thought grimly, singular opportunities; for this was not an element to be faced, but one to be absorbed.

"We all have our characteristics, Carol," he answered evenly.

"Do you like mine, Martin?" Carol's plaintive tone softened the eager, beseeching import of his question.

Again Martin hesitated. He well knew that the middle path was not as the Romans had worked it out—a smooth highway, without deviation. He knew that the middle path must fluctuate with both extremes to deserve the term—which in this case, he observed to himself further with a certain cynical amusement, was between a bitch and a son-of-a-bitch. He took hold of the young man's arm and spoke to him in a friendly fashion.

"Let's go on up to my place, Carol," he said.

On the dark stairs Carol followed close at his heels. Martin could feel little tugs at his coat as the young man hung on to him in a sort of childish panic and Martin had a distinct impression that Carol was groping for his hand. He could feel the boy's breath on the back of his neck as they continued to climb; and when they reached the dark landing just outside Martin's room, Carol was still hanging on to him feverishly. Martin fumbled for the keyhole, succeeded in finding it at last, opened the door and turned on a dim light. Carol followed him into the room, sighed with relief and closed the door quickly behind them.

He stood there, just inside, his hand still on the doorknob, gazing around him with wide eyes and obviously taking notes. There was a pallet on the floor in one corner, an old couch across from it and a writing desk in the center of the room. He could see a T-square, erasers and jumbled pieces of paper on the desk beside a miniature of Deane. He turned his head away suddenly at sight of the picture. In another corner of the room was a washbowl with a screen half around it. There was a general air of carelessness about the place which apparently made him nervous. Martin could see him straightening up things in his mind.

"It's really more comfortable than it looks, Carol," he said, trying to put his guest more at ease. "They keep the rooms warm and that bed sleeps better than it appears." He unbuttoned his pea-jacket and hung it on a nail on the wall. "Take off your coat, Carol, won't you?—and tell me what it's all about. Two o'clock's an odd time to go creeping after people. Why didn't you call out?"

"I was afraid you wouldn't like it," answered the boy, biting his lip. He removed his thickly woven plaid overcoat, looked for a moment at the nail where Martin's jacket hung, then folded his own coat meticulously, gave it a final pat and placed it with the utmost care over the back of the rocker.

"I don't like it, when it's handled that way," said Martin, keeping his voice smooth. "I prefer a 'hello.'"

Carol spoke softly.

"I had to follow you. Deane told me where you worked."

"You asked her?" For the first time, Martin was genuinely annoyed.

Carol smiled unhappily.

"I had to, Martin. I think you're wonderful." His round face was ruddy and glowing and his eyes, bright and intent, were fixed on his host.

"Sit down, Carol." Martin opened the window, pulled his own chair from under the desk and sat down facing him. "That's strange," he went on, a bit puzzled. "I thought you disliked me." He brushed back his hair where the cold wind had rumpled it and sat quietly, staring out the window into the darkness.

Carol shuffled uneasily.

"I did at first. You were mean. I nearly hated you." He sat forward, well on the edge of his chair. "But I don't now. I'm different now."

"Not at all," said Martin, shaking his head quite seriously. "You'll feel the same at the last as you did at the first. I'm sure of it."

"I won't change, dear Martin. I think you're God," the boy answered solemnly.

Martin nodded. Through the insufficient light within the room, the bronze tints of his skin deepened.

"Perhaps I am," he said.

"Please don't joke," said Carol. His voice had acquired a pathetic, pleading quality. "I mean you really are—to me." He shifted his position so that he could not see Deane's picture.

"She won't bite," said Martin bluntly.

Carol twisted his hands.

"Can't you see it my way a little bit, Martin?" The boy spoke now with a definite urgency, his words forming an aggressive prayer. "Can't you change *some*?"

"No," Martin answered. "I can't see the advantage."

"*I* know the advantage," said Carol softly. "I wish you'd try and change just a little bit." He hesitated, his eyes shining. "I can't tell you—but I could teach you, Martin."

"How did this begin, Carol?"

The boy gave him a fond, acquisitive glance.

"It began that afternoon at Deane's. You took my part. And then, at the drag, you were so beautiful in your yellow gown that I fell in love right away. How did you do your hair? It was perfect!"

"Damned if I know," said Martin. He stared out the window again.

Carol lowered his head, pouting.

"But it wasn't fixed the same way after you came down with Drew."

"No?" asked Martin absently.

"No," said Carol. "It was pinned different."

Martin smiled.

"Are you sure," he asked, "that it wasn't Drew about whom you were concerned?"

"Oh!" said Carol, flushing, "I never felt that way about Drew. I just *love* to talk with him and be a pal; but I never felt about him—like this—" His lips trembled a little. "Maybe I was a little flirty—he's been so sweet to me; but then I've been that way before, and I've never been in love. It was all puppy stuff before."

Martin slumped down in his chair.

"I've changed quite a bit in my opinions about things too, Carol," he said. "But it hasn't boiled over and I don't believe it ever will. You know, Carol, that I love Deane."

The boy leaned forward eagerly.

"Oh, I know lots of boys that like girls," he replied, nodding his head wisely. "But they like boys, too." With a timid gesture he reached out and touched Martin's hand. The back of Martin's scalp tingled and he felt like shivering; but he did not move.

"It's no go, Carol," he said, with finality. "It damned well gives me the creeps."

Carol leaned back against the wall and closed his eyes.

"God," he said, "I wish you'd try." He bent forward again, making no attempt to restrain his sorrowful desire.

Martin jumped up, a kind of dull horror building into rage. He took Carol roughly by the shoulders.

"God damn you! What's wrong with you? What the hell's wrong with all of you? Don't you like the feel of a woman's breast? Don't you like a mouth that's soft and sweet, instead of a god-damned beard?" He noticed that he was shaking Carol and stopped. He moved back a pace, his face shaded, the perspiration pouring from his brow in streams. "Do you think it's smart to be this way? Do you think it's clever?" He closed his fists. "Give me Eve, god damn you! Give me Eve, and take your Adam!"

Carol was weeping softly.

"God," he said. "I don't think it's smart.... Oh, Martin, I'm so lonely. I can't help how I feel.... Don't be mad.... I won't do anything.... Please—" He was rocking back and forth in his helpless grief.

Martin sat down again. His face, which had hardened in the previous moment, lost its straight lines and the color came back to his cheeks. He ran his hand, which was trembling slightly, across his eyes. He sat very straight and stiff.

"I'm sorry, Carol," he declared sincerely. "I lost my head. I understand."

But Carol cried out, his palms against his temples, "You understand? *You?* You don't understand at all.... The days! The long, wet days!—I can't stand them alone again!... You don't know how I was born. How I was raised. My mother died when I was born—Oh! I'd have loved her.... My father took me to a mining camp. There weren't any women. Even the cook was a man.

They played with me, and gave me money.... After my father died, there were more men.... It's my first thought, and my last.... I wish you *did* understand. Then you'd just *have* to love me."

And Martin looked at Carol, at the tears running down his cheeks, at the pain that locked his face into the unknown agonies. He looked at the desk, at the picture of Deane and back again at Carol. And to himself he said repeatedly, "What good is compassion now!—What good is compassion now!"

Strangely, he went to Carol, a dark line between his eyes, although there was no frown except one for himself. For a moment he stood facing the boy so steadily and patiently that Carol wet his lips in nervousness, waiting in a kind of stolid anticipation for whatever was to come. Slowly, but with no hesitation, and still regarding the boy with an indefinable expression, Martin raised his hand and laid it on the other's with such feeling, yet such weight that Carol stepped away and bent his knee as though he had been struck. Then, unresistant to Martin's comprehensive look—a look so full of search, and surely pain, and perhaps knowing—and calmed by a hand that had found kindness in its power, Carol stepped forward again and held himself as though he were bemused—for so he was, with all his innocence and limitations conflicting with desire. And all the hopeless libido went out of him before this other one who was so straight and quiet and held him like— Carol thought, and thought again—like—and then quite swiftly it was revealed to him; like one man holds another. This chemical transmutation within him was so rapid that even Martin failed to see it. Just the same, as Carol, firmly gripped by Martin in equality, knew himself another man, he lifted his shoulders, stiffened in his new pride as he beheld new vistas; and in an immediate beauty smiled, unknowing that he had left Martin, who dropped his hand, bewildered.

Martin helped the boy on with his coat.

"Carol," he said, his arm around him, "I want you to know that I'm your friend." Impulsively he went to his desk and searched through a drawer. He drew out a snapshot and handed it to Carol. "Here I am," he said, "climbing a king post at the beginning of a bad day." It was a plain little picture of a ship at a crazy tilt with the sea, and Martin hanging tightly as he worked with a lashing; but Carol put it carefully in his pocket and smiled happily.

CHAPTER XXI

The days were getting warmer. Rio stopped by Martin's house in the early afternoon and together they walked to the Battery where they sat down on a bench out of the sun. People were pouring in and out of the Aquarium. Boats leaving for Bedloe's Island whistled and grunted against the docks. Liberty herself, as statuesque as ever, shone from her spring cleaning and seemed to hold her torch still higher and more independently.

Turning away from the water, Rio glanced at Martin's hand, his attention called to it, perhaps, by a ray of sunlight which fell slantingly upon a flat block of black onyx with a point of ruby in one corner which Martin wore upon his middle finger.

"I've always wanted to ask you about that funny ring you got there," said Rio, yawning. "Where'd you find it?"

Martin twisted the ring until it caught the sun more evenly before he spoke.

"In the Red Sea," he finally replied.

"Sounds like somethin' back of it," persisted Rio.

"There is." Martin locked his hands around one knee and leaned forward in an attitude of tenseness. "The year before I met you, Rio, I got hurt on the old *Silver Cross*. She's being scrapped now, and this was when she made her last trip to the East. I was pretty bad in the Indian Ocean, and the weather didn't help any. I was worse at Aden; and they had to take me off at Massaua. When I was getting well I met a fellow named Nahrinja who was agent for a man who owned a pearl-fishing fleet. I wanted to get out on one of the boats to see how the boys went about it. So when I was better he gave me a knock-down to one of the Arab skippers and we set out.

"The Sudanese divers all seemed to like me, for I took to their native lute as though I'd played it all my life. In a few days I could do their ancient chants on the tamboura—somehow, understanding this sad, lost music. One Sudanese in particular, a boy named Sali, used to squat silently on the deck and watch me by the hour.

"We were after the finest pearl—the bilbil. And one morning Sali and I launched his dugout and piled in, the natives laughing a good deal, for I wasn't used to their tipsy little pirogues. I paddled, while Sali looked through a glass-bottomed box for a good spot. When he found it, he went over the side with a weight to a depth of forty or fifty feet, while I watched through the box to see if he was all right and kept a lookout for shark. I had tried it once, myself, in shallower water and had got nicely stung by a poison fish for my efforts. Sali had many such scars and seemed used to it. But he told me to be careful of the giant clams, careful of the coral and particularly leery of the whip-tail ray, which can give you a bad cut with their barb.

"Sali worked more than he should; but he brought back good oyster. I was having a hell of a good time in spite of the stinks, and looked like one of the divers with my loincloth and my skin crusted with salt. Then it happened." Martin looked at his ring again and continued.

"Sali had just left the ocean bed when I saw a black fin circle the bow of the boat. From his back, the shark was a big one. I began smacking the water with an iron pole, trying to frighten him away or attract his attention to the other side of the dugout, and to warn Sali, who was coming up fast.

"But just as the boy hit the surface, the shark struck him and Sali's head went under. I jumped over the side and got him by the hair. When I brought him above water and could see his face, it looked as though it were frozen. He didn't say anything or make any effort, and I couldn't get him in the canoe; but when I clamped his hand on the gunwhale he held to it like a child, and I climbed into the boat by the stern, hoping the beast wouldn't come back till I'd pulled the lad in. Finally, I got him by the wrist and managed to haul him in without capsizing. He looked down at his body at the place where his leg had been, for it was off high up next the hip. Then he looked at me and smiled, while two big tears ran down his cheeks." Martin stopped again and choked. "I hope, Rio, it was because he was shocked out of his wits. I stripped off my loincloth and tried, as only a desperate man can do, to get a tourniquet around a place where I didn't even have a stub to work on. At last, I started to shove my fist up the hole where the blood was spurting; and then, realizing that I was going mad myself, I grabbed a paddle and headed for the mother-boat like a demon. A pretty picture, eh, Rio?" said Martin bitterly. "A naked white man, as bloody by this time as the Sudanese, racing through the Red Sea with a dying boy who thought I could make him live—for that was what he kept saying all the time."

"Cut it," said Rio, his face hard. "Did you get him to the boat alive?"

"Yes," answered Martin. "The nakhuda and another Arab hoisted him aboard and we laid him on the deck, out of the sun, with his head propped up. There were only minutes left, with nothing to do but magic; so I rubbed his wrists and whispered the Lord's Prayer to him. It sounded all right on that blistering deck, or must have done so, for Sali kept smiling and repeating the words—the sound of the words after me.... 'Our Father which art in heaven, Hallowed be thy name.' ... Then his face changed—I saw it coming. He spoke thinly to the nakhuda, who knelt down and cut the string around the boy's neck which held this amulet." Martin pointed to the charm on his finger. "Sali took it, and with that hopeless, sweet trust glazed on his eyes forever, held it out to me that death-like second before death."

Martin cleared his throat and looked down at the grass.

After watching him for a moment Rio said quietly, "That's the last time I'll ever ask about a ring. I done it once before, and I ought to know better."

"What happened?" asked Martin.

Rio took his time, and scanned the harbor before he spoke.

"I shipped out of Liverpool," he said at last, "because I had to once, on a vessel bound for the Solomon Islands. My watch partner looked like a Limey, but he was a shanty Irishman from Philadelphia. I never could quite make 'im out. We had two hours in Lisbon on the trip South, and he give a kid two bits American to get off a spittoon in a Portugee gin mill. He told me it made him nervous, seein' a boy sit like that. Well, we had some sour wine and some biscuits before I seen his ring. It was a wide gold band on his left middle finger, and somehow I asked him about it. He grinned and looked pretty sick; but he said it was for Maud. I took another drink and lit up a cigarette because I couldn't see no woman with *him*. He called himself 'Philadelphia Dick,' but the city would've killed 'im for it, since he was the ugliest bastard I ever seen, with a skin like tripe and a red eyelid that hung down like a lantern over his left eye. He knowed I didn't believe that Maud stuff, and that damned eyelid dropped down like he was laughin' at me, while he chewed on a biscuit with the ring wigglin' all the time under his Harp nose.

"We sailed, soon after, for undetermined cargo on the Solomon's. Every man of us got fed up after we got there, for it was 'lay to, and wait for orders.' We had the ship so clean she ached, and finally we got shore-leave. The second engineer hammered me out a barb and Chips fixed an ironwood shaft for me, so I had a good harpoon to try on the bass and some red trout I seen around there. Philadelphia Dick grinned and looked sick again when he heard I was goin' fishin'; but he and a couple of other sailors come along.

"It was a small atoll I picked near the mainland; so we rolled up our pants and waded to the belt of coral to have a look at the lagoon. The water was still; but all the fish I could see was small for my spear. One of the boys though, who was standin' between me and Dick, slapped me on the arm and reached quick for the harpoon; and then I could see the water break a ways out, and a turtle come up from the shallows. It was a big one—about three hundred pounds—and we all got down on our knees and stayed quiet, except Philadelphia Dick. He stood there with his jaw droppin' and his skin turnin' so red that his loose eyelid hung down, limp and white, like a blossom.

"The turtle waded up pretty slow, takin' its own damned way like they always do, till the guy that had my spear seen it was time. He jumped up and run toward the creature, raisin' his arm to let the turtle have it through the eye. But he never made it," Rio added slowly. "Philadelphia Dick hit him in the cheek and then in the nose, which broke so we could all hear it snap—even the damned turtle, who crawled on up like nothin' had happened. Well, we stood there like a bunch of god-damned fools, like the guy who'd been clipped, while the turtle come on till she stood right in front of Philadelphia Dick. By God!—they watched each other till it made us feel in the way somehow, and we got the hell out of there. Once, the guy with the bloody face turned round and looked back at Dick and the turtle. 'She took his eye, Rio,' he said to me, funny-like. And I said, 'Yeah—that's Maud.' 'Maud?' he said, still lookin' funny, and we went back to the ship.

"Philadelphia Dick didn't come back that night; but a native brought 'im alongside the next mornin' and he come up the Jacob's ladder like a snake. The Chinee cook seen 'im first and turned green. For Dick's eyelid was down to his cheek like it had been sewed there, and his good eye was too cold for a man. But the worst thing was the look of his Irish nose that had been tilted up for thirty-five years—till then—but that had bent overnight into a hook as sharp as the creature's we was all thinkin' of. By the mercy of God, we sailed that evenin' for Sarawak. Philadelphia Dick was at the steam winch when I seen 'im last; but five minutes later nobody could find 'im on the ship. When we got to Borneo the Devil himself must've reversed our sailing orders; for we was sent back to the Solomons, though the sailors hadn't no stomach for it, I can tell you. The galley boy, more scared than silly, said somethin' about Maud, and got the back of the hand from one of the men. Most of us, though, took this jinx along with the bugs and the sour bread; but we was all steppin' like the Chief's cat when we hove to about the place where Philadelphia Dick had jumped ship. We was all by the rail expectin' somethin', and we got it. A couple of turtles drifted in about midships and out of the long green we watched two beaks come up. One was Maud, the other a stranger. The god-damned Chinee cook yelled out and pointed. I seen the fella—a wide blue turtle with a heavy, forward shell. He scratched Maud (who looked pretty wise) with his right flipper and lifted the other one at us. The damned Chinee yelled again and we seen why; for there was a gold band like a barrel hoop, high up on that blue turtle's port leg, where no human hand could've put it." Rio stopped.

"And then?" asked Martin.

"And then a film come over that fella's left eye and dropped down like our shipmate's—and sure enough, there was Philadelphia Dick, hatin' our guts, but tickled; and with all of us lookin' on and wonderin', he winked at us again and sounded, with his arm under Maud's belly."

Rio cleared his throat and looked out at the water. For a few minutes, the two men remained quiet until Rio, glancing at Martin, saw that his friend was hunched forward, his head down, still staring at the grass, and that his eyes were wet.

"For God's sake, Martin," he said.

Martin put his hand under his chin and regarded the other with a look so brief and yet so haunting that Rio held his tongue.

A Green Circle ship was leaving the harbor. The word NOMAD was painted on her bow.

"I made a trip on her one time," said Rio, pointing, and changing the subject deliberately. "Old Hungry was the steward. God! What food!"

Martin straightened up and leaned back against the hard, wooden bench.

"I never saw you when you couldn't eat," he said, smiling a little.

"This wasn't no different," replied Rio, grinning with satisfaction. "I got chummy with the galley boy and lived handsome. I ate the Old Man's oranges and drank the chief engineer's ale."

Martin looked amused.

"Did the kid supply you with romance, too?" he asked.

Rio regarded him strangely.

"No," he stated, after a moment, "but that brings somethin' to mind. Maybe you know the answer, my educated friend."

"Perhaps," said Martin, in a dry tone.

Rio shifted his position, moving back out of the sun.

"I was in Santa de Marina last trip, as you know," he said. "There was a girl, and a boy." He stopped talking abruptly and removed his cap long enough to wipe away the perspiration which had gathered on the band. "By God, I can't finish it!" he added vehemently.

Martin was silent.

Rio thought for a moment, then sighed and went on.

"Yeah, it's hard tellin'. There was somethin' funny about the girl. Funny in a nice way. And she was screwy, too." He wrinkled up his nose. "She made me dance pretty, but I could see she wasn't tryin' to."

"In the Street of Curtains?" asked Martin.

"Yeah. But she don't belong there," said Rio, his voice rising. "I don't believe I'll leave her there."

"That sounds just right," observed his friend.

"You ain't heard the story," said Rio quietly.

"That's right. The boy?"

Rio shook his head.

"He's tougher to figure than his sister."

Martin glanced up, interested for the first time.

"His sister was the girl?"

"His sister was the girl," repeated Rio. "The boy—well—I never knowed no kid like him—" He stopped and stared at his friend. "Unless———"

"Unless it was myself, Rio?" supplied Martin, a hard smile on his lips.

"Since you've said it—yeah." Rio looked out at the harbor again. "I give the girl all the money I had, and went back to the ship with the boy. On the way, there was a tree in flower—" He turned sharply on Martin and took hold of his shoulder. "Say," he said in a low, intense voice, "what the hell's wrong with me, Martin? By God, I want the truth!"

Martin could see astonishment and resentment in Rio's face; also a desperate sense of fear.

"There isn't anything wrong with you, Rio," he said calmly. "I've been afraid, too. And I've been sick with anger at the extremes. But if God Almighty granted you one precious moment, as I believe He did, and you didn't spend it, you can get down on your damned knees with the rest of the dilettantes and say your A B C's to Heaven the rest of your life without getting another." Martin's face was now so flushed with an anger he could not understand that it was as dark as Rio's.

The frown had left Rio's face. Infinitely puzzled, yet reassured, he stared at his friend.

"You can still talk, can't you, Martin? You can still make me believe you. Yeah, even when you lie, you make me feel better."

"Yes," said Martin, "I can still talk. For I have a problem myself. Perhaps you can help me with it."

"Shoot," said Rio, relief in his voice.

"It's about Carol. I'll try to make it quick for I know you don't like him."

"D'you?"

"Never mind about that. Here's the point. Things are getting a little mixed up in our fashionable set. Drew kept down the friction, but he went away and I can't say that I blame him."

Rio grinned.

"He didn't cut down the friction on me," he said, patting his back and grimacing. "But I'm not sore at him." Rio laughed out loud. "He's too damned pretty. Anyway, what about Carol?"

Martin leaned over and spoke confidentially.

"I can't tell you now, but I saw it," he said, in a low voice. "Carol's bound for it," he went on moodily. "What a shame!"

Rio swung around to stare at his friend. His own mouth was open, and his soft brown eyes were as wide, as honest and as startled as those of a besieged mare.

"I'll be god-damned!" he whispered, and turned away from Martin to stare out to sea. He stuck out his tongue and pulled at his ears. Then, after a moment, he settled back on the bench and regarded Martin with a worried expression. The sun disappeared behind a sailboat and in the bay, Liberty grew darker. A salt wind came up from the harbor and the shadow of the Aquarium now covered all that section of the Battery.

CHAPTER XXII

It was uncomfortably warm in the room where Martin was working on his type. He tried it awhile longer, then put aside his papers and went to the roof.

There were two women lying on a blanket taking a sun bath. They were in bathing suits and had the straps pulled down over their shoulders. Martin had to pass them to get to the opposite side of the porch. So he excused himself and only glanced at them briefly. But his presence apparently irritated them. One of the women, dark-haired and older than the other, seemed particularly annoyed. She laid her hand on the younger girl's arm and whispered something audibly and caustically to her friend. The remark was in such bad taste that Martin turned around and surveyed them coolly.

A dog was lying on the blanket with the women. He was little and white. He was young and curious and friendly. He trotted over to Martin, observed his white slacks, then looked back at his own coat. He sniffed at the slacks and raised his head, and all the while, Martin stood quietly and looked at him. The dog's eyes were brown. His legs were sturdy. Martin wanted to put his hand on the little head. He had done it before with animals. It was a sort of blessing. He wanted to say, "I like you. Don't let yourself be destroyed by these people." But he did not move. The women would object. They would speak sharply and the puppy would be ashamed.

Blood filled Martin's head. He had worked late the night before and he was tired. Anger shook his mind. Once more he looked across the roof at the women. Then he knelt to the dog. Holding the nervous head between his hands he watched the brown eyes. In his own was reflected an heroic poem—an attainable star. Martin did not beg nor did he demand. He showed the small one something greater than pettings and soft food. He showed him hard winds, ice and sun; his wolf-like ancestors—their smoky, torn fur. The dog became quiet, watching intently. He made no sound.

Martin held him patiently, listening with him to the soft pad of feet on the leaves above and around them. The dog's brown eyes grew wider, older, and became lost....

Martin stood up and regarded the women, thinking, "Symbols of a denatured civilization! Men linked together are strung, it is true, on the rock of a fool's evolution. But in them tragedy, strength and beauty neutralize the distortion—while across from me, on the roof, grope the clowns, the mimics, playing music they can never understand. The chords they touch turn black...."

The older woman called the dog to her. She put her arm around him and called him "Willie." It was not the word. It was her eyes, and her mouth, and the way her hands worked. "It is an indictment of womanhood," thought Martin. The woman looked at him; and seeing him stand so cold and full of hatred, she held the dog tighter. She held his fur and his body tighter; but Willie had gone. He was standing by a campfire. His hair was singed and there was a red line across his shoulders. His eyes were tired and glad with dreams.

Every woman feels biological change. It is her first lesson and her last. Although she often misinterprets her intuitive strength, she possesses it. This woman looked at Willie. She could not smell the singed hair nor see the red line; but she did see his eyes. A sadness, a real sorrow was in her. She turned from the dog to Martin who stood contemptuous and erect, and she turned away.

"Now am I right," Martin asked himself, observing in spite of his anger this dark woman's passion, "to condemn the ovary that cries out for its sister?— and absolve by ritual the formulated counterpart in man?" He stood there, pondering in this procession of new thought. "And am I wrong, that I can't feel the love that topples ethics, puts wire in soft fingers with one breath!... Why can't I feel the music of one breast upon another? And why do I call such music 'black,' when I might taste much softer lips than mine upon much softer lips?... These dismal cries—two sheer stockings ripped from their garters and one frightened voice saying, 'God! Make it straight with me!'— while the other, frantically tries syntheses and fluctuating pose...." Martin watched the slender clouds beyond the black roofs for a moment, then went below.

Martin was drowsing on the couch in his room when there was a rap at the door which he had left open. He glanced up sleepily. Roberts was standing there, an attempted smile only accentuating his moroseness.

"Come on in," said Martin cordially, sitting up. "Have a chair. That one's the most comfortable." He pointed to the rocker.

"Damn comfort," replied Roberts, nevertheless sitting down. He was thinner. There was an harassed expression on his face which Martin had never seen before. "I dare say you're surprised at my coming here," he continued.

"No," said Martin, frankly good-humored. "And I'm glad to see you."

The adviser waved the words away.

"Don't be social, in heaven's name. It isn't in your make-up. And if *you're* not surprised, I am, considering the attitude you've taken toward me lately."

Martin laughed, stood up and stretched and offered him a cigarette.

"Don't be a damned grouch, Roberts. You never got an attitude you didn't ask for. Light up, and I'll show you some work I'm doing. It's too hot to fight."

"Stop talking like a hussy," said the adviser as he took the cigarette. His face was damp and his hand was shaking.

Martin half-closed his eyes and there was a curious line about his mouth. Then he laughed again and held out a lighted match.

"What's so amusing?" asked Roberts, holding his hand against his cheeks which seemed to be burning. "Is it this squalor you're living in, or is it I? You're steeped in sin, Martin; but this is the first time I've felt the flatness of hypocrisy." There lay his mistake. He'd struck a heel softer than he knew. For with every flaw Martin had, he hated the word just spoken the most. His entire appearance changed and his cheeks became as white as Roberts' were red.

"Are you here as a friend?" he asked.

The changed timbre of Martin's voice seemed to stabilize Roberts.

"As a friend." The adviser was serious. "I have something that should interest you vitally." He regarded Martin, who still seemed unresponsive. "Don't underestimate this," Roberts continued severely. "I happen to know that Carol is following you." He waited intently for the effect of this speech upon his listener.

"I suspected as much," answered Martin. "In fact, I found him at it one night and asked him up."

"What?" cried Roberts, shocked, amazed, with every thread of jealousy burning in his face. "Good God, Martin! The man's dangerous. I know him better than you do. He's pathological. He'll stop at nothing. And you permitted him—you saw him here, alone?"

"Yes," said Martin dryly. "All, all alone."

Roberts stood up, propped his stick in a corner and walked the length of the room. His head was lowered; he was absorbed as if debating with himself. At last, he turned swiftly.

"You don't want to die, do you?" he asked, staring.

"No."

"Then watch out."

"For what?"

"For that kind of impudence which incurs my displeasure."

Martin leaned back against the head of the couch, put his chin on his hands and looked solemnly at his visitor.

"Have you lost your mind?" he asked.

Roberts' mouth opened and shut as though he were in rarefied air. Then he sat down again and looked at his hand which was still shaking.

"Martin," he whispered, "I'm frightened."

"I'm not astonished at that." Martin sat up. "Roberts!" he cried earnestly. "It's imperative that you get your thoughts out of this channel!"

"There *is* no other channel," interrupted the adviser. "I'm humiliated, degraded—but there is no other channel."

"Very well," said Martin. "I won't try to persuade you to think differently then. But I do ask you to give me the real purpose of this call."

"I came to warn you."

"Against Carol, or yourself?"

Roberts did not answer. His face was set and all the color had drained out of it.

Martin observed him closely.

"You've had some bad nights, my friend."

The adviser wiped his forehead.

"Yes. Bad nights. That I should live—for this!" He looked about him wildly.

Martin sat up straighter.

"Overlook the This, my mad companion, and look for That!"[4]

Roberts stared at him with amazement rising to horror.

"Destroyer of words!" he said. "My God! You destroyer of sand and clay and rock that make the brilliant hills!"

"Yes. Destroyer." Martin nodded in agreement.

Roberts got up, holding unsteadily to the arm of the chair.

"I'll leave you to your destiny!" he cried with savage vehemence.

"Unless it's interwoven," answered Martin coldly.

The adviser's eyes grew bright as though with fever.

"Again, your hatred in your words."

Martin nodded once more.

"That's right."

"What will you do if I don't permit you——" Roberts stopped.

"Propose something," commanded Martin, rising.

"I do." The adviser picked up his stick and walked uncertainly toward the door. As he turned, he seemed to be smiling. "I *have* proposed something."

With an easy stride Martin went to him. He took the stick from his hand and placed it against the wall. He reached for the door and closed it. Deliberately, he caught Roberts by the waist and bent him backwards until he fell. Then he poured one bitter kiss after another—his teeth cutting the adviser's tender lips and cheeks, his sweat falling like molecules of light.

Roberts screamed and turned his face away.

CHAPTER XXIII

One quiet evening Deane and Martin walked down to a street Exhibit in the Village. Since Roberts' visit to Martin, Deane had felt a melancholy restlessness about the man she loved; and on this evening, with small stationary clouds in the west prolonging the summer twilight, she tried with careful intrigue to bring him back again.

They walked the long way—past odd, forsaken streets; past streets with checkered, foreign signs; past junk shops, curio shops; past streets where old furniture, silverware and books were on display within the dusty, ill-kept windows; past lending libraries; past a little half-street with quiet, mysterious houses; past streets that wandered helplessly about until, faced with some busy thoroughfare, they paused abruptly, bewildered, and of necessity came to their end. There was one street built like a dagger, with a single row of trees across it for its hilt. There were crooked streets, dirty streets, smart streets; streets attempting to be gay and failing miserably; streets falling over themselves; scrambled streets; streets running pell-mell at last into Greenwich Square.

The Exhibit centered around Eighth Street and meandered, after various aimless shambles, along MacDougal Street and into the somewhat limited security of MacDougal Alley. Countless easels which held oils or studies in crayon, finished or unfinished, were scattered about the sidewalks. Odd bits of craftsmanship hung on the walls of buildings or were placed for sale on the curbs. Caricaturists and cut-out artists in their batik smocks were hawking their talents to the crowd, not with the loud, raucous voices of sideshow barkers at a fair, but with proud and careful gestures, and an occasional remark about art in general which most of the crowd took seriously.

At the end of MacDougal Alley a hard, slim man who looked like Popeye was daubing wildly at his canvas. Martin grinned and pulled Deane back by her elbow, stopping her suddenly.

"Look at that old boy," he said under his breath, all his melancholy abstraction leaving him in an instant. "He's mad as a hatter, and dreaming of a Dutch ship he took one time out of Sumatra. See, honey?" Martin grew more excited and pointed to the painting. "She's built like a sabot—equally stable in the North Sea or the South Pacific. The Hollanders knew how!" He nodded wisely. "By God! I have a little of their blood in my own veins," he continued with pride. "The painting's bad. But the thing's there, all right. The man has memories." He jigged Deane's arm again. "I'm going to tell the old chap I'm a steamship man. Watch him blow up. *He* never sailed under anything but canvas."

Deane grew concerned.

"Don't make him angry, Martin," she said, holding back.

"I won't. Come on, darling," and pulling her after him, he walked up casually behind the old seaman.

"Ah!" said Martin, as though speaking to Deane, "*there's* a fine ship!"

"Ye don't know her stem from her stern," said the painter, turning round to observe the speaker, then dabbing a ferocious spot of sea under his ship's bow.

"She's beautiful," insisted Martin. "That is—she would be, if she had just a touch of steam." He paused for a second. "There's nothing like steam in a calm, or if you need a head in the wind."

The brush dropped out of the painter's hand and his face turned the color of brick.

"Steam!" he snorted. "*I* went round the Horn with just me hat spread, boy!" He picked up his brush, wiped it carefully and jabbed at the canvas again. "I took me own ship round the Cape durin' a gale! There was less time than you'll get in your liner—and it gave me a belly at fifty *you'll* never see at thirty!"

Martin nodded.

"Canvas had its points, all right," he agreed.

"Steam!" repeated the old master scornfully, not in the least mollified, and spat upon the ground.

"Well," persisted Martin, "I wish I could have tried your square-riggers. I never quite trusted steam, myself." His voice sounded a little regretful.

The old master looked at him, suspicion in his eyes. Suddenly he stepped nearer and brought his face up close to Martin's.

"Do ye know where the Scylla Deeps be?" he asked mysteriously.

"A sea no sailor has found, sir," answered Martin.

The old master continued to peer at him with mistrust.

"Where did me best rope hang, boy?"

"From the yardarm, sir." Martin gave him a slow smile. "And it's not all that hung from there, sir," he added, knowingly.

The master's face turned into a series of amused lines and crevices. He grabbed Martin's arm and his white lips puckered into laughter.

"If I could've had ye as cabin boy, me lad, ye might've made a sailor!—But no more steamship gab!" he warned, shaking his finger. He turned once more to the painting. "Now ain't she a beauty?" He pointed with pride to the ship and over his ravaged face came a sorrowful and faraway expression. "She was trim as a herring," he said, so low they could scarcely hear. "Trim as a herring, me boy."

Martin spoke soberly, with an infinite respect.

"She was, sir. And she is. I'm glad you're bringing her alive."

The old master stared at him. His eyes seemed flaked with salt and he brushed one rough hand across them.

Martin took Deane's arm once more.

"Good-by, sir. A good trip, sir," he said, pulling Deane along. But the old master just kept staring as the two walked away.

"Why did he look like that?" Deane whispered, her own eyes full of tears.

"That ship went down, honey—and the master, also," answered Martin.

On the next corner, standing in an erect, unnatural posture, was a man with a full red beard. In one hand the man held a comb which occasionally he used on his chin with a gesture at once contemptuous and desperate. In the other hand there was a ragged paper upon which something was written— and this, he wore as though it were a part of him. When any passed too close he would draw back the manuscript, hastily covering the words, the beer stains and perhaps tears with his palm. His bold chin under its red blanket would jut angrily; he would hunch his shoulders, and his eyes, which were a little blurred, would narrow in agony and hatred. Martin, ashamed for all mankind that it had shamed this artist and his work, walked by with an impassive glance, understanding full well the torment of beauty which must be held within itself. But the man, sensing some kinship within Martin, or feeling some belligerent contempt, held out to him the sheaf of paper containing all the golden words born of himself in adoration, hunger and distrust. His speech was rapid, barely articulate.

"Twenty-five cents, *sir?*" he called out mockingly. "A block of my heart for twenty-five cents!"

Deane pressed against Martin and he knew that she was frightened. He tried, without speaking, to tell her not to be, and walked on with a strolling deliberation, eyes ahead without expression, minimizing as far as possible the high chain of laughter behind them. He visualized the rotten teeth—the long hysteria——

And then they came upon a flower man, a small Sicilian with an olive skin and a charming, wistful face. He was standing by his little cart, his hands down by his side as though in a mild passion with his lot among the flowers. There were cornflowers and mignonette; crisp French marigolds and early cosmos. Deane made her choice.

"Buy me the marigolds," she asked of Martin. "You remember?—they were your first gift to me."

The little olive gentleman bowed and smiled; and carefully selecting the freshest marigolds from his stock, twisted a strip of tinfoil around their stems before handing them to Deane.

Shortly after they left him, Deane looked back. He was standing by his little cart, still smiling, his hands down by his side in gentle obsequiousness.

Touched deeply by this profound and infinite patience, Deane thought of all the things she had seen that day—one man with a phantom ship, one with a poem, and one—She glanced sideways at Martin, and suddenly, unnoticed by him, the tiny bunch of marigolds which she was clutching fell from her grasp....

Later, in the soft candlelight within the apartment, Martin sat on the arm of Deane's chair, quietly twisting the ring upon his finger. The small red stone on its field of black looked at him speculatively. The tender perception which had been Deane's all that evening now gave way to a definite and fearful prescience.

"What is it, darling?" she asked, for Martin had not spoken in some time.

"I love you," he said simply.

"I love you, too. But what disturbs you, Martin?"

He avoided her eyes.

"It was only a dream," he said at last. "But it has worried me. I dreamt I died and found myself at the crossroads of Heaven and Hell—there to make my decision as to which path I should walk."

"What? A dream—worry you?" Deane sighed with relief and ran her hand across his cheek. Then she arose and led him to the divan. One by one the candles had gone out and like a specter, the pallid light of the full summer moon crept into the apartment. "Go on, my darling," she whispered, half closing her eyes and stretching luxuriously against him.

"I died," he repeated. "And I found myself at the crossroads of Heaven and Hell. I was undecided as to which road to take. Then suddenly I knew the answer. I knew they diverged only for a time."

"What do you mean?" In Deane's voice was a note of dismay.

"I knew that whichever road I took, it would end in pain."

"Oh, no!"

"Yes, I knew that the end would be the same; so, impudently, I took the road marked HEAVEN. I walked for days among winding mountain paths. Giant trees sang to me in the wind, and the air was fragrant with pine and wild rose. Little creeks ran past me, twisting over mossy rocks; and there were narrow falls of water spinning white and silver. In shadowy places where the water eddied dark green and gold, I stopped to rest and drink. A long time I walked through this country. By day, the sun struck blindly through the limbs of trees; and at night, a moon showed. Then I came to a valley where I saw broad fields of grain, shining yellow, and checkerboards of green pasture and plowed field. I was confused by the intermittent sound of bells which rang through the air.

"On one block of green pasture there was a great multitude. I went down the trail, leaving the forest behind, and descended into the lowland. As I approached the congregation, I saw to my amazement that they were all children. I wondered at their quietness. They were so silent and unmoving that I would have thought them dead had it not been that they were facing me, a sweet, desperate expression on their faces. The macabre quality in these little ones gave me an unpleasant thrill. No murmur sounded from this congress of children—no movement of arm, knee or head.

"Full of a presentiment of evil, I walked closer and looked down into their eyes. Row after row of these spectral organisms were before me, reaching, it seemed, to the horizon. Thousands of bright, curly heads shone faintly in the haze of the sun. Their wide eyes, blue or brown, were directed at me.

"My mouth was hot. I tried to smile.

"'Have I reached Heaven?' I asked them.

"The answer seemed to be projected from a thousand throats, but it reached my ears as a whisper. This tired wind, blowing so, held only compassion. It was unbearable. And it said—'We love you.'"

Martin's face became severe and rigid as he told this.

"Go on, Martin," Deane urged.

"I can't."

"It was a dream, Martin. Finish the dream."

"It was destiny!" he cried. "I murdered ten thousand innocents! I asked them if I was in Heaven, and they answered that they loved me. To wheedle, to coax a smile into their weakening, passive faces, I asked a question...."

"They told me that they loved me," Martin repeated tiredly, and once more, Deane felt a prescience of terror.

"I wanted to raise my hand," Martin went on. "I wanted to shout, to jump into the air, to sing a song—anything to dissipate the irrevocable impression of death that carved each face into the appearance of a dying flower.

"I was desperate and I felt that I was wrong.

"'Children,' I said, 'I have hurt you. Tell me the poison, the action, or the mood that has brought you this pain.'

"I can't explain how they looked. It wasn't sadness, nor was it condemnation. It was a death's joke and I was horrified. Again the wind of their minds moved restlessly in my ears.

"'Pain you prophesied,' it said.

"'It was a prophecy of pain for myself,' I told them. 'I didn't mean to condemn you.'

"This time," said Martin, "there was no answer; no audible answer. But for the first time the children moved, dropping gently on their knees. They lowered their eyelids, accentuating the pallor of their faces.

"I cried out to them. I begged their forgiveness. I cursed myself, tore open my shirt and looked for a weapon, reasoning that my death would bring life to the children."

As Martin said this, he caught his breath and projected a swift pain into the woman. Deane held him gladly—drawing in his venom—half fainting.

But Martin, pressing deeper into his mind, continued furiously.

"At each of my gestures—at each syllable, the children sank closer to the grass. Their eyes closed with precision until only the fringe of lash showed where the eyes had been. Watching this slow death of thousands, I stopped speaking and stood rigid, my jaws locked. I glared at them. I saw each movement become fainter until each tortured flower-face lay on the ground, their chins propped up to me. Their cheeks were like wilted petals, their white, reedy arms were extended above them, and each child-finger was pointed toward me."

Martin stopped speaking. Deane lay quiet within his arms. She felt his face against her throat, felt her own arms pinioned and her agony intensified. Compassionately she kissed the thick perspiration from his forehead.

CHAPTER XXIV

Martin pushed his chair away from the linotype, waiting for copy. He leaned back and spoke to Rio who was sitting on the windowsill behind him.

"Smell that sulphur?"

"Yeah."

"It's from the plant across the way. Gets sweet about this time every night. You've probably noticed it before."

"It don't make no difference," said Rio. "This is one hell of a place any way you look at it. Noise and dirt." He spat out the window.

Martin yawned and stretched in his chair, but made no answer.

"It ain't no place for me," continued Rio grimly. "Some of the boys look restless. Is it the strike you're worryin' about?"

"The strike may not come off, Rio. There's always a lot of talk. And if it does, it's no worse than the waterfront."

"Well, anyway, I'm goin' out for a smoke." Rio walked into the little hallway, calling back over the banisters to Martin to find out how much longer he had to wait.

Martin glanced at his watch.

"I'll be through in twenty minutes," he said. "We can stop down the street for a nightcap."

"I'll be outside," Rio mumbled, and went on down the stairs.

He was sitting on the steps when Martin joined him. His huge frame filled the doorway and as he arose lazily, Martin wondered, as he had wondered many times before, at the harmony of his movements.

Far beyond the reaches of the sulphur fumes, the soft tread of these men, accustomed as they were to the intricate, woven fabric of the sea, made scarcely a sound in the night.

Rio sniffed.

"New York," he said, as they walked along. "It smells different this time of year."

And Martin, through his friend, felt a definite, new motion in the color of the air—a deliberate music brought by the full season. In both retrospect and in the moment, Martin watched Huysmans, that frightened older brother, break the skyline into small patches of dim lights between the darkened buildings.

So still was the atmosphere that the two friends felt annoyed at the sight of a lighted tavern. But they stopped in for a drink nevertheless, then went on slowly toward Martin's rooming house.

"Say, Martin," said Rio finally. "I been thinkin' over that act you pulled with Roberts. I don't get it." He laughed. "It's funny, though."

"It really wasn't an act," replied Martin.

Rio looked at him through the darkness.

"You mean———"

"Good Lord, no!" interrupted Martin. "I'll admit, it's difficult to understand—even for me. But the way he stood, the way he smiled, and his new threat (remember, he's carried them out before!) made me break loose. I kept thinking, as I looked at him, that he'd always asked me for something that he didn't want. When I called him, I must have known he wasn't real. For when I pretended a consummation he was frightened and ashamed."

Rio shook his head.

"You're a brave lad. It makes me sick to think about it."

Martin's tone was peculiar.

"I was poisonous," he said.

Rio looked at him again and shrugged his shoulders.

"Well, I guess it cured him."

Martin thought a moment.

"I don't know. I suppose that when it comes down to it I don't understand him at all.... By the way, Rio, what made him take such a dislike to you?"

"Nothin' much. I asked him about you once and when I found out he lied, I shook him up." Rio closed his fist in the dark. "I wish I'd shook 'im harder now," he added, half under his breath.

"Damn it! That's the pay-off!" said Martin angrily.

Rio turned to him.

"If you mean you're fed up messin' with this queer outfit, I'm with you." He began to walk more rapidly. "I wish to God I was back———"

Martin interrupted.

"I know. Sometimes I wish we were at sea again."

"What about Deane?" asked Rio.

Martin's voice was as even as his steps.

"I wouldn't mention her name, Rio," he said. "We never think about a little thing like that the first time." His voice was trembling now. "But I wouldn't ever see her, or mention her name again."

They walked along Eighth Street without speaking for a few blocks until Rio turned to his friend.

"Is that all you're goin' to say?" he asked.

"Yes."

"I'm a miserable bastard, Martin. I wish I was in Santa de Marina. By God!— I think I'll go."

Rio sounded so unusually plaintive that Martin had to laugh.

"I don't blame you. Why don't you return to the family? Your money won't last them forever and you could make out all right down there."

They had reached Washington Square and were about to turn down Martin's street when Rio stopped him.

"Let's go in and sit down for awhile, buddy. There's a few things I'd like to ask you."

Martin walked beside him until they came to the large circular rim of the fountain. They sat down on the low concrete wall and Rio put out his cigarette, grinding it under his heel on the pavement. It seemed difficult for him to speak.

"Y'know," he said, finally, "I been around more than most men. I been places and seen funny practices, and ugly ones, among the heathen. And I know Berlin better'n I do New York. The same goes for a few other cities. I thought I'd scraped most people and most happenin's. Then I had the luck of bumpin' into you."

"Good, or bad?" asked Martin.

"Bad, I guess, or I'd have missed it."

"Why bad?"

"Well, because I had a few ideas that I believed in. Somehow, you've managed to mess 'em up."

"That's all right," said Martin, emphasizing his words with a quick movement of his hand. "If you were on a weak foundation you shouldn't mind having your opinions reversed. If you had a strong one I couldn't change it."

"It ain't one or the other," said Rio in disgust. "You can take an idea, right or wrong, and squeeze it like butter." His tone grew deeper and Martin felt that he was frowning in the semi-darkness. "I'm goin' to ask you a question, Martin. Don't get sore; and I don't mean it hard. But I got to know. We've kidded each other a lot since we met. You stood by me—" Rio's voice faltered. He swallowed and stopped for a moment. Martin could hear his heavy breathing.

"Get rid of it, Rio," he said.

"It's god-damned crazy," said Rio, swearing to hide his embarrassment. "But listen, Martin. Are you———"

Martin half closed his eyes.

"Oh," he thought. He watched his friend struggling through this viscous medium in a painful attempt to absorb most of its ugliness himself. But he gave the man no clue, no help. He merely closed his eyes tighter and listened.

"Are you—" continued Rio. Then, his voice stronger and more demanding, "Are you a god-damned fairy with your god-damned eyes and the way you look at people? You looked queer in that draggy dress at the party, and you acted queer." Rio hesitated. "Oh, I know you took care of me afterward. But when I seen you leanin' on the piano like a girl, I went crazy. If you're a queen, tell me!" His voice had become so husky that he could scarcely speak. "And if you ain't—what are you? Let me know. Let me know damned fast!" He was breathing still harder and Martin could hear his hands rubbing against the concrete.

He slipped off the side of the fountain and faced Rio. In the quiet night, without a moon, the open stars drew their icy shine across his eyes. He lit a cigarette and in the brief flare, Rio could see the drawn lips, the contemptuous silhouette and the sharp lines in his face.

"Time doesn't count, Rio. Kindly don't be in a hurry." Martin spoke softly. "And remember, I'm talking about myself and not you, so don't be anxious. You've asked me a question in your manner, and I'll answer it in your manner, Rio. I am."

"Damn you, you're not!" Rio cried out.

"Then it's for you to judge."

"I don't judge nothin', Martin," said Rio, standing and facing him. "But if you ain't, why d'you hang around them?"

"'Them'?" asked Martin, with a bleak smile. "If you could see yourself standing there, frightened of yourself, frightened of me, frightened of symbols——"

"I tell you, I'm not like that!" interrupted Rio, his hands back of him.

"Perhaps you are," said Martin quietly.

"Clear that up." Rio was leaning slightly forward in dignified, yet dangerously immobile restraint. "Clear that up fast."

Martin spoke earnestly, without resentment.

"Before you ever ask another man that question, Rio, go to the mirror and ask it of yourself. Perhaps the answer will be—'thou, too'!"

Rio kept the same tense attitude.

"You mean *I* am?" he asked slowly. "You better explain it well this time. Show me your point."

Martin looked at him indifferently.

"You asked me, didn't you, if I was queer; and although you're deathly afraid of it yourself, you hold such people in contempt. Did you think I was going to deny it as though it were intrinsically a shameful thing?"

"You say it ain't shameful?" said Rio, not changing his position.

"It exists," went on Martin calmly. "It's part of life. It has its particular and its important position in the world. It has its stages and its stratas. Thus it is, Rio—this force was created."

"Created for what?" demanded Rio. "For nightmares?" He wiped away the sweat from his forehead.

"No," said Martin. "Created for balance."

"'Balance,' hell!—those upside down bastards?"

"I didn't say they were balanced. I don't know that, because I don't know where the average begins or ends. I said they were created for balance. A necessary people forming a resilient salient between the rigidity of the sexes."

"I don't see it," said Rio heavily.

"Don't bother, then," said Martin. "And don't make an issue of it. I've looked at Carol and seen the reason, the essential purpose of his destiny."

"Go on," said Rio.

"And I've looked at Drew," Martin continued. "He made me wonder what the word 'normal' meant."

"God, you're crazy," whispered Rio.

"I've looked at Roberts," confessed Martin, "until his helpless, sick desire forced me into desperation, and I tasted the germ of his too bright mouth."

"God!" repeated Rio, horrified.

"And I've looked at you," went on Martin.

"Yeah?" breathed Rio, straining forward.

"And I became less blind."

Rio's heavy shoe scraped the pavement.

"And I've looked at myself," said Martin, lifting his voice. And still more firmly, "I've looked at all of us and found us all so different—and yet so much the same."

"Holy Christ," said Rio softly.

"Aye," Martin nodded. "Holy Christ."

They left the park and walked on silently, each thinking more of the other's thoughts than of his own. A wind from the south, carrying a burned, sulphurous cloud, quickly hid the stars and descended until even the solitary street lamps were darkened, became ominous and were worse than none at all. It muffled the occasional sounds of late night and was as forbidding as the attitude of these two silent men; for except themselves, the streets were deserted, and their presence only accentuated the desolation. It was a moment of such stillness that even nature becomes disturbed and ultimately furious, and sharply moving her wing, brings down a sudden and a violent sound.

A block away from Martin's room an ambulance rushed past them, its siren full and piercing. It drew up quickly before the house and an ambulance doctor with white cap and trousers bent over a man who was lying on the curb. A thin group of spectators had gathered. They were quiet, looking on curiously. Martin's landlady was standing by, shivering and crying. Martin went to her and touched her arm.

"What is it, Mrs. O'Brien?" he asked.

"I don't know, Mr. Devaud," sobbed the woman. "I heard a noise. I guess it was a shot. So I looked out the window and there he was."

Martin hurried back to Rio.

"What does it look like?" he asked nervously. "I can't see."

Rio struck a match.

"I dunno. He can't get no pulse."

The doctor was still kneeling between them and the figure. At last, he moved to one side and opened the man's shirt, throwing a point of light on a small, discolored spot under the heart. The man's face was in bas-relief. But above the wound, in a broken curve, lay a delicate, golden necklace....

Martin leaned over swiftly and started to speak; but Rio stepped in front of him.

"The guy's dead, eh, Doc?" he asked solicitously, glaring at Martin all the while over his shoulder.

"Get back," said the doctor brusquely, to the crowd. Then he called out to the driver. "Come on, Jim. Lend a hand."

Rio took Martin by the arm and they walked up the steps quickly.

"You god-damned fool," Rio kept whispering to him. "You god-damned fool. Keep your god-damned mouth shut."

In Martin's room they sat down and faced each other. Rio continued to swear at him.

"So there you are," he said mockingly. "Carol's knocked off and you want to butt in."

"Oh, for Christ's sake, shut up!" said Martin miserably. Then seeing the expression on Rio's face, he went over to him and put his hand on his shoulder. "I didn't mean that, Rio. I know well enough you saved me a lot of trouble out there. I'm just trying to figure it out."

"Don't be so dumb," said Rio, and put his cap on backwards.

"Yes. It must have been Roberts. I suppose that's what he meant when he said he had proposed something. I knew it. I was slow. Damn him. Why?"

"Why not? Carol was in his way," said Rio philosophically.

Martin stood up.

"Rio!" He spoke swiftly. His voice was harsh and a terrible light burned in his eyes.

"Take it easy," Rio answered calmly. "He won't hurt Deane to-night. He's weak, some ways. This one job's enough for his stomach this time. He's in bed—cracked up. Puking his guts out. But later, I dunno." Rio was growing thoughtful.

"How did he get away with this, Rio?"

"He's a clever son-of-a-bitch."

"Clever?" repeated Martin. "I wonder." He moved toward the door. "Rio, I'm going to see him."

Rio went to his friend and held his arm.

"Don't stick your chin out, Martin," he said earnestly. "Maybe I got an idea myself." He righted his cap, and without further explanation left the room.

Martin pulled up the rocker in front of his small radio which he turned on softly. There, his head in his hands, he sat and rocked until morning. Then he took a train uptown to Deane's.

CHAPTER XXV

Roberts woke up with a sticky feeling in his mouth. He felt his wrist. It was still throbbing. With difficulty he repressed a sudden panic brought about by his full consciousness of this last and most horrible link forged in the confused entries of his life. He got up, put his feet in a pair of slippers and went to the mirror. He stuck out his tongue and looked at it carefully. Walking away, he stopped suddenly and glanced over his shoulder at himself. Then he rang for his breakfast and went into the bathroom.

Although he was accustomed to this pale Orient, an atmosphere of mauve with the suggestion of a darker tone enhanced by lights, direct and indirect, it seemed to stimulate him now as though it were a new experience. He took a crystal flagon from its glass shelf and shook the bottle slightly, watching the opalescent liquid as hungrily as though he were going to drink it. Removing the stopper, he closed his eyes and drew in a deep breath, shivering; and as an afterthought, carefully shook two drops upon his fingers and rubbed them into his temples. The astonishing scent filled the bathroom and Roberts leaned against the wall as the odor of stable frost arose about him. Slowly, he removed his pajamas, white as his skin, and let them fall around his feet. The warm water from the shower sprayed off his head. He stuck out his tongue again and swallowed a little of the water. It tasted salty and he spat out what was left. After a careless shave he put on a dressing gown of deep red corded silk, and staring vacantly, sat down in front of the coffee table in his living room.

The boy knocked and entered with his breakfast.

"My paper?" Roberts looked up inquiringly.

"Yes, sir. It's on your tray, sir," answered the boy.

"That's right, my lad. Always a paper with one's eggs." The adviser laughed sententiously.

The boy put down the tray.

"Will that be all, sir?"

Roberts looked up again, severely.

"Is that all? Most certainly. Do I ever digress from this routine?"

"No, sir," said the boy and left.

Roberts mused, his lips spasmodically making little ticking sounds.

"Is that all? What else could he want? The scamp—he acted as if he knew something. A pretty lot *he* could know—or anybody, for that matter." The adviser looked around the room, smiling shrewdly. There was a single scarlet geranium on his tray. He picked it up with a caress and held it briefly under his nose before he tore off the petals. Then he looked at his eggs.

"Cold, as usual," he said bitterly. "And what's this?—a spot?" He put his spoon into the eggs. "The nucleus, no doubt. Good heavens!—does fertilization confront me even in my breakfast?" He tried to control his anger and nibbled at a piece of bacon and toast. The hot, black coffee he drank greedily.

A short article at the bottom of the front page of his paper attracted his attention. He read through it swiftly. A murder in Greenwich Village. He smiled again, this time his right eye winking slightly.

"Definitely a bad neighborhood, Mrs. Twitchett," he said amiably. "People who go down there must expect such things, my dear." Then, with a start, he brought himself up. "You ass!" He spoke harshly to himself. "You giggling, impossible hermaphrodite! Hush!" But unable to repress his amusement he laughed aloud, pressing his finger to his lips secretively. After awhile he picked up the paper again. "What was the name? ... Carol?... Yes, Carol Stevens. A young chap, so the papers say. But he'll be a long time down there. It will bring maturity.... Unfortunately, he might be connected with Martin Devaud? That would be scandalous." Before the smile reappeared on Roberts' face he looked at the article once more. Certainly, it would not involve himself. Being merely decent to a homespun lad like that. There couldn't be any connection there.... He spoke aloud again. "There isn't any connection, you bloated bunch of rags! You confounded, grayish bunch of rags! This is the time of year to remain in one's own department."

He went to the desk and took a sheet of paper. Meticulously he wrote:

To the Police:

Using a small caliber automatic and under the pretense of friendship I approached and shot Carol Stevens. The motive was jealousy.

Signed:

William Roberts.

He permitted a slight smile. Then, taking a box of matches out of his pocket he struck one and lit a corner of the paper. After the note had burned he dropped the ashes into the wastebasket.

He took another piece of paper and wrote the same message, stood up and looked at it from a distance, taking his eyes away from it at intervals, for a second at a time. Then he picked up the paper, and waving it around, walked to the other end of the room. After a few moments he walked back, humming, and slowly burned it, too.

Again he wrote the message. This time he left the room. A moment later his face appeared in the doorway. It was tense as he walked rapidly to the desk. But when he saw the message, undisturbed, he smiled again. He picked it up, crumpled it into a ball and threw it across the room. Leaping after it and retrieving it with a desperate, sweeping motion, he unrolled it with quivering fingers. Hastily he read the words and again the satisfied smile lessened the tension on his face. Then he rolled the paper once more and walked to the inside wall. He stood with his back to the room for a long time, at last throwing the wadded note as far over his shoulder as he could, one hand covering his eyes. Turning around, he looked on the floor. The paper was not there. He began to walk back and forth swiftly, looking on the divan, on the chairs. The message was not to be seen. Finally he stopped in the center of the room, a curiously stupid expression on his face. He felt slightly dizzy and the room seemed to be turning. He walked hesitatingly to a chair, his titubation increasing. Leaning over the chair, he looked at the room from this angle. The paper had apparently vanished. He felt his pulse and was alarmed by its rapid beat. In an attitude of half-fear, half-anger, he went hurriedly over the room again, lifting the pillows from the divan and from the chairs. Then he went to a mirror and looked at himself. The pupils of his eyes were large and startling, set in a pale, grayish face lined with anxiety. Panic-stricken, he ran to his clothescloset and took down another dressing robe. This he hung over the mirror in the living room. Animal-like, he fell to his knees, and crawling around the floor, peered under the fringe of the rug. His shoulder bumped against a chair and he tipped it over angrily. His movements became more and more frenzied. At last each article had been closely inspected, and still there was no message. He ran to the door and locked it securely. Suddenly, he looked at the window. It was open. He drew his hand across his forehead which was covered with perspiration. His knees trembled. He sat down abruptly, the upset furniture swaying around him.

Within this desperate sense of fear he quickly regained his balance. He went to the buffet and drank a small brandy. Unsteadily, but seriously, he dressed. He started to leave the room, hesitated, and as an afterthought went to the window. He leaned out and looked down at the alley-like space between the buildings. Unable to distinguish anything, he closed the window, went out into the hall and rang for the elevator.

Downstairs, he crossed the court, climbed over a low fence and walked down the space under his window. One crumpled white paper drew his attention, but it was an empty cigarette package. Toward the sidewalk he saw another wadded paper. People were passing close by and he picked it up self-consciously, not daring to hope that it was the one he wanted. Walking back to the court he opened it feverishly. His eye caught the first line. It said, "To the Police:—" He read no further, but jammed the note hastily, though carefully, into his pocket and folded his hand around it.

In his apartment, came the reaction. He lay on his back on the upset divan, his hand still gripped around the paper, and wept softly and bitterly. When he had stopped shaking he went to the desk, smoothed out the paper and read it, a definite horror on his face. Then anger relieved his fear and he struck the note repeatedly with his fist. Throwing it into the metal wastebasket, he tossed burning matches after it until the confessional was alight with flames. Methodically he straightened the room and took the robe from the mirror. Looking into the glass, he held out his hand and with amazing swiftness struck the side of his face.

Later, in the bathroom, he saw with satisfaction the purple outline of his fingers on his cheek.

CHAPTER XXVI

Deane answered the telephone nervously. A voice, thin and unsteady, came over the wire.

"Deane? This is Roberts."

With difficulty Deane restrained a sudden feeling of panic.

The adviser spoke quickly, without waiting for her acknowledgment.

"This is rather unusual, but I assure you the situation is imperative enough to justify its obvious lack of convention."

Deane's anxiety increased.

"What situation, Roberts?" she asked.

"A situation so delicate that its discussion by phone is impossible. Won't you do me the kindness to have dinner with me?" Roberts' voice had taken on a strange, beseeching quality.

Thoroughly frightened by the implication of drama, Deane tried to remember that she had once been attracted by his intelligence, amused at his suavity. She accepted his invitation.

What could he want of her? She was glad that Martin had gone home. He would never let her meet Roberts if he knew. She recalled how frightfully upset Martin had been that morning.

While she was dressing she kept wondering what urgency had prompted the adviser to contact her so quickly after the tragedy. Surely no guilty man would do such a thing. Perhaps Martin and Rio were wrong. Perhaps Roberts wanted to help.... Did he know about that picture of Martin the police had found in Carol's pocket? Thank God, Martin had had an alibi. Or—did alibis really count!... Poor Carol! Was she responsible for his death? It was true that she had introduced him into this ill-assorted group of men who, more experienced in the conflicting currents of human emotion, could anticipate and often avoid such danger. She remembered little phrases and gestures of Carol which in retrospect seemed touching and child-like. She remembered the day she had gone to lunch with him—his earnest, immature face as he reflected the thoughts and effusions of this man whom she was meeting. What blindness of hers that she had not foreseen an approximate outcome of this relationship! Deane's eyes were full of tears. She felt the tremendous sorrow of the immaculate woman for the spikes and chains which bind humanity's certified incompetents. Too, for herself, there were tears of indignation—resentment over being drawn into this formidable unity. She finished dressing and hurried uptown.

In the restaurant, Roberts leaned slightly forward, over the table, his hands together.

"Deane," he said, "I didn't ask you to meet me because of Carol's tragedy. The child was drawn into a significantly dangerous vortex. But it is about this uncompromising whirlpool itself, which may engulf others whom I love, that I want to speak. There is something here—some sinister thing about us that is in deadly earnest. Do you sense it, Deane?"

"Yes, Roberts. Particularly now."

"Martin," continued the adviser, "does not appreciate the undercurrent of this danger. It is for this reason—for this one reason I begged you to see me."

"Yes," Deane repeated, feeling her skin tighten as it does under a great and hopeless fear.

"I have but one thought in mind—" Roberts proceeded, "Martin's future. His temperament is one that will not adjust itself to the inevitable."

Deane's hand closed over her bag. A swift feeling of revulsion changed as quickly to one of anger.

"The inevitable?" she asked, controlling her voice.

"Yes," said Roberts. "The inevitable routine of this world. I have it on good authority that he is about to lose his job at Miller's Typographical. You know his history. He came to me a transient—a common seaman. I found him a good job. I made contacts for him in this respect which he used, or rather abused, with an amazing recklessness. I do not understand his lack of appreciation. But these things are unimportant. Regardless of his inconsideration, I feel that there is definitely something worth saving."

"That's good of you, Roberts," said Deane, inclining her head a little, the large hat shading her eyes. "Martin would be pleased to know that you consider his regeneration a possibility."

Roberts' lips tightened at her irony. His fingers moved constantly over the white tablecloth, touching a cup—a spoon——

"I appeal to you, Deane," he said finally. "I recognize your influence over him."

She remained silent.

"Have you no answer?" he asked.

"Of course not." Deane's moist, red lips closed tightly.

Roberts picked up a spoon and tapped it nervously on the table.

"I have always respected your antagonism, Deane, but I am somewhat unprepared, just now, to face a personal issue. By coöperating with me, I feel that we can bring about some satisfactory adjustment on the part of Martin that will give him success and happiness." The adviser waited, quiet and intent.

Deane's eyes paled, the color fading into clearness. She looked at Roberts abstractedly. To her it seemed that an unhealthy whiteness moved now under his skin. His handsome face seemed trembling, disintegrating and forming anew, misshapen under the pressure of his mind. His cheeks appeared alive with white nerve roots, moving uncertainly, like microscopic serpents. The lens of Deane's eyes penetrated through flesh into the dark coils of blood, visualizing curiously the spiraling, pallid germ.

Roberts jerked in his chair. He leaned sideways, holding to the table. His cuff brushed a tumbler and a little of the water spilled upon the cloth.

"Deane!" He spoke sharply. "What are you looking at?"

Her eyes grew deeper, lost their transparency.

"I was wondering."

Roberts' voice trembled. His words were insecure.

"You were wondering.... You were wondering at what? What are you looking at?"

Deane took her eyes from him.

"Please go on, Roberts."

He hesitated.

"I was saying—I was saying that you have a remarkable influence over Martin. Doubtless he has told you of our early misunderstanding—a misunderstanding based on the assumption that I was instrumental in having him fired. As an intelligent woman you are probably aware of the fact that he lost his position because he neglected his work. He is not incompetent, but his social program affected his efficiency."

Deane spoke without looking at him.

"Do you mean that I caused Martin to lose his position?" Her lack of resentment, her cold, unemotional question disconcerted the adviser momentarily.

"Indeed not," he answered. "Please believe that I have valued and approved his friendships for certain people. Martin tends toward introspection and celibacy. It is most important that he cultivate the social quality. That is why I was so astonished that he should, of a sudden, become so interested in what constitutes society."

"I do not constitute society, Roberts. I love him."

Roberts lifted his eyebrows.

"Deane," he said anxiously, "I hope that you do not believe that I have intended to invade your personal affairs. I am concerned only with Martin's development. I truly desire his life to be a complete and happy one."

"Then please tell me what you want." Deane made an uneasy little gesture.

For one lost moment, Roberts' pallid cheeks were covered as though by the light of a beautiful, dark flame and he leaned across the table with a desperate, hopeless lust.

"You know what I want, Deane. *You have always known*." Now, he was breathless and the color left his face, leaving him whiter and more distraught than before.

Deane sat erect. There was more than anger in her expression. There was the fury and the cruelty of all her sex against what she believed to be the pitiful, crippled shade of themselves—against the mist of a forever-damned kinship which thought as woman thought, desired with woman's desire, and still was mist, without substance, without gratification. Deane's voice was barely audible.

"Never," she whispered.

At her expression and her exclamation, Roberts wet his lips and trembled slightly in his chair, gazing at her as though in some enchantment.

"Never?" he asked, in a voice as low as her own, but with the quality of a protesting and bewildered child.

"Roberts!" Deane spoke so sharply that he was shaken from his spell and sat more normally, looking at her now with quiet speculation. "What is it you wish me to do? I see no reason to protract a conversation so unpleasant."

The adviser met her glance with restraint.

"My motives are misconstrued," he said slowly. "You will forgive my naive desire to lend Martin my support?"

Again Deane's eyes dimmed and faded. Catching his own reflection, Roberts' pallor grew even more death-like. And again he gripped the table, his knuckles white under the transparent skin. In the opalescent mirror of the woman's eyes he saw his image—saw the pale movement within himself.

Deane, her face cruel, drove her thoughts in swift waves, building and clarifying the image until the naked picture of the man and his disease rose clearly in her mind. There was an odor of decay. Roberts half rose from his chair, slipped back into it, and leaning sideways on the table stared fixedly at her.

Terrified, she arose. In Roberts' face there was no blood, no expression. His eyes were set and the cords of his throat made ridges in his white neck. Deane put her hands over her eyes. She knew now. Her thoughts raced.... "*He killed Carol. He wants to kill me!*" ... Without excusing herself she left the restaurant and hurried to a cab.

Roberts, his hands limp on the tablecloth, stared before him. He felt Deane's movement as she left, but he remained as he was.

"Take your eyes, too!" he said aloud. His voice rose higher. "I say, take your eyes!"

Other diners looked curiously at him, smiling and nodding their heads. A small, dark woman exchanged glances with her escort.

"He's had plenty," she said. "I watched him and the woman. They had an argument. The man's tight."

Her escort regarded Roberts earnestly.

"I don't know. It looks as though he has the horrors."

Roberts gazed steadily at the translucent eyes floating across the table.

"All right, my dear. Stay there," he said loudly.

The dark woman's escort glanced at him worriedly and beckoned to a waiter.

"Say, waiter, there's a chap over there with the jitters. He needs looking after."

The waiter approached Roberts warily.

"Is there something you wish, sir?" he said, deferentially.

Roberts still watched the eyes. He stood up and spoke quietly.

"Very well, I shall go. You remain here." Turning to the waiter, "My hat, quickly."

Outside, the adviser hailed a taxi, climbed in unsteadily and directed the driver to his apartment.

Dropping his coat on the divan in the living room, he went hurriedly to the mirror and stared into it. The light on the glass wavered, a shadow appeared, and Deane's eyes, large and transparent, materialized before him. Roberts cried out sharply.

"I told you to stay!"

He jerked around, went to a chair, sat on the edge of it and put his head in his hands, rocking gently on his toes.

"My God, Martin!—to think that I could have loved you! After all, Devaud, you're nothing but a sailor. A hostile, bestial—" Roberts' head jerked back and he jumped to his feet, breathing heavily. "Deane," he panted, "you're in this room! It won't help to try and hide. I can locate you by your eyes. They're in that glass there." He pointed. "You think you know my secret. It's a lie! It's a dream, and you're a lie!" He leaned against the chair, his cheeks darkening. "I'll find Martin. Martin will be fair.... Martin—you always liked me. You didn't deserve a job.... Take her away, Martin! I want to sleep. I can't sleep while she's hiding here." He stopped speaking, a crafty expression changing his face. Tiptoeing into the bathroom, he pulled the mirror from the cabinet and holding it under his arm, crept back to the living room.

Approaching the larger glass which hung at the end of the room, he quickly drew the other mirror from under his arm and held it so that the two of them reflected into each other. Then, bursting into short, sobbing laughter, he shook the smaller glass furiously.

"There! Look at yourself! You're sick, too!" His laughter became fiercer until his body rocked from its violence. Suddenly he stiffened. The mirror dropped from his hands, the glass splintering, and Roberts fell.

CHAPTER XXVII

Martin and Rio walked along the waterfront in silence. All activity seemed suspended. It was a lonely and a menacing panorama to both men who realized that the very heart of the city had been pierced. Imported goods and products for exportation were lying quiet, slowing up the commerce of the world. Union longshoremen and truckmen had walked out with the striking seamen; and the desperate efforts of independent groups could not compensate for the loss of regimentated teamwork and good fellowship, so vital. Policemen patrolled each pier to prevent acts of violence between organized and unorganized Labor. Between the entrances, the scattered trucks rolled about like confused ants.

"Damn the governors!" said Rio, thrusting out his jaw.

"Who?"

"*Who?*" repeated Rio, in exasperation. "Capital, you bastard! Capital! *You've* eaten their sour pudding and slept on their lousy blankets!—and you ask *me* 'who'! It's Capital that smashes Labor!"

"Money and work," said Martin serenely. "Money and work."

Rio turned on him nervously.

"Cut out that speakin' in tongues, or whatever the hell it is, Martin. I've heard you damn the Companies from Shanghai to Port Said. Anyway, what about the printin' plant?"

"It's closed. The boys walked out. That's all."

"Why?"

"The same reason they're walking out everywhere—for better hours, better conditions."

"When do they open?"

"I don't know. There'll be arbitration, of course. Most of the men though, have put away enough chips to ride it. I haven't."

"Well," said Rio, "what are you goin' to do?"

"I don't know that either. I have enough left to run me for a few weeks. Then if things haven't opened I'll have to ship out."

"And leave Deane with Roberts around? You told me not to mention her, but I guess it's O.K. now."

"Deane will be all right," Martin nodded. "Roberts had a stroke. He can't move."

"Roberts? A stroke?" Rio looked pleased, and there was a definite satisfaction in his voice as he continued. "Maybe that's why my idea didn't work. I went to his place that night, and the next. The second time he was home, but there was lights...." Rio shook his head wisely. "And I work in the dark," he added, looking at Martin. "But about the plant—can't you get another job ashore?"

"I doubt it. I don't know another trade."

"Then what the hell good did college do you?"

"College? That's another one I can't answer," said Martin. "I was too young. The world turned backwards. I hated my young, fresh hair and the child in my face. I needed the forest and the open sea—an insane wind that held my breath. I hated pedantry, and the inquisitive eyes of girls."

"What else?" asked Rio.

"It's too old to hurt now," answered Martin.

"Go on," said Rio.

"It wasn't much. It taught me to drink incredibly bad gin—corrosive enough that it's a wonder I have any guts left. Why go on?"

"I know," said Rio. "You had it your way, and I had it mine. But it was all the same.... I had the wind you longed for, and it put scissors in my throat! Let's forget it. Look!" He pointed to a wharf near them. One group of men walking along it held signs in the air. Another, grimly silent, stood by the entrance to the warehouse pier, watching those who came out and those who entered. "We'll forget our trouble in *that* scramble, Martin! It looks like our boys have tied up a ship."

"Let's see. That's Pier V7. What ship's that?"

"The *Leana*. She makes Pedro, and Puget Sound, I think."

One of the men who were carrying signs stopped when he saw them.

"Howdy, Rio."

"Hello, Brick. What's the jibe?"

"They paid us off an' are tryin' to ship a fink crew," answered the man, hitching the sign a little higher. "We dumped the mattresses over the side last night comin' in. The bedbugs had made 'em Snug Harbor. I slept on the hatch off the coast of Mexico. And God!—what roaches!"

"Hmm," said Rio, and he and Martin walked on.

They had started uptown when a man came out of the warehouse. One of the union men who was watching the doorway ran after him and knocked off his cap with the flat of his hand. The other tried to fight back but was smothered with punches before a policeman broke it up.

"Like old times," said Martin.

"Yeah. Let's go up to the Hall," suggested Rio.

They reached South Ferry, walked to Pearl Street and went up the stairs into an old building. The room was crowded with seamen. Some of them, in chairs tilted against the wall, were sitting quietly or exchanging stories. Others were playing cards. The air was full of tobacco smoke, stale and close. Rio and Martin went to the desk. A jumpy-eyed man behind it knew them and nodded. Martin took out his book. His dues were paid to the following month, but he laid down eight more dollars.

The nervous fellow looked at him, then took the book and examined it carefully.

"I see you ain't got in no picket duty since you left the west coast," he said.

"No."

"We could use a man on the line to-night."

"I'll be there."

"Put me down, too," said Rio. "I need a good sleep."

"Yeah!" snapped the agent. "This ain't Frisco, nor Portland, where they bat their scabby brains out. Here, the Company takes these fink bastards from the ship by car and leaves 'em in town. The boys make a few clap joints, meet the transportation and are brought back to the ship." The agent licked his lips, showing perfect teeth, shining and yellow. "It's silk—till they sail under." He bit a fingernail and turned to another man.

Rio was growling when he and Martin left the Hall.

"God damn the finks," he said.

"That's right," agreed Martin. "They struck me midships once. They nearly sank me."

"You know," said Rio, angrily, "I like you. But for Christ's sake, don't give me your end of the sea! You're about as salty as lard."

Martin smiled.

"Yes, they nearly sank me," he repeated. "The ship was listing fourteen degrees when the bos'n ran into the fo'c'sle in his dirty underwear. He danced the ise-odori with a bottle of Saki under one arm and an ordinary seaman under the other, on a deck that would have frozen grandmother's mittens. Now Rio, do you figure yourself a deep water sailor? Because you've pulled in the log on a cold night and lashed barrels to a hatch with your butt to the wind—are you sure of the ocean?... Have you ever curled a sea egg around your elbow?—kissed a barracuda over black water?—raced a shark in a harbor full of battle-wagons dumping garbage, with your own boat forty feet away against the wind? Have you winked at a sea spider and made him shuffle backwards till his legs ruffled slow sand in your face?"

"Well," said Rio, laughing, "I told you once you were the 'part of.'"

They were back at Pier V7. Other men were concentrating from the Hall to relieve the day pickets.

"They brought in two cars full," said a tall fellow who had been heading the day men. He turned to Rio. "You take care of the night gang. We'll bring down coffee. The Company is usin' black sedans—some of the blinds was down when they pulled in. A couple of cops is standin' by the gate so you can't do much there. But if you divide your gang and send half of 'em up the alley a ways, you can get a sign. Hop on the runnin' board, an' you know what to do. Another thing. All the deck officers walked out when we was paid off except the third mate. That's one Company man I'd like to see you get. The finks may not get no leave to-night, but the *Leana* don't sail for four days. If we keep a good lookout, maybe we can get a couple of the bastards. That's all, except don't do no drinkin'."

"What's that on your breath?" asked someone. "Orange juice?"

"I can hold it," said the tall fellow.

The pickets laughed and the day men left. The night gang joined around Rio.

"I'll take a few of you up there." Rio pointed to a pile of dunnage. "The rest of you watch the gate. If a Company car comes, give me a light three times and get out. We'll take care of the rest of it. Don't talk to the cops unless they talk to you first. Keep your distance from the gate. Have you got a torch you can signal me with, Billy?"

"No, I ain't."

"I got mine here," said one of the men, pulling out a flashlight.

"Give it to Billy," said Rio. "He's worked with me before. Remember, Billy—burn it at me three times."

"O.K."

It was almost dark and Rio selected his men, including Martin. They walked up the street to an old pile of lumber by a dark pier.

"Get this, boys—no knives. A club's best, but not a piece of pipe. Work on 'em hard, but don't kill 'em. You, Eddy—and you, Martin—an' me'll hop the runnin' board. Smash the glass an' bring her to the side. We got to work fast before brass-buttons shows up."

"What if they're Company officials?" asked Martin.

"*They* won't be here," said Rio, amused. "But if they are, give 'em two, instead of one."

"What's the matter with ye, sonny?" asked a dwarf-like man with immense shoulders. "Is yer belly soft?" He glared at Martin.

"We'll find out soon, my muscle-bound patriot," said Martin walking toward him swiftly.

Several seamen jumped between them.

"I'll hear one more crack from either of you, an' I'll bat your thick skulls together," said Rio quietly. "Our union is split already. We got work to do, an' you start a parade. You ain't fit to work."

"I'll work," said Martin.

"Me, too," said the heavy seaman.

"Shake hands," said an older man with grizzled hair and an intense, strained face.

"It was my fault," said Martin.

"Naw, it was mine," objected the squat fellow sheepishly as they shook hands.

"You don't need to kiss," said Rio sharply. Then he held up his hand. "Get this straight," he continued. "It ain't no joke we're playin'. Maybe this'll help." He took a bottle from his pocket and passed it around, each man taking a shot of the liquor. Rio finished it and tossed the bottle under the dunnage. "It's about time for the rats to come out if they're goin' ashore," he went on. "Keep an eye to the pier." He turned suddenly to one of the younger seamen. "You ain't got no club."

"My brother was killed in Detroit that way, Rio. Lemme use my fists."

Rio turned his face aside for a moment. When he looked at the boy again it was like metal.

"Get yourself a club, buddy."

Hesitatingly, the seaman took up a knotty piece of wood. He held it in his hands one way and then another, his face white.

One of the men came up to Rio and took him to one side. He said something in a low voice and Rio nodded. The man returned his nod and left hurriedly.

"*This is the time, dear Mother*—" hummed a seaman.

"Shut up," said his partner.

They waited silently, watching the pier for any light. Suddenly, a man came upon them, startling them as he shuffled in and laid down a large package.

"Here it is, Rio." The man was panting. "It's me—Al."

"Beer!" The men exulted quietly, peering through the early darkness.

Al now took a short automatic from his pocket and handed it to Rio.

"Drink up," Rio said to the men.

Each man took a bottle and waited in turn for the opener except one seaman who, impatient, knocked off the cap of his bottle against a block of wood.

"Take the rest down to the men at the pier," said Rio to Al, who shambled away noiselessly.

Someone struck a match. In the flare Rio saw Martin regarding him steadily. He grinned. It was a painful, smashing look and he didn't take his eyes away. The match flickered out and Martin came up to him slowly.

"Watch for the lights, Eddy," cautioned Rio, as he and Martin walked a few yards away from the lowered sounds of the men.

"So you believe, Martin, that I'd pull this?" Rio twisted the automatic in his hand. "Al got this for me. He'd eat out of my hand. Never mind why. This—belongs to Roberts. It was used one night. I got it for you."

"You told the story?" asked Martin.

"I told no story. Al's a thief. He does what I say, but his heart is finer than yours."

"I don't doubt it," said Martin, feeling the gun and Rio's hands in the dark. Breaking it under Rio's wrist, he suddenly threw back his arm and spun the automatic into the river.... Vaguely he heard Rio say there were lights....

Martin looked toward the pier and saw the headlights of an automobile coming upon them. The car was gaining speed as it passed the pile of lumber. Martin, faster than the others, leaped for the running board and swung himself against the windshield glass, holding to the door-handle. His head was turned just enough to see Eddy jump behind him. Eddy missed the board. His body spun vertically against the rear fender and crashed on the pavement. Behind him, Rio was running frantically. Martin smashed his hand through the side window, feeling slivers of glass against his arm. He caught the driver by the throat and, through the sound of the motor, could hear the dark gurgle under his fingers. There was swearing and shoving inside, but Martin hurt too much to care. He pushed steadily against the lower part of the wheel until the machine swerved and tilted toward the river. It came around in a wide arc, breaking heavily on the shoulder of the pier. Then Martin heard Rio's voice and knew that he, himself, was falling. He turned so that the back of his head would not strike the paving, and felt the rush of hot blood as his nose and mouth hit first. Instead of putting him out, it cleared his brain. He lay quietly, watching Rio swing his fist and then his club. Abstractly, he watched the other men in the crew go into action against the finks. He didn't care....

The gorilla-like sailor with whom he had quarreled, held a bottle as though it were a club. He was snarling as he pulled a man from the car.

"So it *is* ye, ye finkified mate! I been lookin for ye!" Martin heard him say. "I been lookin' for ye, an' yer damned long finger ye've pointed at me like a dog! God!—I'll git that finger now!" he added hoarsely, bringing the bottle down on the fender of the car until it was split across. Savagely he threw the mate on the ground, held him by the collar and stepped on his wrist. Then, separating the man's forefinger from the rest of his hand, he brought down the split edge of the bottle sharply above the middle knuckle.

"Wife—Wife!" cried the mate softly.

The seaman picked up the severed finger, shook it in the man's face and flung it on the ground beside him.

"Splice it, Jack! Splice it!" He was cursing the fallen man brokenly. Martin looked away....

Then he saw the boy whose brother had been killed in Detroit. "Automobiles," thought Martin. The boy had no club and was on his back, fighting desperately with a large man from the car. Martin crawled to his knees, not feeling his injured arm or his split chin. He stood waveringly for a moment and got to them just as the man's broad hand was spearing the boy's face. Martin knew that he was falling again, not fighting, as he reached them; but he dug his teeth into a fleshy neck and held on as though he were killing a snake, while the body beneath him thrashed and cried. A hard hand pulled him off. Rio was standing above him.

"It's over, Martin. We got a car.... Come, men!"

Martin spat out blood and climbed into the automobile along with the others.

CHAPTER XXVIII

Martin went slowly to Roberts' apartment house, his head lowered. His right arm was in a sling, the lower part of his mouth was bruised and split. His nose was swollen. He went up in the elevator to Roberts' rooms and rang once. A doctor came out into the hall. For a moment the two men regarded each other speculatively. Martin saw the blue, introspective eyes, the strong turn of the chin and the gray hairline, receding deeply at the temples. The physician saw a young man with a broken, illusive face.

"I'm Martin Devaud, Doctor. I'm Roberts' friend. I heard he asked for me."

"I can see you, Martin," said the physician kindly, "for I'm Roberts' friend, too."

Martin rubbed his cut arm and turned his eyes away.

"You can see? How far?"

The physician shook his head, but did not answer.

"This stroke," Martin continued. "Is it serious? Is there any time to help?"

All this while, the doctor had been watching him, noticing his bruised face and strained expression, his bandaged arm.

"You seem to have been in something of a mix-up, yourself," the physician smiled faintly. Then, of a sudden, his face became divisible with the old, tired pains and the new, sharp ones as balance. "Do you know Roberts' condition?" he asked seriously.

"No," said Martin. "Roberts and I quarreled, and I haven't seen him lately." He ran his hand over his tender chin.

The doctor looked off down the hall, and in his eyes there was now restraint born of his intimacy with pain.

"He mentions your name continually, Martin," observed the physician. "The thought of you seems to make him desperate in the moments of lucidity which unfortunately attend his madness. And from the strange way he talks at times, one might think you had had a part in the cause of this grave illness. But such is not the case. His illness took root years ago."

One word cried out to Martin.

"'Madness'?—you say?"

"Yes," said the physician. "It's like the putrefaction of albumen. Almost like the expansion of gasses within a closed chamber. This disintegration must go on. It's what we have here."

Martin felt himself turning sick.

"'Putrefaction'? Doctor?"

"Yes. Putrefaction of the cerebral mass, that most delicate and most amazing structure—a powerful gift to man." The doctor was grave.

"What can I do?" asked Martin, horrified.

In answer, the physician shook his head and Martin knew that all was futile.

"May I see him?"

Again the doctor regarded Martin thoughtfully. It was as though he wondered whether this man's agitated mind could view the spectacle which was soon to be presented. And Martin, waiting quietly, understood and respected this professional skepticism. At last, the physician spoke.

"Before you go in, Martin, remember that you are looking at the demanding, expansive form of paresis. Be careful!"

As Martin entered the bedroom he saw a disorientated face—a deflective rapport of Roberts with his environment—a clouding of consciousness. And as he went closer he knew that Roberts had no comprehension of detail or of situation. Martin felt completely helpless. It seemed to him that the translucent, attenuated skeleton of the adviser had wrapped its arms around him, instead of the disease. The sick man's lips, dry and split, opened and closed in an effort to speak. The guttural tones reached Martin's ears as though from a great distance—the words moving gently, like a broad leaf without wind.

"Martin! Martin!" Roberts' expression became clear and defined. The immobile muscles of his face relaxed. "Martin!" he repeated. "Are you there?"

In the room was a terrible pressure.

Again he called—"Martin! Martin! Are you there?"

"Yes, Roberts, I'm here."

The pitiful, decayed mask upon the pillow broke like a free tide. It spilled in diluted, semi-conscious tears against the linen. Roberts tried to shake the covers; but his hands stood out perpendicularly from the sides of his waist. They remained there, insensitive, incoherent, until Martin took them gently and laid them on the sheet.

Again, momentary consciousness lighted Roberts' face. Its brightness and shrewd study shocked Martin more than any act of tension could have done.

"Do you want a confession, dear boy?" called out the sick man. "Do you want my signature?... Ha, ha!—Ho, ho!—Hee, hee, hee!..." The ghastly cry reflected from the ceiling. It wasn't laughter, or hysteria. It was a lachrymose and untidily folded cry of remorse, torn from the swiftly hollowing brain cell.

With his left hand Martin raised his own wounded arm to his forehead. When at last he brought it down, the gauze was wet. In the interim, bright eyes shone through the window. They were mirthful, smoldering and amused—the cancerous eyes of birds. Infuriated, Martin crossed the room and pulled down the blinds. When he turned in the direction of the bed once more, Roberts' luminous eyes were parallel with his hand which was now hanging over the edge of the covers. The constriction of the pupils was so intense—so minute that the eyes seemed blind. But the expression was one of gravest interest.

"Come, Martin! Come, Infidelity! You're my only one. If I don't look grotesque enough for a death scene, give me a nightcap. One with white flaps over the ears and a blue peak—laugh for me, Martin!"

"For God's sake, Roberts—not now. I'm dying with you."

There was a sprawling, unintelligible sound from the adviser's lips, and then silence. Martin waited, amazed at the clarity of Roberts' words, amazed at this strange and powerful mind, still formidable. Again the adviser looked at him.

"Die?" he asked peevishly. Then more firmly, "No you won't, darling. Unhappy men don't die.... Could you give me your strong, brown arm without shuddering? It would mean a great deal to me.... I can see your strong, brown arm where there's heat and dark, flashing clouds. It's peeling a tangerine—cutting a fruit for lips as soft as the flesh in my spine—oh, wicked!... A dark girl's belly—the cup for your mouth. Oh, God, Martin! Your mouth—the stomach—the stench of normalcy. Before that happens, give me your arm—your clean, brown arm...."

Martin went swiftly to the bed, his eyes flickering as he sank to his knees. With his good left arm, and hiding the one stripped with bandages, he lifted the skull-like head until it was level with his own, which had begun to throb and ache.

"Here is my arm, Roberts. It is your protection and your faith," he said.

Vapidly Roberts smiled at him.

"My faith—my own true faith.... No one believed, but I knew that you were mine!... Not even Deane believed."

"Not even Deane," repeated Martin, his wounded arm shaking against the silken counterpane.

Roberts' eyes were becoming glazed.

"They'd all feel cheap, if they could see us now. Your arms around a corpse—a corpse that strikes to prove itself!" His thin hand pushed against Martin's broken nose, falling again and again on Martin's face which failed to recognize the pain. "You love me, though I'm defeated, my dear boy." He raised his hand once more, but this time it dropped limply to the coverlet. Again the torn brain lost all contact, and he wandered, hesitantly.

"I come before the leisured policies of man. I have these tears, these positive notes of cruelty. Do you want to know?... Smash the hidden casket of Carol, and you'll find the first. He fed himself with the intolerable dreams of your isolated sanctuary. He cried out of lips as stale as mine. Our Grail was the same, each futile in its own pride. Carol, the bucket. Filled with the residue of my hatred. Murder?—Death?—That's nothing.... I went to him on a night gray as your eyes. He desired you. His flesh, quite frantically, cried out. Could I stand *that*? Could I stand the corned stupidity of his mind after *you*, most beautiful?... I went to him. Deadly and most honestly I threw the passionate, leaden stone into the vacuum of his heart." Roberts spoke without lips—the ventriloquy of his despair so hurtful and adolescent, so pitifully gay.

"There is a tear for Rio. I've seen him follow you with his eyes—that rollicking, healthy sailor! That bold adventurer with the Mongoloid eyes. His bravado is covered with a native strength to hide his shame." Roberts chuckled hoarsely. "My sinful innocent—never to have seen the colored lechery behind his muscles!... Rio—epitome of flesh—carnality in Mother Goose's shoes—a bundle of white snow—quite terrified.... I've seen his bleak face, whipped by wind and wave, and so have you. But it takes death to bring me the knowledge of his simple, frightened passion. Oh!—he will never fail you, although he doesn't know why.... Enough of him—enough of his cautious, boastful gallantry which makes one sick when one is well, and makes one laugh when one is sick." Again the adviser hesitated. Slowly and painfully he turned that he might look at Martin.

"The next tear is for Deane—the one you think you own. You don't possess her. You hold an empty vase—the artificial movements, smiles and anguish of the woman—all of them as brazen as I, when I first met you. I thought you were the spindle, I the thread. I thought that you were life—an intoxicating bubble in a heavily filled glass. Deeply and amusedly I drank, too late to feel the poison."

"I've saved a tear for Drew. He thought that he was strong enough to escape. But it isn't 'escape' to avoid the thing one loves the most. And so, *I* know I had the strength *not* to escape—and I am happier than he....

"The last tear is in a vial that I give you. A tear to use when abstract sorrow's not enough—a potion you may pour on blistered flesh to lift the crust of tender skin that each swift-moving piston and fast-spinning wheel of man can drive and curve before your fond excitement.

"On myself, you didn't use a tear. Your hands and mind tore my integument until the bone shows. Watch this!" Roberts, weakened, but fierce, reached for Martin's hair. There was a brief silence as Martin, his head bowed over the bed, felt the momentary spasm of twisted fingers on his scalp. He did not speak or lift his eyes. As in a dream, he felt the fingers that had clutched his hair so frightfully, become more feeble. There was a gentle, automatic patting against his forehead and he heard deep, horrible sobs....

Roberts put his hands across his eyes.

"Martin, you are like my desperate, dead mother, she being the more selfish and adored though, of the two. It's why I've loved you both, though you the less. She is the most important now. She is the greater." The adviser raised his head in a final gesture of triumph. "Speak! Why don't you speak, Martin? Your tongue's been loose enough before. But now that each mad syllable could match the inarticulation in my own vast lungs, you sit dumbly—like a passive Christ. Have you reformed?—or, are you a dead man waiting for my company? For I'm a King. I have great powers. Shall I have you tortured in my dungeons, or thrown from my domain?—But no! I have no rack, no bed of agony to meet your own inventions. And my domain's a joke. You own it all, from the boiling center of the earth unto the farthest, coldest star."

Martin held him closer. He stared at Roberts until the sick man's eyelids lifted, showing the brief, unfocused glance. There was recognition, but complete indifference. The vacant, polite smile was only a slight movement of the lips. Had Martin not been blinded by his own fine helplessness—his deepened affection, he would have seen another thing. He would have noticed the oddly rounded chin with its slackness—its hint of cogent lechery below the hungry bones that stretched the cheek of the adviser. He would have seen the newly tapered lines, out of silhouette, and the dense eyes, gaping; or the fibrous hair, the cocked head and gently fluttering tongue. Instead, the generalities—vague outlines were predominant. This swiftly perishing mask, to Martin's eyes, could have been a sallow apple—a melon broken from the vine—or an older moon in autumn. There was no individuality or ego. There were damp breathings, sonorous emanations from the bed and the faint, orgastic music of white flowers in a tomb. Martin held his breath, held his own head lower and asked for some release.... When he looked up again this blended, spectral motion was gone forever. This mixture of sound and color, so horrible to him, now drifted from the gently closing door.

CHAPTER XXIX

Martin knew that it was time to work again. He knew that there must be some expression of his own to erase the unending march of Carol and Roberts in his thoughts. The evolution of his type design had stopped, each pattern seeming worse than the preceding one.

He was disturbed and hesitant upon regarding the sun. The clouds were no longer poems and the sunset meant only darkness. Within himself alone could he feel the yearnings and the beauty, the life chord pulling, insisting. He was tormented with dreams. Sounds grew from the ground. Proud women with dragons on their white shoulders walked in a death-like mist. Behind the retreating curve of mountain he could hear Deane laughing. Brought with the wind, the laughter became monotonous—something at which to strike.

In the early morning there was peace. In the early morning when even the birds were silent and the stars white, Martin would awaken and stand by the window. During these moments he was elated and alive. But when he went to sleep again, he fought among dreams that seemed both real and unreal.

One daybreak he awoke and threw his arm across his eyes. The night's monsters were growing larger and more demanding. Perhaps it was impossible to kill them by bending them into symbols—by throwing them on paper. The units of the living and the dead must be presented to daytime and the mind's curiosity. He worked soberly, breeding the straight line with the afflicted. He tried the medium of words, changing every character, crossing their susceptible hands. He danced the ugly noises with the sound of roses and blew a splintering rock into a wreath of silver hair. Bravely he went to the night's agony and blinding sweat until he felt himself confused by so meaningless a gallantry that once again he turned to Deane.

They sat beside each other in her home that night. Deane saw that he had changed—she saw his quietude, the patient line between his eyes.

He kissed her lips.

"It's restful here, darling," he said. "A sweet, domestic anodyne—the sweetest I have ever known. The transition has been swift. I ran with wild men, smashed machines, climbed, waded and struggled toward an impossible ideal. I was hard when Carol was murdered; and though little chips were broken from me, the planets remained in their orbits—heat meant one thing, and cold another. This is still true in one sense; but my relationship to them has changed.... Roberts died in my arms. He thought I loved him. Diseased, humiliated by our artificial sexual codes, he made his own world. Quite happily he lived and dreamed in this chimerical condition until unfortunately, I entered his last kingdom. It had to be myself—the one man whose bitter defenses remained impregnable to Roberts' bold demands. However, as the albinic, antagonistic germ bored into his brain, this mind became detached, severed; and I felt the pent-up hatred of his frustration. I didn't mind that—but suddenly, consciousness was established again through some strange medium, and he told me it was my world—that he belonged to me. He told me of my cruelty. And that's how he died.... I love you, Deane, but I'll go back to the midstrip of the world where my toes bubble, oiling the hot deck of a ship, before I'll hurt you. That's my country—isolation in body, but not in mind. And when I touch land it will be a dark whore." Martin's face had not changed expression nor had his voice gathered volume. But his self-contempt and his visualizations against the soft, purple shadows of the quiet room and the chained refractions of the woman's beautiful face beside him pressed Heaven and Hell together and there was no breath around them.

Deane held back her tears.

"You're bleeding yourself, Martin," she said, "and for no reason. I'm in love with you, too, and I love your fantasies. But please don't talk of things which are absurd—of the South Seas—of dirty ships and dirtier islands. Your sound effects about black women are not dramatic, darling—they're just a little irrational. Oh, no!—Martin, I'm not trusting your libido or your discrimination. To be candid, it isn't a question of trust. You must have your stage, your setting and your actors. I don't mind that—and I'll be part of the whole scheme although I don't understand it. I've run wild, too, though in a different way. But I found out how meaningless it was, how much it hurt me without helping anyone else and I've stopped, just as you'll do. There will always be violence in your dreams, and that will be some outlet. And there are gymnasiums and little fishing boats where you can break your neck in a more restrained fashion." Deane closed her hands on his, and spoke with a desperate gravity. "And you can always swear loudly to me about the world's tyranny—perhaps I'll swear a little, also. But you can't go back to bad ships and worse men, and be part of an organized brutality. I want you here with me. I want you to work on your beautiful ideas and build a solid foundation for both of us. You look different, Martin. You look more mature. I think you're tired of that other world. Dearest," she went on, touching her lips to his cheek, "we can't dismiss our life together even though it has been brief." She turned to Martin with a sudden passionate insistence. "Let's go on from this point together, darling. Let's dismiss philosophy, ideals that can be forgotten in a night, other people's helplessness and drama." She held Martin more tightly. "We must stop thinking about these terrible people," she repeated. "What do we care about them?" Deane's lips trembled. "Carnality!" she exclaimed. "The vile, damnable beasts! Pouncing from house to house and bedroom to bedroom like a disjointed Roman carnival. Give them any veil of understanding you possess and they still exist in the flatlands—the tilted, undernoted lowlands where not even slime comes to birth! A driveling code of introduction from one land to the other and a rotten horde of Young America comes alive! What have we to do with that?" Deane was weeping; and as though symbolical of her blazing words, her hair had spread over her shoulders—had spread, thought Martin as he touched it, "like the flame of a torch in the dark waters of a lost lagoon."

"'What have we to do with that?'" he repeated. "Nothing, Deane. Nothing can touch us now. But first I have to go from you. I don't know for how long, or how far. It's part of the scheme. And remember, I didn't build it; but I know the undertows, the ebb tides and the breakers. There is a distant sun on our horizon, and I won't go into happiness or unhappiness until it's reached. Don't you think I'll miss those lights?" He pointed out of the window. "But I'll have stars around that will bring this room to me. I'm a dreamer, and they have luck. So forget the dull months or the aching ones. Give my picture a bath once a day until it's white; and I'll stay that way." Martin's voice broke and he stood up. "I can't say 'Good-bye, Mrs. Smith—' and bow and strain until my sharp, black coat sticks out, nor turn and smile 'It's been a pleasant afternoon—I'll call you soon.'"[5] His voice became harsh. "These fools' farewells and wet good-byes are as thick and viscous as a glue pot, Deane. Sentiment rises in me easily and I'm ashamed that my hand seems blurred against the dress that covers your knee. That's why I curse such weakness and yearn to leave my beloved with my hat over my nose, yelling blasphemously at a wall-eyed, pot-bellied moon."

"You sound like a drunken Irish tenor," exclaimed Deane, covering her celibate pain at once with the same quick irony.

"By God, I *am* drunk!" cried Martin. "Drunk on your hair and the moisture of your lips and the way you look at me. Drunk with hatred because I won't see them or taste them again until the same dark wind that takes me away brings me back."

A wraith-like smile hovered on Deane's lips.

"The wind that brings you home, Martin, won't be dark. It will be light and gentle and perhaps will carry a few white clouds on its back."

"No." He shook his head. "I want it dark and heavy and raging. I want it so fierce it will bring me home much faster."

"Let me have it my way, Martin," she urged softly. "I want it gentle so that no part of you will be hurt. I've never been patient about most things; but I will be—about this." Deane spoke so tenderly that the cool night wind stopped blowing, and a moment of such stillness ensued that all outside was hidden—all sound, all waves of sound and color—everything was hidden.

"Almighty God!" whispered Martin, staring at her—staring at her coral cheeks and swollen bosom. "The Scylla Deeps—a sea no man has found—" Aloud he cried, "It will be done your way, Deane. In the end, it will always be your way." The tears were coming into his eyes without restraint. He opened the door, saw the silhouette of the woman sitting quietly on the couch, looked for a moment through the window at the lights which seemed to be nodding to him and went into the hall.

Outside, in the street, he hesitated, then turned toward the river. For a long time he wandered about the waterfront. Wearily, at last, he sat down on one of the piers and watched the moon set. When dawn came he got up stiffly and went to the Seaman's Institute.

CHAPTER XXX

Martin went into the large main room of the Institute, found a vacant chair, sat down and looked at the men. He couldn't recognize a single face although the seamen were going through the usual formulas. Some of them were lined up before the marble bar, drinking coffee and eating doughnuts. Others stood in groups, talking to each other; while a few, like himself, sat quietly, knowing themselves on the fringe of the stream. Some of these few were regarding their history—pressing their falls and errors out of the past. Some were rubbing the small change in their pockets, wondering whether to buy "smoke" and for a brief period drift into the senseless drunkenness and blindness of the poison, or to try again—to use this precious remnant of their money for getting to a pier already lined with men as desperate to ship out as themselves.

A man walked in, brown-skinned, alert. He went, in turn, to several groups of seamen. They welcomed him and he shook their hands. "I wonder how long he'll last," thought Martin. "A week, I guess, if he's paid off." He heard the men question the newcomer about the ship—the food. Had he seen Ella in Coconut Grove?... Was Charlie's Punch Bowl as alive as ever?... Had he paid off?... The man grinned when they mentioned Ella, nodded his head vigorously about Jamaica; but said "No!" about paying off.

"I can't get that way again, boys." He pointed to a few deadheads, snoring in their chairs. His finger swung to Martin. "For Christ's sake," he said, walking rapidly to him. For a moment he stood in front of him, shaking his head, his hands on his hips. "You look like one of them crawlers we used to swat in Morocco. Is your short-arm jammed?"

Martin managed a thin smile.

"I've spent a winter in New York—that's all."

The sailor bent over him.

"Listen—I been up at the Hall. I heard what you done the other night. There's two ships in you can make. One is your old pal, the *Verda*. We need two men. Can you get Rio? I still got his oilskins."

"What happened to the little ordinary, Al?" Martin asked.

The sailor looked puzzled.

"The ordinary?" Al thought a moment. "Oh—you mean that little screw that was aboard when you and Rio piled off. Damned if I know. He only made one more trip. Say," he said, looking at Martin queerly, "we sail at five. There ain't no time to lose. Git hold of Rio and beat it to the Hall."

"All right," said Martin, getting up. He went out quickly, nodding to the policeman by the entrance, then hurried to Rio's room and knocked on the door. Rio opened it. He looked half-asleep.

"What's up?" he asked, rolling back on the bed. "James don't bring coffee till eleven."

"I'm shipping on the *Verda* this evening. Do you want to come along?"

"Nuts again, eh?" said Rio, yawning.

Martin turned to go.

"Wait a minute," called Rio, sitting up. "How do you know we can make her?"

"We're the fair-haired boys after the other night. Al told me about the ship. But we have to hurry."

"Are you leavin' Deane?" asked Rio incredulously.

"Don't ask me that," said Martin, his face turning white.

"But I don't want the damned *Verda*. I'm going to Santa de Marina."

"Rio," Martin opened the door, "this is the last trip we can ever make together. I don't want the *Verda* either, but she'll get me to Panama. From there I can make it to the East Indies. And as far as Santa de Marina is concerned, the *Verda* goes to Puerto Colombia. You can swim from that point."

Without a word Rio got up and began to put on his clothes. His bag was packed and Martin didn't ask him why. When he was dressed they went to the Hall and saw the agent again. This time he greeted them more cordially.

"I was hopin' you boys would come. That was great stuff," he said, looking significantly at the end of his own nose. "You earned this jelly." He made out two forms for the mate of the *Verda* and gave them to Martin and Rio. "Get there by three P.M. drunk or sober." One of his eyes twitched nervously.

"O.K.," said Rio.

He and Martin put their slips in their pockets and left the Hall.

"Is your gear ready, Martin?"

"It won't take long. But I have a note to write, so we'll make it fast."

Once in his room, Martin packed his clothes with Rio's help, saw that his sneakers were rotten and threw them away. Then he sat down at his desk, folded his drawings and put them in an envelope addressed MRS. IDARA. For a few moments he sat there, staring at the name, a shameless grief upon his face. After a little, he took a piece of paper and a pen and wrote:

"Dearest...."

Rio walked up and down, smoking one cigarette after another, stopping at intervals to glance somewhat anxiously at Martin.

When Martin finally got up, his eyes were red; but he looked straight at Rio.

"That's that, my bonny friend. We're going to the *Verda*."

On the deck of the *Verda* they found the mate. He looked at the papers sent from the Hall and at the men's discharges and lifeboat tickets.

"You can take the eight to twelve, Martin. And you, Rio, the four to eight. The bos'n won't mind. He's sleeping some of it off. We sail at five and if you go ashore, for God's sake don't get too drunk. Somebody has to handle those derricks. Al and Pete's ashore, and the ordinaries came from Mr. Fizz in the office. They won't know a block from a winch."

"I'm not going ashore," said Martin.

"Me neither," said Rio.

The mate looked at them in some astonishment as they went aft. Then he shook his head.

It was like all ships at sailing time. The sailors cursed the lines and the mates cursed the sailors. The ordinaries didn't know what to do, but they hopped gallantly from one side of the deck to the other in a cold sweat of pretense. Pete's arm was nearly pulled from its socket when Al gave the winch too much steam. A linesman on the dock shook his fist at the ship and the captain walked up and down the bridge, saying little, but looking at his watch frequently. A longshoreman got his finger caught, working at one end of the hatch, and yelled frantically in Italian.... But finally it was done, as it is, always. And the *Verda* backed into the current with a tugboat pushing against an impossible weight and barking angrily through her whistle. It was almost eight when the last hatch had been battened and the lines coiled. Martin went back to the fo'c'sle and washed his hands and face. Then he rubbed his back and chest, put on a clean shirt and was on the ladder to the bridge in time to hear eight bells struck.

Martin grew into the relativity of time. Was it a day?—a month?—a year that he had been in these warm waters?... The stars grew deeper in the night; the constellations spread their tails above the ship; the moon, more arrogant than ever, called from the sky and filled his eyes with dust. It was the same. The dark, fast knife of cloud that ran at him was welcomed as a friend. This monster might blot out, in mercy, the silhouette of Deane.... When pressure, rain and cracked, dry lightning burned his eyes, he held his hands—his arms into the wind, that it might bring him solitude from dreams.... And when the squall had passed he turned to Rio.

"That entity was beautiful and clean. It swept out all the clammy, dirty things.... You see that cloud?" He pointed to the swift, retreating sky. "It had more tears in one brief moment, Rio, than both you, and I, and all our comrades in a lifetime. And once again, when life is sticky—seminant with lies, we'll find a ship, and find that cloud and hold it...."

Rio sighed.

FOOTNOTES

[1] *Dynamic Symmetry*, by Dr. J. Hambidge (Yale University Press).

[2] Stravinsky.

[3] Music by Charles T. Griffiths, based on the poem by William Sharp.

[4]

"How long, how long, in Infinite Pursuit
Of This and That endeavor and dispute?"
—*Rubáiyát of Omar Khayyám*.

[5] Allusion to mood of *Portrait of a Lady*, by T. S. Eliot.

www.ingramcontent.com/pod-product-compliance
Lightning Source LLC
Chambersburg PA
CBHW031434160426
43195CB00010BB/730